MAN AND HIS MUSIC

VOLUME ONE

This book is published also as Part I in a one-volume bound edition, which contains all four volumes. The cross-references to Plates refer to that edition and should be disregarded here.

MAN AND HIS MUSIC

THE STORY OF MUSICAL EXPERIENCE IN THE WEST

ALEC HARMAN
with Anthony Milner

VOLUME ONE

BARRIE & JENKINS
COMMUNICA - EUROPA

© Alec Harman 1962

First published in paperback in 1969 by
Barrie & Rockliff (Barrie Books Ltd)

Reprinted 1973, 1977 by
Barrie and Jenkins Ltd
24 Highbury Crescent, London N5 1RX

ISBN 0 214 66580 1

Made and printed in Great Britain by
J. W. Arrowsmith Ltd., Bristol 3

CONTENTS

PREFACE

In the Preface to a later volume of this history Wilfrid Mellers remarks that a music historian should approach his task with both "circumspection and humility". He is undoubtedly right, for when one considers what is involved in such an undertaking one should be extremely chary of adding to what has already been achieved in this sphere; indeed, it is doubtful whether the attempt should ever be made unless one is convinced that the kind of history one has in mind is sufficiently distinctive to justify the writing of yet another.

In this series the authors have been guided by three chief aims, and we believe that it is in the combination of these aims that the distinctiveness of this particular history lies.

To begin with, we have tried to convey something of the feelings aroused in us by the music we write about and to give as many aesthetic judgements on individual works and composers as is possible in a work of this size and scope, for although we realize that such feelings and judgments are purely personal and that therefore it is hardly likely that everyone will agree with them, we believe that a history which does not seek to arouse a critical enthusiasm for each and every period and in which there are few or no aesthetic judgments to guide the taste of those less familiar with the music in question is not fulfilling one of its functions.

Our second aim has been to write a history that would be of use in both schools and universities, and while conscious that there is a marked difference in ability and attainment between those studying music in their last two or three years at school and those specializing in the subject at university level, and that hence this history will provide more for the one and less for the other than is needed, we hope that both will find something of value.

But a history of music should do more than stimulate enthusiasm, or assess greatness, or pass aesthetic judgments; it should do more than present facts and reasonable deductions, or include well-chosen examples and quotations, or give accurate analyses of styles and techniques, important as all these are; it should also (to quote *The New Oxford History of Music*) "present music not as an isolated phenomenon or the work of a few outstanding composers, but as an art developing in constant association with every form of human culture and activity". This has been our third aim, and in pursuing it we have tried, by giving what we hope is sufficient relevant information of a general nature, to set the stage, as it were, for each successive scene and (to continue the analogy) by out-lining the principal characters involved (religion, painting, literature, etc.), to show in what ways and to what extent they influenced or were influenced by music.

This attempt to present music as an integral part of western civilization is essential, we believe, because all creative artists are influenced by the spiritual and intellectual environment in which they live, and so it follows that the more we know about a particular period the more we can enter into the creative minds of that period and hence appreciate more fully their aims and achievements. This may appear, and indeed is, obvious enough, but it is all too often forgotten, because each of us can enjoy and even be profoundly moved by a work of art knowing little or nothing about its creator or general back-ground. Nevertheless, it remains true that every creative artist gains in significance when his work is related to the conditions in which it was created, whether he be someone whose name is a household word, like Mozart, or a comparatively obscure mediaeval composer, like Pérotin. Thus, knowing something of the rationalism, the sophisticated sentimentality, the polished elegance of society in the latter half of the eighteenth century, of the delicate sensuousness and exquisite refinement of Watteau's and Boucher's paintings, we marvel more than if we knew nothing of all this, not so much at the utter perfection of Mozart's style and sense of structure as at the undercurrents of emotion that pervade his work and which at times amount almost to romantic passion.

Compared to Mozart, Pérotin gains in significance to a much greater extent when we know something about his background because the time at which he lived and the style in which he wrote have far fewer points of contact for us today than is the case with the eighteenth century. At first hearing, his music may well sound bare, monotonous, and meaningless, but when it is realized that the systematization and reiteration of rhythmic patterns, which are the main features of Pérotin's style, not only represented a new development in music, but also reflected, as did the solutions to the structural problems of Gothic architecture, the intellectual awakening of the twelfth and thirteenth centuries, an awakening that was stimulated by the discovery, through Arab philosophers, of the works of Aristotle, and which led men like Peter Abelard and St. Thomas Aquinas to believe and teach that faith can only be wholly assured when founded on reason; when it is further realized that, apart from the octave, the fourth and fifth were the basic intervals because they were as satisfyingly sonorous to ears accustomed to unison singing and playing as thirds and sixths are to us; and, lastly, that the music was intended to be performed as an act of devotion in a cathedral rather than listened to as an aesthetic experience in a concert hall—then the significance of the man becomes apparent and, after adjusting our ears and minds in the light of what we have learnt, we can begin to understand, assess, and (because he was in fact a fine composer) enjoy his music, with its marked contrast between the lively, bouncy rhythmic figures in one part and the sustained or slower-moving notes in another.

But writing alone cannot give an adequate account of any period, especially with regard to the fine arts, and if there had been no considerations as to cost this history would have included many more reproductions, some of them coloured, of buildings, paintings, sculpture, etc. Nevertheless, we hope that all those who read it will want to discover more of the achievements in other fields and that some will wish to pursue in greater detail the development of the music itself.

It is obvious, however, that the greatest value from knowing something about the background of a particular art can only be obtained if one has experienced or has the opportunity of experiencing that art, and because much of the music written in the Middle Ages is so different from that which we normally hear and, moreover, is performed so infrequently I have included, in the first five chapters of this first volume, a fair number of complete compositions, together with suggestions as to performance and with the original words freely translated. Even so, it has been impossible, for financial reasons, to include as many examples as I would have liked, and I have therefore given a number of references to Vol. I of *The Historical Anthology of Music* (*H.A.M.*).

Because it is seldom possible to be dogmatic about what was typical of England rather than, say, Scotland, especially in the Middle Ages, I have in most cases used the term 'British' when referring to the music of The British Isles. Admittedly the bulk of what has survived was written down, if not actually composed, by Englishmen, but this does not necessarily mean that the style or type of composition was peculiar to England: it must be remembered that the ability to write music was largely restricted to centres of learning such as monasteries and, later, universities and the Chapel Royal, of which centres there were, even proportionally, many more in England than in Scotland or Wales (St. Andrews', the oldest university after Oxford and Cambridge, did not open until 1412). Furthermore, in Scotland, where there was a flourishing musical tradition second only to that of England, the destruction of music, particularly of part-music, during the early years of the Reformation was far greater than elsewhere in Britain.

R. ALEC HARMAN

MUSIC IN THE EARLY CHURCH:
CHRISTIAN CHANT

Most people would agree that it is perfectly natural and proper for music to have a place in Christian worship. Natural because music and religion have been associated from the earliest times, and proper because the Bible sanctions its use. But there would be and always has been far less general agreement as to the *kind* of music that is suitable in religious services. If the suggestion were made that hymn texts should be adapted to popular 'hits' and accompanied by a cinema organ, very few people would tolerate the idea for one moment. Yet this suggestion gives us some idea of the problem facing the early Christian leaders or Church Fathers, as they are usually called, for although the problem was not so serious during the first two centuries when persecution was severe and the number of Christians small, and music not only sustained the converted but was an aid to conversion, it became acute in the third, fourth, and fifth centuries when the Church expanded rapidly, especially after its official recognition in 313, and the host of new converts brought with them their own cultural and philosophical traditions. Then it was that the Church Fathers had not only to combat the infiltration of pagan ideas, but also to decide whether music, with its strong worldly associations, was in any way suited to take part in Christian worship. To understand their difficulties fully we must remember that music was an essential part of Greek and Roman entertainment, for from as early as the sixth century B.C. there had been an instrumental 'class' in the great Greek contests (of which the Olympic Games is now the most famous), and by the early centuries A.D. the Romans, who adopted most of the Greek forms of entertainment, but in a coarser and more spectacular manner, had caused music to be largely associated with debauchery and immorality of all kinds. Small wonder, then, that the Church authorities were in a quandary and felt it imperative to draw the line somewhere, but exactly where was another problem. Some insisted that all instruments should be excluded from the service, others admitted only those mentioned in the Bible, while still others allowed any instrument, regarding each symbolically—the trumpet, for instance, being the power of God's message, the drum the conquering of sin, the cymbals the soul thirsting for Christ, etc. The first of these three attitudes eventually won the day, with the result that the music composed for the Church during the first thousand years or so was sung unaccompanied. As regards singing, however, practically all the Church Fathers decided that it was a good thing; indeed, they would have flouted all natural instincts had they decided otherwise, but, like the old Greek philosophers, whose influence on them was considerable, they realized that music can either ennoble or debase man's moral fibre and that therefore all church music must be associated with devout words—another reason for the rejection of instruments. In the words of St. Basil [*c.* 330-387], "God blended the delight of melody with doctrines in order that through the pleasantness and softness of the sound we might unawares receive what was useful in words. . . . For this purpose these harmonious melodies of the Psalms have been designed for us."*

What were these harmonious melodies? Unfortunately we do not know, for they were not written down in any shape or form until about the sixth century, and not until the middle of the twelfth century was a system of musical notation invented —that is, a system of symbols which show the exact pitch of the notes, but not necessarily their values. Hence the original melodies, passed down orally from generation to generation, must have changed a great deal both from careless alteration and deliberate variation, particularly during the first four or five hundred years, before the Church began to organize her repertoire (see p. 8).

Although we know very little of the actual music of the early Church, we do know that psalm-singing was the core of its services, the core from which radiated most of the songs now usually called plainsong. This name comes from the Latin *cantus planus* and was used by some thirteenth-century theorists in order to distinguish between the 'plain' notes of these

* Quoted from O. Strunk, *Source Readings in Music History*, p. 65.

melodies, which had no definite values, and 'musica mensurata', in which the notes were 'measured', i.e. had exact values. A better name, however, and the one we shall use, is Christian chant, for plainsong can be and is used to describe any un-measured music that consists of only one melodic line.

We also know that there were three main types of melody which are usually called syllabic, group, and melismatic or florid. These are distinguished by their underlay—that is, by the way the syllables of the text are fitted to the notes of the melody. Thus the syllabic type has mainly one note to each syllable. (An accented syllable here and elsewhere is shown by an acute accent. The notes printed small are sung lightly, Ex. 1):

Ex. 1. Hymn *Ut queant laxis* (1st verse)
Modern transcription.※ (♪= MM c.120)

Ut quéant lá - xis re - so - ná - re fí - bris Mí - ra ge - stó - rum fá - mu - li tu - ó - rum,

Sól - - - ve pol - lú - ti lá - bi - i re - á - tum, Sánc - te Jo - án - nes.

The group type has from two to four notes to most syllables (Ex. 2):

Ex. 2. From Mass XI - Vatican Gradual
(♪= MM c120)

Sán - ctus, Sán - ctus, Sán - ctus Dó - mi - nus Dé - us — Sá - ba - oth.

While in the melismatic type some syllables are sung to a great many notes (Ex. 3):

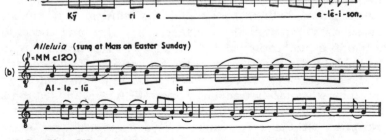

Ex. 3. From Mass III - Vatican Gradual (*Kyrie Deus sempiterne*) (♪= M.M.c.120)

(a) Kӯ - ri - e e - lé - i - son.

Alleluia (sung at Mass on Easter Sunday)
(♪=MM c120)

(b) Al - le - lū - - ia

* See Plate III.

These three types, either separately or mixed, can be applied to any song that has ever been composed, and in general it is true to say that the first type is used when the text is regarded as more important than the music, while the third type shows the opposite point of view; in fact the 'alleluias', with their long flourishes on a single syllable, were really a contradiction of the official teaching that music was only permissible if directly associated with holy words, and were the first examples in Christian chant of the delight in singing for its own sake; the Church Fathers, however, duly pointed out that such singing praised God in a way no words could possibly express! Melismatic chant, however, was not the earliest type, being preceded by syllabic chant, and this provides one of the many examples of the so-called 'wave-theory' of art—the crests representing (in this case) a high degree of conscious elaboration and the troughs simplicity, either natural when the artist is unsure of or experimenting with his medium, or deliberate when he is pruning excessive ornamentation or trying to achieve a balance of expression. But the earliest Christian chants were simple not only because of this artistic wave progression, but also because the service itself had to be both simple and secret, owing to the ever-present threat of persecution which, under the Emperors Nero [37-68], Domitian [reigned 81-96], and Diocletian [reigned 283-305], was particularly severe.

The central act of the service or liturgy was the Eucharist (Greek for 'thanksgiving') which, like the Holy Communion in the Church of England, is based on the Gospel accounts of the Last Supper. At first this was held on the Jewish Sabbath (Saturday), but was later transferred to Sunday morning after 'vigils' or 'watches' had been held during the previous night. Although the Eucharist never lost its central position and importance, local variations of the service sprang up all over Christendom, both in ceremonial and musical performance, and it was not until the fourth century that any successful attempts at unification could be made. The reasons for this are twofold. Firstly, the division of the Roman Empire into eastern and western empires in 314 fostered existing liturgical differences between the eastern and western Churches and led to the formation of five main groups: the Syrian, Byzantine, and Egyptian in the east, where Greek remained the official language, and in the west the Roman (with its offshoot, the

Ambrosian) and Gallican (with its offshoot, the Mozarabic), in which Latin replaced Greek in the liturgy. This split encouraged a greater degree of unity within each group, but it is with the western groups only that we shall be concerned from now on. Secondly, the official toleration of Christianity in 313 by Constantine the Great [reigned 306-337] made public worship possible, and by thus openly exposing local variations stressed the need for greater uniformity. It also made possible the building of churches and encouraged elaboration of the service through the introduction of greater pomp and ceremonial, in the performance of which music took an active part, and the next five hundred years saw both a rapid development in the organization of the liturgy and the creation of most of the melodies we now call Christian chant.

We do not know who composed these melodies, but some of them were certainly adapted from Greek and Jewish sources and possibly from folk-song also. Which had the greater influence, Greek or Jewish music, was a bone of contention until recently, but although Greek was the accepted language in most of the churches during the early years—hence the words 'eucharist' and 'kyrie eleison' ('Lord have mercy' —originally a hymn to the Greek sun-god!), which were retained even after the Roman Church had changed over to Latin—and although the Church Fathers were greatly influenced by Greek thought, it now seems certain that Christian chant owes more to the Jewish synagogue than to the Greek temple. For one thing, the chant melodies as they have come down to us are much more closely allied to Jewish than to Greek music, and as the texts are nearly all taken from the psalms (which are of course Jewish, not Christian) it seems very probable that many of the psalm melodies themselves were adapted from those used in the synagogue. In fact, it has been shown that many such tunes sung to-day by Jewish communities who have been completely isolated since pre-Christian times are strikingly similar to those of the Christian Church. Furthermore, the different ways of singing the psalms were the same in both church and synagogue; these are now called direct, responsorial, and antiphonal psalmody. Direct psalmody means that part or the whole of a psalm is sung in syllabic style without any additional matter, the verses being alternately performed by either a soloist (cantor) and chorus, or else a divided chorus (men *versus* women and children in the early days). In responsorial psalmody§ the entire psalm was originally sung also in syllabic style by the cantor, while the congregation 'responded' after each verse with a single word like 'Alleluia', or 'Amen', or even a short phrase; later the music became more ornate and only a few verses were sung, while the 'response' grew longer and often preceded the psalm as well as being sung between each verse and at the end.

Antiphonal psalmody§ developed from direct psalmody, the distinction lying in the introduction of a short sentence which was sung before the psalm by the entire congregation, this new melody and text being known as the 'antiphon'. At important feasts this was sung both before and after the psalm and in some cases the psalm was omitted, the antiphon thus becoming an independent chant.

So far we have only dealt with chants based on the psalms, which are poetic in feeling but written in what we can call lyrical prose. The pure prose parts of the Bible, however, were recited by the priest in a manner borrowed from the synagogue and called 'cantillation'. This simply means chanting on a monotone or one note, but complete 'monotony' is avoided by the introduction of a few ascending or descending notes ('inflections') at the beginning, middle, or end of the phrase. Another important type of chant was the hymn, also of Jewish origin but influenced to some extent by Greek models. The first Christian hymns were written (in Greek) for the eastern churches, where they became extremely popular, and were eventually introduced into France by St. Hilary of Poitiers [d. *c.* 367]. St. Hilary's hymns were in Latin, and as all but one are lost, his younger contemporary, St. Ambrose, Bishop of Milan [339–97], is usually regarded as the father of western Christian hymnody. The Ambrosian hymn texts differed from those of all other chants in that they were not taken direct from the Bible, but are poetic paraphrases of Biblical passages written in a regular metrical pattern of short-long syllables, like Greek verse (see p. 29). They were meant for congregational singing and in fact were expressly written by St. Ambrose in order to strengthen the morale of his flock, who were being divided by an heretical sect. The music therefore, though it has not survived, must have been simple, with mainly one syllable to a note. This use of the hymn—which can be described as political in the sense that it was used to attack heresies and encourage orthodoxy—was one which lasted right through the early history of the Church; indeed, it was still a powerful weapon in the hands of Luther and others during the Reformation in the sixteenth century. Only four definitely authentic hymns§ by St. Ambrose have come down to us, of which three have been accorded places in the Roman Liturgy, but a great many more were written in imitation, and these are all called Ambrosian hymns, while the other chant melodies composed for and still used in Milan are called Ambrosian or Milanese chant.

As regards the chants of the other two western groups (excluding the Roman), the Gallican§ flourished (as its Latin name, *Gallicus*, implies) in Gaul, but its influence extended as far as Ireland, whose missionaries brought it to Britain in the late fifth century, where it was sung until Roman chant was introduced in 596 by St. Augustine [d. *c.* 604]. In Gaul itself, however, Gallican chant continued in use until it was banned by the Emperor Charlemagne [742-814], who decreed that it should be replaced by Roman chant. Mozarabic chant§ was sung in Spain, where, during the Moorish conquest from the eighth to the eleventh centuries, Christians were called 'Mozarabs' or 'would-be Arabs'. It had a longer life than Gallican chant, being farther from the authority of Rome, and partly as a result of this its liturgical practices often differed considerably (they actually danced during divine service in Toledo!); not until the eleventh century was it officially forbidden. Thus the chants of these three Christian provinces, northern Italy (Milan), Gaul, and Spain were ultimately replaced by that of Rome, and although this city was the obvious centre for western Christianity there is no reason to suppose that its chant, before the sixth century at any rate, was in any way superior to the others—in fact, in some ways Rome was conservative in its attitude to new ideas (a rôle she continued to play in later centuries) and, for example, antiphonal psalmody as well as hymn-singing were only admitted some time after they had become well established in Milan.

The reason why Roman chant eventually supplanted the other western chants was due to the organizing zeal of a number of Popes from Damasus I [366–84]—the patron of St. Jerome [*c.* 340–420], who was the translator of the official Latin Bible, the Vulgate—to Gregory III [d. 741], and to a lesser extent the Emperor Charlemagne. The most ardent organizer, however, was Gregory I [c. 540-604]. Elected Pope in 590, he intensified the efforts to establish a uniform liturgy and chant which would serve the whole of western Christendom, and by his death he had largely succeeded, for the classification and repertoire of Gregorian chant,§ as it was called in honour of him, have remained largely unchanged to this day. At present Gregorian chant consists of nearly 3,000 melodies, the great majority of which were selected and 'edited' under Gregory's authority and which the Church regarded and still regards as the only official ones. But the creative spark takes little account of officialdom, and although Gregory's reforms may have curbed they did not kill the urge of later composers to write new chants or embellish old ones, and while from the fifth century to the eighth may be called the Golden Age of Gregorian chant, there was also a Silver Age from the ninth to the twelfth centuries in which a whole host of new melodies and texts were composed.

This renewed creative impulse in the realm of Christian chant was no isolated event, but simply the result of a general flowering of the human mind and spirit that affected all human activity, and which manifested itself in the four Crusades, ending with the capture of Constantinople in 1204, the struggles for and against authority (Magna Carta, 1215), the final separation between the eastern and western Churches (1054), the Norman Conquest of England (1066), the organizing of communities into towns, the formation of guilds of craftsmen, the intensive study of classical literature and philosophy, the establishing of universities (Paris and Bologna, c. 1140; Oxford, early thirteenth century), the increasing use of the various vernaculars (e.g. Old English, Provençal, etc.), the beginnings of western science (a school of medicine was founded at Salerno, near Naples, c. 1000), the magnificent achievements of the Romanesque and Gothic architectural styles, the birth of European drama, the first blossoming of secular music (troubadours and trouvères), the rise of part-music, and so on. The culmination of this renaissance came in the twelfth and thirteenth centuries, but this takes us out of the realm of Gregorian chant and into the new and rapidly expanding territory of polyphony (Greek, *polu*=many; *phone*=voice), and so discussion of it must wait until Chapter 2.

In all these different branches of human learning and action the Church was the dominating influence; it could make or mar a man's career and help or hinder the discovery of new knowledge; indeed, as a body the Church was an educational institution, research station, and library, and her buildings were places of worship, theatres, and opera houses. This may appear to be a sweeping claim, but we shall try to justify it by beginning at the heart of the Christian religion and then, so to speak, work outwards.

By the middle of the eleventh century the Eucharist had become enshrined in an elaborate ceremonial both spoken and sung which was eventually called the Mass and which has remained unchanged to the present day in the Roman Church. The various items of the Mass are divided up into two categories: the Proper, in which the texts of the items vary according to the day on which the Mass is celebrated; and the Ordinary, in which the texts are invariable, although they are not all sung at every celebration, the Gloria, for example, being omitted during Lent, and the Credo being only sung on Sundays and the more important feast days. The order and names of the sung items can best be shown as follows:

PROPER§	ORDINARY§
Introit	*Kyrie eleison* ('Lord have mercy')§
	Gloria in excelsis Deo ('Glory to God in the highest')
Gradual§	
Tract or Alleluia§	*Credo in unum Deum* ('I believe in one God')
Offertory§	*Sanctus, sanctus, sanctus* ('Holy, holy, holy')
	Agnus Dei ('Lamb of God')
Communion	*Ite missa est* ('Go, the congregation is dismissed')
	or
	Benedicamus Domino ('Let us praise the Lord')

The Proper of the Mass is the oldest part, and all the items are taken from or were originally connected with the psalms;

they thus represent the three types of psalmody mentioned earlier, the Tract being an example of direct psalmody, the Gradual and Alleluia of responsorial psalmody, and the remainder of antiphonal psalmody, except that in the Offertory and Communion the psalm verse has been dispensed with and therefore only the antiphon is sung. (In the Mass for the Dead or Requiem Mass however, the psalm verse is retained in the Offertory and Communion.) The items of the Ordinary were added to the service at various times from the sixth to the eleventh centuries, and except for the Ite missa est, which was nearly always sung to its original chants, have been set to music literally thousands of times from the thirteenth century onwards, for the simple reason that as the words never changed, composers were encouraged to write new settings which would be performed far more often than, say, a setting of an Introit text which was only sung once a year in memory of a particular saint; in fact, when we speak of a Mass by So-and-so we mean a composition based on the five main items of the Ordinary.

In addition to the Mass, short services called the Canonical Hours or Offices took place at various times of the day and night. These developed from the vigils held before the celebration of the Eucharist (see p. 4), and with the addition of other vigils adapted from the eastern churches became a complete and independent system by the fifth century, consisting of Nocturns, later called Matins (the original vigils), at midnight, Lauds at daybreak, Prime at 6 a.m., Terce at 9 a.m., Sext at midday, None between 2 and 3 p.m., Vespers at about 6 p.m., and Compline at 7 p.m., at each of which psalms, antiphons, and hymns were sung. Nowadays the Offices are rarely observed in their entirety except in monastic communities, and it was in such communities that they were first strictly organized and performed.

The founder of the first monastic order in the west was St. Benedict [*c.* 480-*c.* 547], although the seeds of monasticism had been sown in the days of persecution, when groups of Christians sought refuge in wild and lonely parts. This enforced isolation came to be regarded by many as the ideal expression of the Christian life, and even after Constantine's edict of 313 the number of such groups continued to grow all over Christendom. Some system of organization became essential, therefore, and St. Benedict, whose devoutness and self-denial were widely known, after establishing a monastery on Monte Cassino (destroyed, alas, in 1944, but since rebuilt as before), wrote the first monastic Rule in which the details of daily life and worship were laid down. The Benedictine Order eventually spread to the rest of Europe, and during the following seven centuries gave rise to a number of other dedicated brotherhoods, such as the Knights Templar, the Dominicans, and, perhaps most well-known of all, the Franciscans.

At first the monasteries were poor and the monks spent most of the daylight hours in manual labour in order to be self-supporting. Later, however, as the result of rich endowments, the intensive study of both Christian and classical authors was made possible and many monasteries became centres of learning; indeed, they were the only centres before the universities came into being. Here most of the more important earlier manuscripts were copied, annotated, or translated, a fact which disproves the common belief that interest in classical culture was first shown in the Renaissance, for the great secular awakening in the fifteenth century was largely prepared by the study and preservation of the ancient authors in the mediaeval monasteries. But such learning was by no means wholeheartedly approved of by the Church leaders, and such eminent men as St. Gregory, St. Benedict, and St. Augustine, bishop of Hippo [354–430], condemned it strongly; their views however, only affected Italian monasteries and explain the fact that not until the late Middle Ages did Italian scholarship compare favourably with that of other countries, although paradoxically enough the two men who most strongly advocated the study of classical literature and thought were both Romans. The first of these, Cassiodorus [*c.* 477–570], established a monastery on his own estate in the southern tip of Italy, where he insisted on the study of pagan works in order to confound pagan philosophy, and by thus subordinating secular knowledge to Christian theology set an example which most other monasteries outside Italy quickly followed. He also wrote many books, one of which, the *Institutiones*, contains an important section on music—in fact, he was one of the two most influential writers on this subject between the ancient Greek authors and the Middle Ages, the other being the second great Roman scholar, Boethius [*c.* 480–524]. Unlike Cassiodorus, Boethius valued knowledge for its own sake, not merely as a means to an end, and before he was brutally done to death at an early age on a false charge of treason, he had written voluminously on a wide variety of subjects, his most important work for our present purpose being *De Institutione Musice*. This is typical of its author's main purpose—namely, to transmit to Rome the wisdom and culture of ancient Greece, for it summarizes all that was then known of Greek musical theory, and such was its popularity and authority that it became the prime theoretical source for all mediaeval and most Renaissance musicians.

The amount of time, ink, and paper that has been spent in writing about Greek music in the last 1,000 years or so is past computing, but if we are to understand much of the mediaeval attitude to music as well as its practice, some of the more important aspects must be mentioned.

To begin with, music to the Greeks was largely a matter of speculation—that is, they were not so much concerned with melodies and intervals as with their effects on man or their imagined relationship with the heavenly bodies, each of which was supposed to emit a musical note as it revolved round the earth, and while they admitted that we never heard these notes they explained this awkward fact by maintaining that as they were always sounding in our ears we were therefore unconscious of them! This fantastic idea, known as 'the music of the spheres', was first put forward by Pythagoras [sixth century B.C.], who also claimed that man, as part of the Universe, was similarly constructed, the soul, mind, and body all being 'consonant' with each other, and such was his reputation and that of his advocate, Boethius, that not until the thirteenth century were these speculations seriously criticized, although they persisted in popular belief very much longer, as, for example, in Shakespeare's *The Merchant of Venice*, Act V, Scene 1, where Lorenzo informs Jessica that—

> There's not the smallest orb which thou behold'st
> But in his motion like an angel sings,
> Still quiring to the young-eyed cherubins :
> Such harmony is in immortal souls;
> But, whilst this muddy vesture of decay
> Doth grossly close it in, we cannot hear it.

On the other hand, most of the results of Pythagoras's mathematical investigations into music have remained to this day and are the basis of modern acoustics.

The belief that music affected man in different but very definite ways was much more fundamental, and explains why the study of it was such an essential part of Greek education, for each melody, rhythm, and instrument was thought to exert its own special influence on man's character, a belief which, as we have seen, the Church Fathers also subscribed to, and indeed so do we in a sense if we say that a major chord is brighter or happier than a minor one, or that a trumpet is martial, or an oboe mournful. The first great advocate of this doctrine was Plato [*c.* 427-347 B.C.], who associated each of the Greek 'modes', rhythms, and instruments with a definite emotional or moral effect. Thus the Mixolydian 'mode' made men sad, while the Dorian ennobled their minds; the rhythm short, long, long (˘ – –) was suitable for drinking songs, but not heroic ballads; the aulos, a reed instrument of piercing tone, was only fit for feasts and virtuoso performances, while the kithara, an instrument of seven strings (in Plato's time) which were plucked, was regarded as more refined and moderate, and was in fact approved of by nearly all the Church Fathers, especially for music in the home, because King David was supposed to have played it. It is easy to dismiss the idea that music directly affects men's actions, but we would do well to remember, firstly, that Plato, to put it mildly, was no fool in matters concerning the human mind, and, secondly, that Greek music was entirely monophonic (*monos*=one): in other words, although a song might be sung simultaneously at different octaves, or varied slightly on an accompanying instrument, there was only one melodic line, and it is therefore only natural to expect—in fact, it has been proved conclusively—that in such a musical culture slight differences in melodic structure and rhythmic design expressed far more than they do to us, whose ears have become melodically dulled by incessant harmony, and limited harmony at that. Furthermore, the Greeks used intervals smaller than a semitone, as indeed do many Asiatic and other races today, thus increasing the flexibility and expressiveness of the vocal line. All this is important because European music was also entirely monophonic until the rise of part-music in the ninth century, and not until the thirteenth century did part-music begin to oust monophony to any great extent. This fact explains the seemingly incredible (to us) stories and legends concerning the power of music, from

Orpheus to the Pied Piper of Hamelin, and when we read of the kithara player of a certain Danish King in the twelfth century who boasted of his ability to drive his royal master into a raging madness and, on being challenged, succeeded so well that the King slew four men before being overpowered, we may allow for exaggeration, but should not dismiss the story as completely fantastic. After all, when comparatively sophisticated adolescents of the mid-twentieth century are transported into a state of near-ecstasy by the virtuosity of a jazz ensemble or the mellifluous tones of a male crooner it is perfectly credible that in an earlier and far less sophisticated age people were aroused to a high pitch of emotional excitement by music that we would regard as simple or even naïve.

We used the word 'mode' in the preceding paragraph and put it in inverted commas because we have no proof that Greek music was in fact modal, for by mode is usually meant an arrangement of notes within an octave which is regarded as having a distinct and separate existence from all other arrangements. Our major and minor scales for instance represent only four of the many modes possible (major, harmonic minor, ascending and descending melodic minor), another important one being this example of a pentatonic mode (*pente*=five) (Ex. 4)—

Ex.4.

which is the oldest and most widely used, for it was known to the Chinese at least 2,000 years B.C., is found in many folk-songs all over the world, and is almost certainly the basis of a great many Gregorian chants, the gaps (*d'-f'* and *a'-(c")* in our example)* being filled in later in most cases. However, when we talk about the modes in general we mean the twelve commonly recognized in the late fifteenth and sixteenth centuries. These were divided into six main modes called authentic, which range from the lowest and most important note—the final—to the octave above, and six dependent modes

---

* Throughout this book roman letters are used either when the exact position of the notes is immaterial (e.g. 'the perfect fifth C-G') or when they are qualified (e.g. 'middle C', 'violin A'); italicized letters refer to Helmholtz's pitch notation in which *c'*=middle C, *c"* and *c'''*=the octave and double octave above respectively, and *c*, *C* and *C₁*, =the octave, double octave and treble octave below respectively.

called plagal, each being 'part' of an authentic mode and ranging from the fourth below the final (the dominant) to the octave above (hence the prefix *Hypo-*, a Greek word meaning 'below'). Here are the twelve modes, the final of each being shown by a black semibreve (Ex. 5):

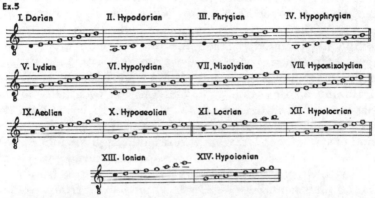

Ex.5
I. Dorian   II. Hypodorian   III. Phrygian   IV. Hypophrygian
V. Lydian   VI. Hypolydian   VII. Mixolydian   VIII. Hypomixolydian
IX. Aeolian   X. Hypoaeolian   XI. Locrian   XII. Hypolocrian
XIII. Ionian   XIV. Hypoionian

Modes XI and XII—Locrian and Hypolocrian—were not used in practice, as the important interval between final and dominant (B-F or F-B) is not a perfect fourth or fifth and was in fact called 'diabolus in musica'—'the devil in music').

Of these twelve modes, only the first eight (the 'ecclesiastical modes') were recognized and applied to Gregorian chant, and 'applied' is the word, for, as practically always happens in the realm of art, theory merely classifies and clarifies previous practice, and there seems little doubt that many chants composed before the eighth century (when the classification of melodies began as a result of Gregorian reform) were later altered in order to agree with the modal system. This system was not, as is sometimes supposed, taken over from the Greeks, nor did it achieve completion until the tenth century; moreover, the usual definition of 'mode' already given only applies to the tenth century and later, for it is almost certain that melodies were originally classified according to their *symbolical* significance—that is, their suitability for definite types of expression, praise or lamentation, for instance—because not only Greek (as we have seen), but Syrian, Jewish, and other chants went through a similar stage. Later the melodies achieved importance in their own right and were classified according to their *musical* significance: in other words, their melodic differences.

This would obviously necessitate melodic analysis, the first stage of which would be the recognition of certain characteristic groups of notes, and the frequency and position of one or more of these groups in any melody would distinguish it from other melodies. Analysis would also extend to the groups of notes themselves, and this would lead to a study of the scale in which the notes forming the groups were the most important, especially the notes which began or ended a melody, for in antiphonal psalmody—much the most popular of the three types of psalmody—the join between the antiphon and the psalm or vice versa was nearly always made easier by ending or beginning on the same note, and this led eventually to the classification of scales or modes according to their end note, i.e. their Final. In their attempts to organize the modes into some kind of system the mediaeval theorists, through the influence of the writings of Boethius and Cassiodorus, turned to Greek theory, their misinterpretation of which proved as fruitful as the misunderstanding of Greek drama by certain Italian gentlemen at the end of the sixteenth century. The confusion that reigned in the mediaeval camp concerning Greek theory is not surprising when we consider that even now we are unable to form a complete picture of how it worked in practice, for the simple reason that not only have a mere handful of melodies been preserved, but the theory itself changed at various times. It is clear to us, however, though it was not so 1,000 years ago, that the differences between Greek and mediaeval theory are greater than their similarities, as the following brief discussion will try to show.

The Greeks had only one important note and one important scale, which, like all their scales, was reckoned from top to bottom, the highest note to us being the lowest to them. This definition of pitch may have resulted from the way the kithara player tilted his instrument, the lowest sounding string (to us) being the highest in position, just as in the Italian method of writing lute music or 'tablature' in the sixteenth century, in which each string is represented by a horizontal line, the symbols representing the notes of the lowest string being placed on the top line, thus giving a clear, visual picture to the player, because the instrument was always held so that the lowest string was uppermost. On the other hand, it may be that the characteristics of highness to us were those of lowness to the

Greeks. The important note was *a*, called 'mese', the middle of a two-octave scale ranging from *a'* down to *A*, the central octave of which—*e'* down to *e*—was the important scale called Dorian, shown within square brackets in Ex. 6. (The black semibreve here and in the following examples is the mese.)

Ex.6.

The Dorian scale, as can be seen, is built up of two tetrachords or four-note groups separated by a tone, each group consisting of the intervals tone, tone, semitone, thus: T, T, S/T/T, T, S.

By at least as early as the fourth century B.C. there were as many as six different Dorian scales, two diatonic (so called because they need no sharps or flats), three chromatic and one enharmonic. In both diatonic scales the semitone is the same size, but whereas in the commoner of the two scales the tones are all equal, in the other they are not. The most common chromatic scale consisted of the notes *e'*, *c♯'*, *c♮'*, *b*, *a*, *f♯*, *f♮*, *e*, while those of the enharmonic were *e'*, *c'*, *c*'*, *b*, *a*, *f*, *f**, *e*, the asterisk standing for a quarter-tone. As regards the diatonic scale, it is worth noting that the order of the intervals is exactly the same as our *ascending* major scale, a fact which has provoked much speculation, particularly as the Greek idea of high and low was the opposite of ours.

All Greek diatonic melodies used the notes of the Dorian scale but they did not all, of course, keep to the octave range *e'-e*. Now if someone composed a song using these notes (Ex. 7)—

Ex.7

it is quite obvious that the relative position of the mese has changed; instead of being in the centre as it is in the Dorian scale, it is now near the top,* and as the mese was the most frequently used note in any composition, this new position to the melodically sensitive ear would give quite a different 'flavour' compared with a song which used the Dorian range.

---

* Unless otherwise indicated, 'high', 'low', 'ascending', 'descending', etc., are used in our sense, not the Greek.

As there are seven different notes in the scale there are clearly seven different positions for the mese, the highest being shown in Ex. 7, while the lowest is obviously this (Ex. 8):

Ex.8
T T S T T S T

If we put the two scales of Ex. 7 and 8 together, and add to Ex. 7 the low *A* (to which was given the magnificent name of Proslambanomenos, or 'the added') we get the complete diatonic scale shown in Ex. 6.

In actual practice, however, all the scales except the Dorian were transposed so that they lay within the Dorian octave *e'-e*, which was not only the average range of a man's voice (and it must be remembered that only men performed in public, whether at feasts, competitions, or in drama), but was also the range of the kithara, the earliest Greek type of which had six strings probably tuned pentatonically, thus (Ex. 9):

Ex.9

In order to obtain the missing notes *c'* and *f* of the Dorian scale the kithara player had to 'stop' the two strings *b* and *e* by pressing on them firmly with his fingers. Now, when the scale in Ex. 7 was transposed up a fourth so that it ranged from *e'-e* the notes sung or played were these (Ex. 10)—

Ex.10
T T T S T T S
Mixolydian *tonos*
(transposed)

the relative position of the mese and the order of intervals being, of course, the same as in Ex. 7, while the notes *c'*, *b♭*, and *f* were stopped. Similarly the transposed scale of Ex. 8 was (Ex. 11)—

Ex.11
T T S T T S T
Hypodorian *tonos*
(transposed)

c' and *f♯* being stopped, and so on with the remaining four scales. All these scales were called 'tonoi' (*tonos*=tightening) because two or more of the kithara's strings had to be stopped and hence tightened in order to produce all the notes. Each scale was given a name. Ex. 10, for instance, was called the Mixolydian tonos, and Ex. 11 the Hypodorian tonos, the order of the tonoi, from highest to lowest, being shown by the position of the mese in each scale, thus: Mixolydian (mese *d'*), Lydian (*c♯'*), Phrygian (*b*), Dorian (*a*), Hypolydian (*g♯*), Hypophrygian (*f♯*), and Hypodorian (*e*). (Notice that the hypotonoi are a fourth lower than the three main tonoi with which they are linked.)

It was these tonoi, these transposed scales all based on the Dorian scale, which represented actual Greek musical practice and which the mediaeval theorists mistakenly thought were modes. Moreover, they misinterpreted Boethius, for when he stated, as we have done, that the Mixolydian is the highest and the Hypodorian the lowest scale, he was referring to the position of the mese in the tonoi, but they thought, firstly, that he was referring to the untransposed scales (Exx. 7 and 8) because, having different octave ranges, they were more closely allied to mediaeval practice than were the tonoi, and, secondly, that he was judging the pitch of a scale by its lowest note (as they did), but that he used the words 'high' and 'low' in the Greek sense. Thus the order of the untransposed scales, if judged by their lowest note, is the exact opposite of the transposed scales—the tonoi, as a comparison of Exx. 7 and 8 with Exx. 10 and 11 will clearly show, the untransposed Mixolydian (Ex. 7) being the lowest and the Hypodorian (Ex. 8) being the highest; but if 'lowest' and 'highest' are interpreted in the Greek sense, then to the Greeks Ex. 7 was the highest and Ex. 8 the lowest scale. Thus when the Greek names were applied to the mediaeval modes round about A.D. 950 the highest mode was called Mixolydian (*g* up to *g'*), and the lowest Hypodorian (*A* up to *a*). Before the tenth century the modes had been called either 'Authentus Protus' ('First Leader'), 'Plaga Proti' ('Part of the First'), and so on with 'Deuterus', 'Tritus', and 'Tetrardus', or else 'Primus Tonus', 'Secundus Tonus', etc., up to 'Octavus Tonus'; this latter method we still use when we write Mode IV or Mode VIII instead of the more clumsy Hypophrygian or Hypomixolydian modes.

It may well be asked that, even allowing for mediaeval confusion concerning Greek theory, why is it that the modes bear so little resemblance to their namesakes in the untransposed Greek scales (compare the octave ranges in Ex. 12 with their equivalents in Ex. 13)? We do not know, but there are two possible answers, one theoretical and one practical. The theoretical explanation depends on the fact that in the untransposed Greek scales the mese is always the same note, *a*, while the octave ranges vary; thus the four main scales can be shown as follows (Ex. 12):

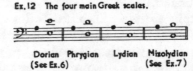

Ex. 12   The four main Greek scales.

Dorian   Phrygian   Lydian   Mixolydian
(See Ex.6)   (See Ex.7)

But to the early theorists it was not the mese but the octave range that was important, and hence they may have argued that in the Dorian octave for instance, as *e* (to the Greeks) was the *lowest* note a fifth *below* the mese the equivalent effect to western ears would be obtained by making *d* the lowest note, for this (*to us*) is a fifth *below* the mese. Similarly, with the others; for example the lowest note (to the Greeks) in the Mixolydian scale was *b*, so that the equivalent to us would be *g*, hence the following, which of course tallies with Ex. 5 (Ex. 13):

Ex 13   The four main mediaeval modes.

Dorian   Phrygian   Lydian   Mixolydian

The second, practical, explanation depends on the fact that Eastern chants in Byzantium and Syria were based, at least as early as the sixth century, on a system of eight 'echoi' (*echos*='sound'). This system probably went through the same stages of evolution as those described on pp. 15-16, but had arrived at a series of scales classified according to their finals, before the west. These scales were divided up into four main echoi and four plagal, thus (the finals are given in brackets), Main echoi: I (*a*, less often *d*); II (*e*, less often *b*); III (*f*, less often *c'*); IV (*g*, less often *d'*); Plagal echoi: I (*d*); II (*e*); III (*f*); IV (*g*). By comparing these finals with those of the mediaeval modes it will be seen that the plagal echoi have the same finals, while the most common finals of the main echoi (except I) are also the same. (The fact that the numbering differs from that of the mediaeval modes is of no consequence.) In view of the great influence of eastern chant on western, it is extremely likely that the echoi played an important part in helping the western theorists to formulate their modal system, particularly as there were four plagal (=hypo) echoi, whereas the Greeks only had three, the Hypomixolydian being absent.

Considering that the only seats of learning before the rise of the universities in the twelfth and later centuries were the monasteries, it is not surprising to find that nearly all the early musical theorists were monks. The most important of these so far as information concerning Gregorian chant is concerned were Alcuin [753-804], Abbot of St. Martin's, Tours, a Yorkshireman and Charlemagne's chief spiritual, intellectual, and political adviser, Aurelian of Réomé [mid-ninth century], Hucbald of St. Amand [c. 840-930], Regino, Abbot of Prüm [d. 915], Odo, Abbot of Cluny [d. 942], Notker Labeo of St. Gall [d. 1022], Guido of Arezzo [c. 995-1050], Berno of Reichenau [d. 1048], and Hermannus Contractus of Reichenau [1013-54]. (Note that the monastery at Arezzo is the only Italian one in this list.)

But the monasteries were not only places of learning; they were also centres of creative activity, and the "host of new melodies and texts" mentioned on p. 8 were composed so far as we know entirely by monks. These additions to the official collection of chants were called 'tropes'§ from a Greek word, which in its Latin form of *tropus* originally meant 'added melody'. The practice of inserting melismatic passages at certain places in some of the chants had been tolerated by the Church long before St. Gregory, but from the middle of the ninth century onwards not only new music was added to some of the official chants, but new words as well.

The most important and popular kind of trope was the 'sequence'§. This came into being towards the end of the ninth century when the long melismas on the final syllable of 'Alleluia' were syllabically underlaid with a new text, partly in order to help the singer to memorize the notes and partly to allay the suspicion with which a number of churchmen had always regarded pure melody (see pp. 2, 4). These additions to

the 'Alleluia' were not tropes in the original sense, because
there was no new music, but the idea spread and was applied to
other chants, notably the Kyrie, Gloria, Sanctus, Agnus Dei,
and Benedicamus Domino chants. Thus, for instance, in Ex. 3,
instead of 'Kyrie eleison', 'Kyrie Deus sempiterne eleison'
('Lord, everlasting God, have mercy') was sung, the added
words being adapted to the melisma on the last syllable of
'Kyrie'. Later the added texts became long poems consisting of
a number of couplets with a 'free' line at the beginning and end
of the complete poem, and while each line of a couplet had an
identical number of accented syllables, this number could vary
from couplet to couplet. These poems were set to new music
and so the sequence became a real trope.

As always in Christian chant, the words of the tropes were
more important than the melodies, and hence the new texts
always had a close connexion with those of the chants to which
they were attached. The music, on the other hand, while
sometimes being a kind of free variation on the chant melody,
was more frequently entirely independent; moreover, it began
to be less elaborate and more clear-cut, and there seems little
doubt that much of it was influenced by music outside the
Church, particularly instrumental music.

The main centres of trope composition were the monasteries
of St. Martial at Limoges, and more especially of St. Gall in
Switzerland, where two monks, Tuotilo§ [d. 915] and Notker
Balbulus§, or the 'Stammerer' [d. 912], wrote many examples,
but did *not* invent the idea. Notker specialized in sequences,
and while we know that he was the author of many sequence
texts we do not know who wrote the music, unless we assume
that he composed the complete chant, a reasonable assumption
and one that probably applies to all the other trope writers,
such as the German Wipo§ [d. *c.* 1048], Hermannus Contrac-
tus§, and the Frenchman Adam of St. Victor§ [d. 1192]. Adam
was particularly important, as he introduced rhyme into his
sequences, and his six-line verses, each with the same number
of accented syllables, are actually hymns; they became so
popular and led to so many imitations that in the succeeding
centuries the sequence threatened to overshadow the official
body of Gregorian chant, a danger that was only averted by
the drastic action of the Church in the sixteenth century, when
the famous Council of Trent banned all tropes and sequences

except four of the latter—namely, Wipo's *Victimae paschali laudes, immolent Christiani*§ ('Let Christians offer praises to the Easter victim'), the late twelfth-century anonymous *Veni Sancte Spiritus*§ ('Come, Holy Spirit'), *Dies Irae*§ ('Day of Wrath'), by Thomas of Celano [d. *c.* 1250], and *Lauda Sion salvatorem* ('Praise, O Zion, thy salvation'), by Thomas Aquinas [*c.* 1225–74]. A fifth sequence, the famous *Stabat Mater*§ by Jacopone da Todi [1230-1306], the great Franciscan poet, was admitted in 1727.

It would seem then that the great creative florescence of the Silver Age came to practically nothing so far as the official liturgy of the Church was concerned, yet in a tenth-century trope prefixed to the Introit for Easter is to be found the origin of a great secular art. This trope was a dramatization in dialogue form of the scene outside Christ's tomb between the Angel and the three Marys and begins:

ANGELUS: Quem quaeritis in sepulcro, O Christicolae?
MULIERES: Jesum Nazarenum crucifixum, O coelicola.

['ANGEL: Whom do ye seek in the tomb, O servants of Christ?']
['WOMEN: Jesus of Nazareth who was crucified, O celestial one.']

The complete trope§ takes about two minutes to perform, yet from this tiny seed stemmed the magnificent tree of European drama, a tree whose roots lie in the soil of Christian ceremonial not, as is sometimes stated, in Greek tragedy, although this too developed from religious rites. To this little scene others were quickly added describing the events both before and after the Resurrection until the whole formed a well-organized series of dramatic episodes. The idea soon spread and other parts of the Old and New Testaments and even the miracles of the saints were similarly treated, particularly the account of the Birth of Christ, the dramatization of which is still performed every Christmas all over the world. These dramatic presentations of Biblical stories are generally called 'liturgical dramas', an unfortunate title, as neither the tropes nor the scenes that developed from them were ever part of the liturgy; moreover, the word 'drama' is usually associated with the spoken word, whereas in actual fact the earliest examples were sung throughout. A more accurate name, and the one we shall use, is 'church operas'§, for this indicates both the place where they were originally performed and the fact that they are partially or

wholly set to music. The texts of these church operas were
taken from liturgical chants, tropes, or else (more rarely)
added specially; the music was that associated with the chant
and trope texts, while for the added passages it was either
adapted from a chant melody, a popular song, or else newly
composed. In the succeeding centuries these operas lost their
symbolic simplicity and became increasingly complex and
realistic, both in construction and in the use of costumes and
scenery. Solos, ensembles, and choruses, processions and
tableaux, and a greater degree of dramatic realism, together
with an increasing use of the vernacular instead of Latin and of
secular song instead of Gregorian chant, resulted in a spectacle
so elaborate and, in the eyes of ecclesiastical authority, so
worldly that in 1207 Pope Innocent III [1198–1216] passed an
act forbidding performance in church, an act that was re-
affirmed by Pope Gregory IX [1227-41]. Thus by the end of
the thirteenth century church operas were taken over by
professional actors, and the stage, originally the nave, later the
steps of the church, now became the market-place. The
subsequent history of the church operas which led to the
Mystery and Miracle Plays of the fifteenth and sixteenth
centuries will be dealt with in Chapter 5, but it is interesting
to note that the musical development of the mediaeval church
operas from short, simple chants in plainsong style to extended
songs of widely differing character was essentially the same as
that which took place in seventeenth-century opera.

But what is plainsong style? This, so far as Gregorian chant
is concerned, is indeed a thorny problem to which there never
will be a complete answer, because the early Christian
composers did not write their melodies down; instead, they
made them up in their heads and then taught them to their
friends; and even when they did eventually put pen to parchment the symbols they used were chiefly an aid to the memory
in showing the shape of a melody, not the exact manner of its
performance; not until the thirteenth century in fact did a
system of notation arise which was based on an exact distinction
between notes of different value. In other words, not one
Gregorian chant of the Golden or Silver Ages was written down
in such a way as to give us a clear indication as to how it
should be sung. Some people would say that this merely
shows the backwardness of the composers, for after all the

Greeks had a notational system, and while admittedly this does not give us the value of the notes either, and only tells us their pitch, one would have thought that by A.D. 1000 somebody would have improved on it and invented a method that was foolproof. Such a view is perfectly justified if we assume that the attitude of the chant composers towards music was the same as our own today; but such an assumption would not only show an unwarrantable conceit and lack of imagination on our part, in that we would be judging according to the traditions in which we have been brought up, but also would take no account of a perfectly obvious explanation—namely, that the freedom in interpretation which a vague notation made possible was preferred for its own sake. Even the later attempts at writing the melodies down did not restrict this freedom; all they did was to define more and more precisely the actual pitch of the notes, not their values; and even those theorists who actually state that the melodies should be sung as a series of long and short notes and imply that the ratio between them is 2 : 1 do not suggest any means whatsoever to show this relationship.

The earliest attempts at writing the music of the chants down crystallized into a definite system just before Gregory's reform. This was no coincidence, but part and parcel of the urgent need for unifying the whole liturgy. This system used various symbols called 'neumes' (Greek, *neuma* = 'sign') which not only aided the memory by showing the general contours of the melody, but also indicated many of the finer shades of vocal expression, the technique of which, though it died out in Europe, is still practised in the East (see Plate II). Thus the neumes provided some sort of safeguard against the deliberate or careless alteration of the official chants, a real danger in a purely oral tradition. This safeguard, however, was plainly not strong enough to ensure that Gregorian chant retained its melodic purity no matter where it was sung, and from the eighth century to the eleventh century various systems of notation were tried, including the use of letters (as the Greeks had done), which, although they gave the exact pitch of a note, did not indicate the up-and-down movement of the music. It was this up-and-down movement that, in the tenth century, began to be shown more clearly by grouping the neumes round an imaginary line, the so-called 'heighted neumes'. The climax came in the eleventh century when Guido of Arezzo introduced a remarkable system which has made him famous ever since. The most important part of this system was that instead of one imaginary line a number of real lines, parallel to and equidistant from each other, were scratched on the parchment by a sharp-pointed instrument, these lines (except the two lowest) representing notes lying a third apart, just as the five-line stave we use today does. On or between these scratched lines Guido drew two red lines representing the notes *f* or *f'*, and two yellow lines representing the notes *c* or *c'*, and on or between any of these lines he placed the neumes, which therefore showed the exact pitch of the notes they represented. His complete system, which extended from the lowest note of the lowest mode (*A*-Hypodorian) to the highest note of the highest mode (*g'*-Mixolydian), was as follows (Ex. 14):

Ex. 14

   (1) *g'* . . . .

   (2) *f* ————————————————————(red)

   (3) *e'* . . . .

   (4) *c'* — — — — — — — — — — — — —(yellow)

   (5) *a* . . . .

   (6) *f'* — — — — — — — — — — — — —(red)

   (7) *d* . . . .

   (8) *c* ————————————————————(yellow)

   (9) *B* . . . .

 (10) *A* . . . .

(. . . . . =scratched line, — — — —=scratched line drawn over in red or yellow ink, —————=red or yellow line between two scratched ones. The bracketed numbers are added for reference.)

Of course, neither Guido nor anybody else used the complete system, but only a part of it when writing down a melody, for very few Gregorian chants exceed the range of an octave, and a great number have a much smaller range (this applies to nearly all early music, primitive songs, folks-songs, etc., and indeed to most voices in part-songs up to the seventeenth century); thus if he were notating the portion of the Kyrie given in Ex. 3, which ranges from *c* to *a*, he would only need to draw the lines (8) to (5). The whole point of the coloured lines was to catch the singer's eye and make the notes F or C stand out, and the reasons why these two particular notes were chosen were (*a*) that they occur more frequently and play a more important part in Gregorian melodies than any other notes, and (*b*) they are the only two notes in the diatonic scale which have a semitone beneath them. This latter reason in itself is remarkable enough, for by stressing the importance of a note because of its sub-semitonal approach Guido was not only ahead of his time, but was also at variance with modal practice, as this progression to an important note (e.g. E to F—the final of the Lydian mode) was the very one that was most avoided.

Guido also advocated the use of clefs—that is, letters placed on or between the scratched lines which provide the 'key' as to what note the line or space represents. We do not know how many or what letters he used, but in theory any of those between A and G were possible; twelfth- and thirteenth-century writers, however, tended to restrict the number to F and C only, representing the notes *f* and *c'*, and as soon as the importance of these two notes was clearly recognized the coloured lines, having served their purpose, fell into disuse; they were a nuisance anyway, as the writer always had to have red and yellow ink ready whenever he copied a chant. Our modern F and C clefs spring directly from the above two, as they represent exactly the same notes; the G clef, however, did not come into use until the late fifteenth century. As regards the number of lines, it was soon realized that three were sufficient to cover the entire range of Gregorian melodies, depending on the positions of the F or C clef, thus (Ex. 15):

Ex. 15

But three lines did not cover the range of an octave, and although this could be overcome by moving the clefs about, it was obviously simpler to have a uniform stave of four lines all drawn in black or occasionally red ink. This in fact is the stave now used for all modern editions of Gregorian chant, and the notation of these editions is the same as that which developed from the neumes in the thirteenth century (see Plate III). This is called Square Notation, for obvious reasons, the two basic note shapes being the 'punctum' ■, and the 'virga' ¶ ; these were the only two notes that were used singly, but more often they were 'bound' together in different ways and with various other note shapes and called 'ligatures' (Latin, *ligare* = 'to bind'). These showed the singer the number of notes to be sung to a syllable (see Ex. 1, the syllables '*la*-xis', 'ges-*to*-rum', '*sol*-ve'), or the phrasing in a long melisma on a single syllable, or the manner of singing (see Ex. 1, where the middle note of the ligature on '*mi*-ra' is to be sung lightly).

So far so good; everyone agrees with the development and meaning of square notation up to this point. But once you breathe the words 'mensural' and 'accentual' the fat's in the fire with a vengeance and the flames that have been burning for nearly a century now show no signs of diminishing. The whole trouble revolves round the answers to two questions. Were the notes of Gregorian chant of equal duration? Were they unaccented? The monks of Solesmes, who represent the official attitude of the Roman Church today, reply 'Yes' to both questions. Another school of thought, usually called the Accentualists, replies 'Yes' to the first question and 'No' to the second. A third school—the Mensuralists—replies 'No' to both questions, at least the majority do. We shall not go into all the pros and cons of these three opposing interpretations, but as this matter is obviously a vital one some attempt at dealing with the problem must be made.

First of all we must define 'accentual' and 'mensural', both of which are used primarily in the discussion of poetry. Accentual means the classification of syllables as either strong or weak, stressed or unstressed, the lengths of the syllables being roughly the same. This is sometimes called 'qualitative' rhythm and is the basis of all early Jewish poetry. An accentual pattern may be either strict, in which an arrangement of strong and weak beats is repeated exactly in two or more lines (which need not necessarily be consecutive), as, for instance, in—

> When he was dead and laid in grave,
> Her heart was struck with sorrow;
> O mother, mother, make my bed,
> For I shall die tomorrow.

where alternate lines follow the patterns . .′. .′. .′. .′ and
. .′. .′. .′. (.=weak syllable; .′=strong syllable), or free, in
which the number of strong syllables is the same in two or
more lines but the number of weak syllables varies (as in
Jewish poetry); for instance, these lines—

> Yes, I ken John Peel and Ruby too,
> Ranter and Ringwood, Bellman and True,
> From a find to a check, from a check to a view,

have this pattern

. .′. .′. .′. .′

.′. . .′. .′. . .′

. . .′. . .′. . .′. . .′

Mensural (or metrical) means the classification of syllables
as either long or short. This is sometimes called 'quantitive'
rhythm and is the basis of all classical Greek and Roman
poetry, the ratio of long to short being theoretically 2 : 1.
A metrical pattern may be strict or free as in accentual
rhythm.

To these two definitions we shall add two facts. Firstly, that
mediaeval Latin poetry from at least the fifth century onwards,
and indeed European poetry in general, is predominantly
accentual. Secondly, that as a result of this there has always been
a tendency in European poetry, no matter what the language,
to stress long syllables, and hence even the comparatively
little metrical verse is also accentual.

To sum up, the text of every single Gregorian chant consists
of accented and unaccented syllables, including the hymns of
St. Ambrose and his imitators and those written under
Byzantine (Greek) influence in the eighth century and later
which are usually regarded as metrical. But the Solesmes
interpretation of the melodies takes no account of this fact, for
they maintain that all notes are both equal in length (except
those at the ends of phrases and at certain other places) and also
of equal stress, but that there is what they call a 'rhythmical
ictus', marked in their editions by a short vertical dash beneath
a note, this ictus being "felt and intimated by tone of voice
rather than expressed by any material emphasis". Whether a
note receives an ictus or not depends entirely on the position of

the note in the melody, unless the chant is syllabic, in which
case the accented syllables of the text have some influence on
its position. In actual performance, however, the ictus has the
effect of an accent—not, of course, a strong one, but no
different from that in a smooth and sensitive rendering of, say,
Drink to me only, hence the melodic accents are frequently at
variance with those of the text. Although this interpretation of
the melodies, together with various other vocal refinements, is
undoubtedly effective and aesthetically satisfying for the bulk
of Gregorian chant, it is most unlikely that it was used for the
majority of hymns and sequences, particularly those intended
for congregational use; furthermore, there is no historical
evidence to prove that it was the only or even the ideal interpretation.

It is this failure to distinguish between the poetic texts of the
hymns and sequences on the one hand and the prose chants on
the other that is the chief weakness of the Solesmes school, for
the former are popular in approach and written in either
strict or free accentual and sometimes metrical patterns, and
the melodies, which are mostly simple and syllabic, would
therefore naturally follow the accentual patterns of the words,
so naturally in fact that the theorists would not bother to
mention it. Another weakness is the refusal to take into account
the statements of several mediaeval theorists that note values
were either long or short, and even though it is most unlikely
that this was a universal practice, and even though we have
proof that in the eleventh century at any rate there was a
strong tendency towards evening the notes out, we do not
know that this evening-out process represented the official
interpretation or was generally accepted. What we do know,
however, is that the way the hymns and sequences were
performed varied in different parts of Europe and depended on
purely local factors. For instance, St. Ambrose, if we assume
that his hymns are metrical, most likely taught his flock to sing
a long note to a long syllable; similarly the abbot of a monastery
who happened to be a great admirer of Greek poetry might
very well have insisted that all hymns and sequences be sung
mensurally; but in both cases there would be an accentual
pattern also. Here, for example, is a rhythmic version of the
hymn *Ut queant laxis* which might well have been sung a
thousand years ago; it should be compared with the Solesmes

version on Plate III or the modern transcription in Ex. 1 (Ex. 16):

Ex.16 Hymn *Ut queant laxis* (metrical accentual version)

Ut qué - ant lá - - xis re - so - ná - - re fi - - bris

Mí - - ra ge - - stó - - rum fá - mu - li tu - ò - - rum, Sól - - ve pol-

- lú - - ti lá - bi - i re - - á - - tum, Sán - - cte Jo - - án - - nes.

('Let Thine example, Holy John, remind us
Ere we can meetly sing thy deeds of wonder,
Hearts must be chastened, and the bonds that bind us
Broken asunder.')*

The prose chants are a more difficult problem, for the texts are not arranged in accentual patterns. Furthermore, they were sung by the choir, which consisted of trained singers, and it is therefore quite possible that the Solesmes manner of performance was practised in certain places during certain centuries. But again we must insist that there is no proof that this particular way of singing Gregorian chant was the official or even the most widely accepted one, and it is just as likely, indeed more likely, that chants in syllabic or group style would stress the notes set to accented syllables and possibly lengthen them also, depending on the factors mentioned on p. 30. The melismas, however, which are sung to only one syllable and were recognized as the most difficult parts of all Gregorian melody, were almost certainly sung in the Solesmes manner. The melisma in fact can be regarded as a miniature vocal fantasia or cadenza, a wordless and therefore rhythmically free outpouring of melody, the structure of which alone determines its rhythmical organization. But it was this very rhythmical freedom that the trope composers of the Silver Age destroyed, for by adding a text, particularly one arranged in accentual patterns as in the sequence, they turned the melismas into hymn tunes. This treatment of melismatic passages was continued by the polyphonic composers of the late twelfth and

* Quoted from *The New Oxford History of Music*, II, p. 291.

thirteenth centuries, as we shall see in Chapter 2, but instead of
adding words they gave the notes exact values and eventually
arranged them in regular groups.

To end this discussion on the performance of Gregorian
chant, an observation must be made that is all too often forgotten—namely, that from the early Church Fathers to the
Council of Trent in the sixteenth century it was the words, not
the way the melodies were sung, that mattered most. It was
the singing of biblical texts that was originally the main
justification for including music in the Christian service, an
attitude which virtually excluded instrumental music during the
early centuries; it was the words of the tropes and sequences
that the authorities objected to and ultimately banned (all but
five), whether they were set to old or new music; it was because
the words were largely unintelligible in the complex polyphonic
settings of the mid-sixteenth century that caused the Council of
Trent to advocate a simpler style and less elaborate presentation. Furthermore, the notation, as we have seen, was not
concerned with values, only with pitch, and the various
additional signs added to or above the neumes in some manuscripts from the ninth to the eleventh centuries that indicate
such things as 'slower', 'quicker', 'longer', etc., not only stress
this point, but provide interesting sidelights on purely local
practices. Provided therefore that the melodies were those
officially sanctioned, the Church did not concern itself
unduly with the manner of performance, whether vocal or
instrumental.

The use of instruments in accompanying Gregorian chant is
another problem that will never be solved, for although the
majority of the early Church Fathers objected strongly to
instrumental participation in the service because of the close
associations with pagan entertainments, there is no doubt that
the organ at any rate was used in later centuries, particularly
during the Silver Age of Gregorian chant. Other instruments,
such as the kithara, trumpet, drum, etc., are also mentioned,
but in most cases it is impossible to tell whether the writer is
referring to actual performance in church or is being merely
symbolic (see p. 2). We shall therefore leave detailed
discussion of them until the next chapter, with the exception of
the organ, the instrument that has always been most closely
associated with Christian worship.

The first organ was invented and built by a Greek named Ktesibios [third century B.C.], who lived in Alexandria, a city then famous for its engineering skill, and rightly so if Ktesibios's organ is a typical example. This instrument consisted of an enclosed tank partially filled with water and divided into three interconnecting chambers. At the back of the organ was a handle which pumped air into the two side chambers, and so forced water from these into the central chamber, thus increasing the air pressure in the wind chest above. The pipes were placed above the wind chest and arranged in two or three ranks, one behind the other, so that each note had two or three pipes; in the latter case the pipes in the front rank were tuned two octaves above those in the back rank and those in the middle rank one octave above those in the back. Air was admitted to or cut off from the pipes by both sliders and valves. The sliders were strips of metal which moved horizontally beneath the mouths of the pipes; each represented a different note (not counting octave duplications) and therefore had two or three holes to correspond to the pipes. When the organist wanted to sound a note he pressed down a 'key' which pushed a slider along so that the holes came exactly below the mouths of the pipes and so made it possible for air to enter from the wind chest. When the key was released, a spring returned it and the slider back to their original positions. But even with a key pressed down the pipes would not speak unless one or more of the valves were open. These were placed at one side of the organ and each affected a complete rank of pipes, just as a modern organ-stop does; thus the player could vary both the pitch of a note by using only one rank at a time, and also its colour (timbre) by sounding the fundamental alone (back rank), or its octave (middle rank), or, if there were three ranks, its double octave (front rank), or any combination of these. This kind of organ was called the 'hydraulis' (Greek, *hudro* = 'water'; *aulos* = 'pipe'), and its loud, strident tone endeared it to the Romans, who increased its size and power and used it at their feasts, spectacles, and other orgies. This almost certainly explains why it was virtually never used in the western churches, for the organs mentioned from the ninth century onwards were all 'pneumatic' (Greek, *pneuma* = 'breath'), in which the wind to the pipes was transmitted straight from the bellows and hence lacked the constant wind pressure which the use of water gave to the hydraulis. They also lacked the key system of the hydraulis, for the sliders had to be pushed in and pulled out by direct manual labour, which in the larger organs was no mean task. Keys in fact were not rediscovered until the thirteenth century, an extraordinary example of how knowledge can disappear for long periods and one that is only surpassed by the gap between Archimedes of 'Eureka' fame [third century B.C.] and Copernicus in the sixteenth century, both of whom believed that the earth revolved round the sun. Some of these pneumatic organs must have been fearsome instruments, and a description of one built at Winchester about 950 states that it had 400 pipes, forty sliders (ten pipes to a slider), and twenty-six bellows which needed seventy men to operate them. The sliders were in two sets of twenty, each set having exactly the same notes and each requiring a player. There were no valves, so that if both organists pulled out a slider twenty pipes sounded simultaneously, and the resulting noise must have been indescribably ear-shattering!

There seems little doubt that instruments were at first used more frequently in churches outside Italy, particularly Germany and England, for, to adapt an old saying, 'While Rome's far away, the churchmen can play'. This, as we have seen, was true of Mozarabic chant and it was also true of British Gregorian chant, the chief collection of which was that originally practised at Salisbury or 'Sarum', to give it its Latinized form, and now known as the Sarum Use; later it spread to most parts of Britain until it was banned in 1547. The deviations of Sarum Use from the official Gregorian repertoire must have been deliberate to some extent, for a number of the chants differ considerably from those in the latter collection; and although such variations, as we have seen, were natural enough before the improved notation of the eleventh century there could have been no doubt after this as to what Rome considered to be the authentic melodies.

The most reliable way of transmitting these melodies before the advent of square notation was through trained singers who accompanied missions to various parts of Europe, and who either taught the newly converted how and what to sing or else refreshed the erring memories of those choirs already established.

These singers learned the repertoire in choir schools, the first of which was probably founded during the latter part of the fourth century. Later Gregory, as a natural outcome of his organizing bent, set aside two buildings in Rome, one housing the trained singers and clergy, the other being a school where orphans were taught to memorize the entire collection of Gregorian chant. This, of course, was not as large in Gregory's day as it is now, and it is a well-known fact that illiterates— which the orphans almost certainly were—have extremely good memories; even so, it was a long and arduous training, the same chant being sung over and over again until it was indeed unforgettable. Neither the use of neumes nor, later on, of lines and clefs helped much in learning a new song, because even with clefs the exact intervals represented by the lines and spaces vary according to the clef and to its position, and the labour of learning what these intervals were for all possible clefs and their positions and then reading the intervals at speed obviously demanded much more brainwork than in merely memorizing. The ordinary singer of today only has to learn the F and G clefs, whose positions on the stave never vary, if he or she wants to sing from staff notation, but many children find even this difficult enough to begin with. Admittedly the mediaeval singing masters used hand signs to indicate when a melody went up or down and by roughly how much, but these signs could not show the difference, for example, between a leap of a major or a minor third; in fact, they were only of any real use as a means of helping the memory over something imperfectly learned or partially forgotten, not as a means of teaching something completely new.

Once again, however, that remarkable monk, Guido of Arezzo, had a brilliant idea. He devised a method of teaching that enabled young boys, in his own words, "to sing an unknown melody before the third day, which by other methods would not have been possible in many weeks".* In modern terms, his method was this. He took the then well-known hymn to St. John, *Ut queant laxis* (see Ex. 1), the first six phrases of which begin on successive degrees of the scale, C, D, E, F, G, and A, and made his pupils memorize it so thoroughly that they could sing both the initial note of each phrase at will, and also the intervals between any of these notes. These six notes were later

* Quoted from O. Strunk, ibid., p. 124.

called the 'hexachord' (Greek, *hex* = 'six'; *chorde* = 'tone'), and in order to cover the entire range of Gregorian chant Guido expanded them into a series of six overlapping hexachords, each hexachord being exactly similar in construction—the first six notes of our major scale in fact. Now, it is obvious that there are only two major scales that need no accidentals for their first six notes—namely, those beginning on C and G— but if we use a B♭ (which occurred in Gregorian chant long before Guido) then we get a third hexachord starting on F. Guido's complete system was built up from these three notes, each of which was the basis of two hexachords, thus (Ex. 17):

Ex. 17

The syllables *ut, re, mi*, etc., are those to which the initial notes of the six phrases in the hymn to St. John are set, and were used to help the pupil to distinguish between the different degrees of the scale. The most important interval in any hexachord is the semitone, or *mi-fa* progression (a fact which underlines what we said on p. 27), and even if the range of a melody necessitated changing from one hexachord to the one above or below, thi, progression was always sung in the same hexachord.

In order to see how the method actually worked we will imagine that we have to learn the part of the Kyrie given in Ex. 3, and that our only musical ability is that we can sing accurately any interval between any two notes in any hexachord. If we had to learn this melody by ear, then the first thing that happens is that our teacher sings it through for us. From this we should be able to find out how far away the last note is from the nearest semitone, which in this case is easy, because the third note from the end is a semitone above the last note. This is our clue, for it means that the final note can only be *mi*, the third note from the end being, of course, *fa*. We can now sing the entire melody, for although we may not be able to remember all the ups and downs, the teacher's hand-signs will tell us where they come and approximately how big the intervals are, and as all the notes will have the same relation to

the last note as the hexachord syllables have to *mi* we shall sing
these intervals not approximately, but exactly in tune. If we
have to read the melody from notation, we first of all study the
clef and discover what notes the lines and spaces represent,
then look for the nearest semitone to the last note, E-F in this
case, which of course means that E is *mi*. We can now sing the
melody much more easily than in the first way because we can
actually see when the melody goes up or down, instead of
having to rely on the much vaguer gestures of our teacher;
and although we do not know the exact intervals by looking at
the notation (we are not musically intelligent enough for that!),
we do know which note is *mi* and this gives us complete
accuracy. Admittedly this second way involves knowing what
the clefs mean, but this knowledge is only applied to the
purely mechanical task of finding at our leisure what hexachord
syllable should be given to the last note of the melody and
not to the much more difficult one of remembering at speed
exactly what the intervals are between the different lines and
spaces while we are actually singing.

Guido's method of teaching spread all over Europe and is
indeed the source of our present-day tonic sol-fa system, the
only differences being the substitution of *doh* for *ut*, the addition
of *te* for the seventh degree of the scale and of various other
syllables for chromatic notes, and, most important of all, the
linking of *doh* with the chief note of a scale, the tonic or key-
note, whereas in the original system *ut* only represented the
chief note in the Lydian and Mixolydian modes (F and G
respectively). An offshoot of Guido's method was invented
some years after his death in which each finger joint and tip of
the hand represents a note, and by pointing to the appropriate
part of his hand a teacher could impart a new melody much
more quickly than by repeatedly singing it over. Later still a
seventh hexachord beginning on *g'* was added to the original
six, thus making the total range *G-e''*.

Guido claimed that he could teach boys a new song in three
days, but if we assume that there were 1,000 different Gregorian
melodies in his day then it looks as though the poor boys would
be hard at it for about eight years! Actually it was not as bad as
this, because most of the melodies are largely built up from a
common pool of note groups (see p. 16), and once these were
learnt they would be easily recognizable in a new chant. Thus

chant composition was more a question of selecting a number of stock melodic fragments and arranging these in a new order rather than the invention of a completely original tune; in fact, the whole idea of originality in art is relatively modern and was quite foreign not only to the composers of Christian chant, but also to those of much later centuries, even including the eighteenth. This is a very important point to remember when studying or listening to early music, particularly mediaeval music, for to the mediaeval composer it was the way a composition was constructed that mattered most, not the parts of which it was constructed, just as in painting new colours were of minor importance compared to the way they were arranged on a manuscript, wall, or canvas. It was no accident, therefore, that of the three main visual arts—painting, sculpture, and architecture—it was architecture, the art in which structure is most important and clearly shown, that dominated the mediaeval scene. Moreover, the attitude towards music which the Church Fathers held—namely, that it was right and proper provided that it served devout ends and did not have a too obviously pagan association—was also applied to the erection of the first churches, known as basilicas, for it did not matter if the stones and pillars were taken from a Roman temple destroyed by the Huns, provided that actual statues of pagan gods were not used. Thus the interior of a completed church was often a most curious mixture of varied marbles and stones, pillars of unequal length and different designs, and (where the looters had been lucky) all kinds of gold and silver ornaments and mosaics (i.e. designs or pictures composed of small pieces of coloured glass or stone). But although the interiors of the basilicas varied greatly, their general plan was both more uniform and utilitarian, being T-shaped with a wooden roof and a central nave with supporting aisles on either side. In this contrast between having the same end in view (satisfying liturgical needs) and providing variety in the means to that end (the elaboration of basic material) the basilicas were like Christian chant, and it was again no coincidence that the next style of architecture—Romanesque—arose at the same time as the liturgical and chant reforms by Gregory and others, for Romanesque architecture parallels Gregorian chant in that it was originally simple and became international. Like Gregorian chant, too, Romanesque style became more ornamental during

the Silver Age, but even so late an example as Durham
Cathedral (eleventh to twelfth centuries) is simple (but what
magnificent simplicity!) compared, say, to the thirteenth-
century Gothic Cathedral at Lincoln (Plates IV and V).
Gothic art, however, is more closely linked with polyphony
than with Gregorian chant, the creation of which lost both its
spontaneity and its purity of style after the twelfth century, and
although we may disagree with the official Solesmes manner of
singing many of the melodies, we owe them an enormous debt
for their researches into and restoration of the original music, a
labour that has revealed Gregorian chant as undoubtedly the
finest single collection of melody ever created. Wonderfully
supple and perfectly balanced, these melodies are not only
historically important in that they provided the basis for nearly
all liturgical music up to the seventeenth century, but are also as
artistically and spiritually satisfying as most later compositions
written for the Church.

PERFORMANCE

(See also pp. 6, 29-32.)

Ex. 1. Full choir. (N.B. It is most probable that the full choir
sang only the simple chants such as psalms, 'Credo's,
hymns, and sequences, the less simple ones being
performed by a 'select choir' of not more than six
singers.)

Ex. 2. The first 'Sanctus' is sung by a solo voice, the rest by
the 'select choir'.

Ex. 3(a). The 'Kyrie', excluding the melisma on the final
syllable, is sung by a solo voice, the melisma and
'eleison' being sung by the 'select choir'.

Ex. 3(b). The first phrase is sung by a solo voice, which is repeated, plus the long melisma on the last syllable, by
the 'select choir'.

2

MUSIC IN THE EARLY CHURCH:
THE BEGINNINGS OF PART-MUSIC

THE desire of the composers of the Silver Age to enrich Gregorian chant was not restricted only to the addition of words to old melodies or to the creation of new ones, but also found an outlet in the simultaneous combination of both old and new melodies, although in the earliest examples, which come from an anonymous treatise called *Musica enchiriadis*§ or *Musical Handbook* (*c.* 850), the new melodies mostly duplicate the old ones at the intervals of a fourth, fifth, or octave, or all three combined, above or below the main melody. This kind of part-music, the oldest that has come down to us, was called 'organum', but we do not know why for certain. The Latin word meant any kind of instrument, not only the organ, and it is possible therefore that this particular type of composition was originally instrumental. Some people believe that it sprang from the organ itself which, as we saw in Chapter 1, was introduced into Europe during the ninth century, for if two players on the same massive keyboard happened through design or accident to play a melody a fourth or fifth apart the effect may have been so attractive as to promote immediate vocal imitation. There is evidence, however, which makes it unlikely that the organ was the source of organum (see p. 41), and in any case the examples in *Musica enchiriadis* are all vocal, the main melody, which is either an original chant or else a sequence, being called the 'vox principalis', and the added melody the 'vox organalis'. There are two main kinds of organum, parallel and free. Parallel organum§ is either simple, with one added part moving in parallel fourths or fifths below the main melody, or two added parts moving in parallel octaves above and below the main melody, or composite, with one, two, or three parts doubling at the octave above and/or below the first of the simple types. In free organum§ the vox organalis moves in parallel, oblique, or contrary motion to the vox principalis. Here is an example taken from a commentary on the *Musical*

Handbook called *Scholia enchiriadis*,§ in which the first section (up to 'Domino') is in simple parallel organum at the fourth, while the second section is in free organum, the brackets marked 'a' showing oblique motion, and those marked 'b' contrary motion in the vox organalis (Ex. 18*):

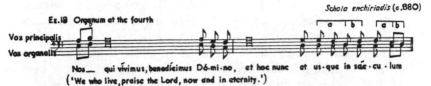

Scholia enchiriadis (c.880)

Ex.18 Organum at the fourth

Vox principalis
Vox organalis

Nos— qui vívimus, benedícimus Dó·mi·no, et hoc nunc et us·que in sáe·cu·lum
('We who live, praise the Lord, now and in eternity.')

Now, it is a well-known and obvious fact that it is impossible to classify anything that is not already fairly stable and well developed, whether it be an animal species or an artistic trend, and the fact that the authors of the two treatises mentioned could present organum in an ordered and rational manner means that it had been practised for some considerable time before. This rules out the organ theory and makes it likely that organum arose outside the Church, because if it did not then we should certainly have much more and clearer written evidence of its use in the service long before the middle of the ninth century. In fact, one theorist definitely refers to its 'popular' nature, and another implies that it was already quite familiar by about 900. As it is, however, the only distinct reference to part-song before *Musica enchiriadis* is by the Englishman, Bishop Aldhelm [640-709], but his account is too vague to be of much value.

Even if we assume that organum was popular in origin, we still do not know how it arose, although it is usually thought that parallel organum was practised first and that free organum was a later and more advanced development. However, it is much more likely that the two types grew more or less simultaneously from two different ways of performing a melody, both of which were known to the Greeks. In the first way, a melody was occasionally played or sung in octaves ('magadizing'), and it is not difficult to see how, in order to bring the melody within the comfortable range of male and female voices, consecutive octaves later became consecutive fourths or fifths, for the normal ranges of a bass, tenor, alto, and soprano are roughly a fourth or fifth apart. This kind of singing

* From O. Strunk, ibid., p. 130.

was classified as parallel organum by the mediaeval theorists. In the second way, a melody was sometimes freely and spontaneously varied, but complete chaos was avoided by everyone singing the same note at the beginnings and endings of phrases. This kind of singing was called 'heterophony' by the Greeks (*heteros* = 'other'), and from it free organum almost certainly developed, for this type of organum is essentially governed by beginning and ending on a unison, while the middle portion of the melody moves in consecutive fourths or fifths—according to the theorists at any rate. Actually it is very doubtful whether in fact organum was sung in as strict a succession of fourths or fifths as the mediaeval theorists make out, not only because it is quite likely that they simplified what was in practice much more varied in order to classify more easily, but also because the few examples that exist outside their treatises and which can be transcribed, while admittedly not earlier than the eleventh century, show a divergence from accepted theory. For instance, in the two-part organa contained in a manuscript fragment from Chartres,§ roughly 32 per cent. of the intervals are octaves or unisons, 20 per cent. are fourths, only 6 per cent. are fifths, and 28 per cent. *are thirds*; moreover, there are seven groups of three consecutive thirds.* Even so, the fourth, fifth, and octave were originally the only intervals which mediaeval ears accepted as fully concordant, other intervals being tolerated only if used as an approach to or as a contrast with these three, which even today textbooks call the 'perfect' concords, while thirds and sixths are classified as 'imperfect'.

These 'perfect' concords were the main ones used in all music up to the beginning of the fifteenth century, except that from *c.* 1150 the fourth, as a fundamental interval, was increasingly avoided, both in two-part compositions and as the lowest interval in three-part writing, until from *c.* 1225 on it was virtually restricted to the upper parts.

Why did the mediaeval musician regard these concords as more satisfactory than the 'imperfect' ones? The answer lies not in the primitiveness of the mediaeval ear, as is sometimes stated or implied, but to the exact opposite—the greater sensitivity to sound compared with our ears today. Before we justify this statement we must make a distinction between

* See *The New Oxford History of Music*, II, p. 284.

concord and discord on the one hand and consonance and dissonance on the other. The former are *musical* definitions of sound; the latter are *physiological*—that is, they depend on the pleasant or unpleasant effect of a sound on the ear regardless of musical context or fashion. Now, the mediaeval ear was no different from our own, for we know that like us they found the octave the most perfect consonance and the minor second the harshest dissonance. They also found, like us, that the fifth was the next most consonant sound, and then the fourth, and that the major second was less dissonant than the minor second. The difference between us lies in our respective attitudes towards thirds and sixths. We find them more satisfying than the octave, fifth, or fourth because they sound richer; but richness of sound (sonority) depends entirely on the amount of dissonance present, and we can prove scientifically that thirds and sixths are in fact more dissonant than the 'perfect' consonances. In other words, we accept as the most satisfying concords intervals which to mediaeval ears were too rich—i.e. too relatively dissonant—to be classed as wholly concordant, just as in some modern music today we judge as relatively concordant certain dissonant passages which would have been excruciatingly discordant to our grandfathers. The history of music, in fact, is also the history of aural development (which is not the same thing as aural progress), for the ear has constantly, though not continuously, accepted as concordant or relatively concordant sounds that in earlier times were ranked as discords. Thus the third and sixth, too rich for everyday mediaeval fare, became the staple diet from the Renaissance on, and the chord of the 'added sixth' (e.g. C–E–G–A), treated with great circumspection in the Renaissance, but with more freedom in the eighteenth and nineteenth centuries, provides a perfectly satisfactory and very popular final chord for many jazz pieces today. The important thing to remember is the musical tradition at any given moment in history; the earliest composers were brought up to music that was sung or played almost entirely in unison or in octaves, and hence they heard and judged any other interval far more acutely than we would, therefore the greater dissonance of the fifth and fourth compared to the octave, though slight to us, provided an increased richness of sound that was as satisfying to their ears as thirds and sixths are to our own. The fact that some compositions contain more thirds than was usual (as in the Chartres organa) is simply an indication of something we would have expected anyway—namely, that there was then as there have been ever since certain composers who were more experimental than their fellows, but this should not be allowed to distort the general picture.

The preponderance of fourths, fifths, and octaves in mediaeval part-music is justified by contemporary theorists on the grounds that Pythagoras had ·'proved' that these intervals were consonant because they have simple ratios, e.g. $\frac{4}{3}$, $\frac{3}{2}$, and $\frac{2}{1}$ respectively. By 'simple' Pythagoras meant a ratio in which the denominator divides into the numerator either exactly ($\frac{2}{1}$) or else once or more with one part over ($\frac{4}{3}$, $\frac{3}{2}$), and by 'ratio' he meant, as we do today, the comparative speed of vibrations of two notes; thus $\frac{2}{1}$ means that the higher note of an octave vibrates twice as fast as the lower, $\frac{3}{2}$ means that the higher note of a fifth vibrates $1\frac{1}{2}$ times as fast as the lower, and so on. By taking four fifths, e.g. c–g–d'–a'–e'' ($\frac{3}{2} \cdot \frac{3}{2} \cdot \frac{3}{2} \cdot \frac{3}{2} = \frac{81}{16}$), and subtracting two octaves, c–c'' ($\frac{4}{1}$), Pythagoras arrived at a major third, c''–e'', with the ratio $\frac{81}{16} \cdot \frac{1}{4} = \frac{81}{64}$, a horrible fraction and by no means simple. The same applied to the minor third ratio, and therefore to their complements, the minor and major sixths, and so he stated that these are all dissonances. But he also found that the ratio of a second or whole tone is $\frac{9}{8}$, and that therefore this was also a consonant interval theoretically, whereas an eleventh (fourth plus octave) was theoretically a dissonance because its ratio is $\frac{8}{3}$ ($\frac{4}{3} \cdot \frac{2}{1}$)! But Pythagoras was primarily a mathematician who let his passion for numbers and neat calculations overrule his ear, with the result that his musical scale differs in several respects from that which exists naturally, as we shall see when we deal with scales and intervals in Part II.

As regards the two main ways of singing in parts—namely, the exact repetition of a melody at different pitches to suit different voices (parallel organum) and the simultaneous ornamentation of a melody (free organum)—it was, as we should expect, the latter which caught on, for the desire to ornament or vary given material is and always has been a much more powerful one than that which merely aims at duplication.

The most arresting thing about free organum is the use of

contrary motion, and although neither the ninth-century authors of *Musica enchiriadis* and *Scholia enchiriadis* nor Guido of Arezzo§ in the eleventh century specially stress this, Guido at any rate seems to prefer free to parallel organum, and some of the examples he gives not only employ contrary motion, but crossing of parts as well; furthermore, the collection of over 150 two-part organa from Winchester which are contemporary with Guido contain a number of passages in contrary motion, particularly at cadences. Thus one of the two essential characteristics of polyphony—melodic independence—had entered music, and round about 1100 the great theorist who is usually called John Cotton and described as an Englishman, but who was almost certainly a monk at the Flemish monastery of Afflighem, near Liége, specifically recommended contrary motion and the crossing of parts. In so doing he advocated using all the concords, not just parallel fourths or fifths, as the theorists before him had done, but a mixture of unisons, fourths, fifths, and octaves, all the other intervals being regarded as discordant as before, and therefore only to be used as approaches to concords.

The second of the two essential characteristics of polyphony—rhythmic independence—can also be found in some of Guido's examples, where several notes of the chant melody or vox principalis are set against one note of the vox organalis, and although later practice reversed this procedure by setting several notes of the organalis to one of the principalis, the seed had been sown, and again we find John of Afflighem strongly recommending what had previously only been allowed. But rhythmic independence inevitably demanded some kind of measuring system if the parts were to be sung or played as the composer wished. So long as the parts moved at the same time there was no difficulty in keeping together, but when, as happened at the beginning of the twelfth century, the chant melody was performed in long-drawn-out notes above which was added a florid organalis part, the problem of ensemble became serious. Admittedly the music was written in score with one part above the other, and the vertical alignment of the notes would give an approximate indication as to how many organalis notes were to be sung to one of the principalis, but the exact point at which the principalis changed from one 'held' note to the next (hence the later name, 'tenor', from the Latin *tenere* =

'to hold') can only have been decided by the choirmaster, assuming, of course, there was an 'exact point', because while accurate ensemble matters to us it may not have mattered to the early composers of organa, provided that certain 'rules' were observed, such as beginning and ending a phrase on a concord.

So far as we know, the earliest school of composers who wrote organa in which the two parts are rhythmically independent came from the monastery of St. Martial§ at Limoges during the first half of the twelfth century. This style of writing is usually called 'sustained-tone' from the way in which the notes of the chant were performed, but, as in the case of Gregorian chant, we do not know the exact values of these held notes nor those of the florid upper part, although it is probable that when the latter is set to words more or less syllabically it follows the rhythmic pattern of the text, and when it is melismatic with many notes to a syllable or else with no words at all it is performed freely in the Solesmes manner. Here is part of a St. Martial organum based on the *Benedicamus Domino* chant melody ordained to be sung at First Vespers on Solemn Feasts, a very popular melody with twelfth- and thirteenth-century composers. (The melody is given complete in Ex. 22) (Ex. 19*):

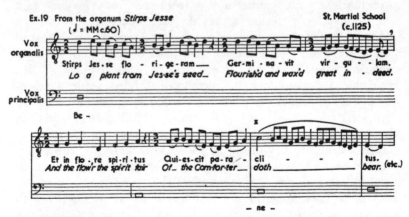

Ex.19 From the organum *Stirps Jesse*   St. Martial School (c.1125)

x   In free rhythm

But not all St. Martial organa are written like this; in fact, Ex. 19 is rather exceptional in that both voices sing different

* Adapted from H. Gleason, *Examples of Music before 1400*, p. 33.

words, for usually the upper part has the same words as the lower, chant-bearing part, although this lower part was often performed by an instrument or by voice and instrument together. Moreover, there was another kind of organum in which the parts move together in note-against-note style. If the parts are melismatic, then the notes are presumably of roughly equal value, but if syllabic, then the notes probably follow the verbal rhythm, as in Ex. 20,* which is transcribed in triple time, although it sounds just as well in duple time:

Ex.20 Organum *Mira Lege*
(♩=MM c.60)

St.Martial School
(c.1125)

Mi - ra le - ge   mi - ro mo - do   De - us for - mat   ho - mi - nem.
By   a law and   in   a   fa - shion   won - der - ful doth   God make men.

Mi - re ma - gis   hunc re - for - mat   vi - de mi - rum   or - di - nem.
But be - hold more   won - der - ful   this   won - drous plan he   forms a - gain.

Re - for - man - dis
Those who share this

mi - rus or - do   In   hoc so - nat   de - ca - cor -
re - for - ma - tion   Sound   the lyre   In   ex - ul - ta -

do.
tion.

* Adapted from H. Gleason, ibid., p. 31.

Four things should be noted about this very attractive little piece. Firstly, the predominance of contrary motion and the frequent crossing of parts. Secondly, the number of thirds and sixths that occur between the parts. Thirdly, the fact that the lower voice, the vox principalis, is not a borrowed chant, but a newly-composed melody—an important feature, as it led eventually to a quite distinct type of composition known as 'conductus' (see Chapter 4, p. 97). Fourthly, that each part has roughly the same number of notes. This note-against-note style was usually called 'discantus' by contemporary theorists, and later (c. 1300) the term 'punctus contra punctum' was applied to it, from which we get the word 'counterpoint'. Strictly speaking, counterpoint means the combination of two or more melodies which are more or less rhythmically identical, as in Ex. 20, but unfortunately it is often used as an alternative word for 'polyphony'. However, we shall use the word 'counterpoint' throughout this book to mean the combination of melodies that are only independent as regards their shape— that is, their movement up and down—while the word 'polyphony' will mean the combination of melodies that are rhythmically independent as well. Thus by the middle of the twelfth century there were two kinds of part-music or 'organum generale'—namely, the polyphonic 'organum speciale' (Ex. 19) and the contrapuntal 'discantus' (Ex. 20). (Whenever we use the word 'organum' in future we shall mean 'organum speciale'.)

The only other important school of composers which flourished in the first half of the twelfth century was that at the monastery of Santiago (St. James) de Compostela§ in the north-west corner of Spain, the only part of the country not conquered by the Moors. The organa of this school are clearly influenced by the earlier St. Martial compositions, but it can lay claim to the earliest composition in three distinct parts that we know. The existence of this school, however, does not alter the fact that from c. 1100 to c. 1400 France was the undoubted leader in European music, for during this period the French genius contributed more to the development and enrichment of music and exerted a greater influence than any other country, an achievement she has never repeated.

But this musical domination was no isolated feature; it was paralleled by the growing importance of France in European affairs, by the achievements of her scholars and craftsmen, and by the fact that Paris, during the twelfth and thirteenth centuries at any rate, was the intellectual centre of the world. Capital of France since the end of the tenth century, Paris had rapidly increased in size, importance, and beauty during the succeeding 300 years. Famous for her university, her teachers, and her architecture, it is small wonder that music too shared in her greatness, and the school of composers who made her musically pre-eminent among European capitals flourished at the same time as the erection of her most famous building, Notre Dame (1163-1257).

By the middle of the twelfth century the florid polyphonic organa of the St. Martial composers had made the introduction of a system in which notes had more definite values a crying necessity, and it is the great distinction of the Notre Dame School,§ as it is usually called, that it formulated the principles of such a system and put them into practice. This system is now known as 'modal rhythm' and consists of six metrical and accentual patterns which are almost certainly derived from the Greek poetic metres, for, as we have seen in Chapter 1 (p. 11), classical culture was assiduously studied in many monasteries, and this eventually led to what has been called the "Renaissance of the twelfth century". Here, then, are the six rhythmic modes reduced to modern note values, together with the Greek poetic metres and patterns (Ex. 21):

Ex. 21

Rhythmic Mode	Pattern	Greek name and pattern	
1.	♩ ♪	Trochee	♩ ♪
2.	♪ ♩	Iamb	♪ ♩
3.	♩. ♪ ♩	Dactyl	♩ ♫
4.	♪♩ ♩.	Anapaest	♫ ♩
5.	♩. ♩.	Spondee	♩ ♩
6.	♩♪♩	Tribrach	♩ ♪♪

By comparing the mediaeval and Greek patterns given above it is obvious that whereas in the Greek system only the first, second, and sixth patterns consist of ternary groupings, *all* the mediaeval patterns were so grouped, in France at any rate, for there seems little doubt that in twelfth-century England the third, fourth, and fifth modes were binary like the Greek patterns, but that this deviation from Continental practice disappeared towards the end of the century. Many reasons have been suggested as to why a ternary grouping was forced on rhythmic modes III-V, but it was probably due to the belief, held long before the twelfth century, that the number three was a symbol: of perfection together with the strong desire for an ordered, logical system, a desire that affected all branches of learning during this period. Thus as the first rhythmic mode (the most common and probably the earliest in time) is naturally ternary, the naturally binary modes were altered so as to bring them into line, and as three cannot be divided into two equal whole numbers one of the short notes had to be doubled, hence, for example, ♩ ♫ became ♩. ♪ ♩. There were now therefore two basic note values, both derived from the notation of Gregorian chant (see Chapter 1, p. 28), the 'long', ¶ which was either ternary as in the third, fourth, and fifth rhythmic modes, or binary as in the first and second modes, and the 'breve', ▪ (Latin *brevis* = 'short'), which was either normal and equalled a third of the ternary long, or else 'altered', when it doubled its value as in the third and fourth modes. These differences in value, however, are not explicitly shown in the notation, and the only way in which a composer could ensure that his music was performed in one particular rhythmic mode and not another was by grouping his notes into ligatures of two, three, or four notes and by arranging them in a certain order; for instance, a four-note ligature followed by a series of three-note ligatures indicates the sixth rhythmic mode, while a single note followed by a series of three-note ligatures indicates the third rhythmic mode, and so on, each mode being written down in a different way from the others. All this was admirably clear provided composers used only the six rhythmic patterns given above, but artistic creation never has been and never will be bound by a rigid set of rules, and composers therefore varied what might otherwise have become rhythmically monotonous pieces either by making a note longer than it would be normally or else by breaking it up into notes of smaller value; thus a binary long might become ternary, and a breve be divided into two. But despite the fact that modal rhythm makes no written distinction between the different note values, it was a tremendous step forward in the development of notation, for whereas the notation of Gregorian chant neither indicates nor implies exact note values, although such values were almost certainly applied in practice to syllabic chants, the notation of the Notre Dame School, while it too does not indicate differences in note values, definitely implies them by means of a well-ordered system.

The history of any art shows among other things that when one aspect of an art is being developed other aspects tend to suffer. This was certainly the case in the part-music of the late twelfth and early thirteenth centuries, for mainly as a result of their preoccupation with rhythm the melodies of the Notre Dame School were definitely inferior compared to those of Gregorian chant or of the contemporary trouvères and troubadours (see next chapter), just as the melodies of Stravinsky's early works are compared to those of Brahms or Wagner, and for the same reason. This melodic inferiority is particularly noticeable in three-part writing which became common round about the beginning of the thirteenth century, because it is obviously more difficult to add two interesting parts to a borrowed chant melody than one, especially when the ranges of the two parts are identical (as they normally were) and certain rules of concord and discord have to be observed. In theory the only concords were the unison, fourth (but see p. 42), fifth, and their octave duplications, although thirds and sixths were sanctioned by some theorists; in any case these last were certainly used in practice, as indeed was the tritone (e.g. B–F or F–B). Not until after *c.* 1425, however, were thirds and sixths generally recognized as essential constituents of part-music. In theory, all intervals on strong beats had to be concordant with the tenor, although what we would call accented appogiaturas were permissible provided they were short and resolved on to a concord, but in practice discordant intervals which are not appogiaturas and do not resolve on to concords also occur on strong beats, particularly in three-part writing, but it is unusual for both added parts to have different discordant notes with the tenor.

The inability or perhaps the disinclination of the Notre Dame composers to write continuous melodies resulted in their chopping up the added part or parts of an organum into short sections called 'ordines' (Latin, *ordo* = 'row' [of notes]), and it is worth noting that this constant interrupting of the melodic flow was an important characteristic also of the 'New Music'

composed around 1600 and of the instrumental compositions
of the mid-eighteenth century which preceded the symphonies
and sonatas of Haydn and Mozart, the link between all three
periods being that each followed and, to a greater or lesser
degree, reacted against a tradition in which the melodic line
was the dominant factor: Gregorian chant before 1200,
Renaissance polyphony before 1600, and the Baroque operatic
aria and instrumental fugue before 1750. The composers of the
two later periods marked the end of their sections by cadences
which consist of certain conventional chord progressions; such
a procedure, of course, was out of the question for the Notre
Dame composers, as harmonic considerations did not begin to
enrich (and impoverish) music for another 250 years or so, and
what they were largely concerned with was the interval between
one accented note of an added part and the tenor, not with
the effect of a succession of such intervals nor, in three-part
compositions, with the simultaneous sound of all three notes;
instead of cadences, they indicated the end of an ordo by
drawing a short vertical line through the stave; this mark—the
first ancestor of our modern system of rests—tells the performer
to pause, usually for the duration of either a breve or a long,
depending on the rhythmic mode. In three-part pieces the
sections for the two added parts nearly always tally, thus
making it easier for the singers to keep together, particularly
if the normal notes of the mode are lengthened or broken up
into smaller values. (The added part written immediately
above the tenor in the original MS. was called 'duplum' and
the part above this—if there was one—was called 'triplum'.)

Like the earlier St. Martial School, the Notre Dame
composers wrote not only organa, but discanti§ as well. Both
types of composition are divided into short sections (ordines)
and both are based on a Gregorian melody in the tenor, this
melody being only that portion originally sung by a soloist
(cantor). Thus from the following *Benedicamus Domino* melody
(the same as that used in Ex. 19) only the notes set to the first
line of the text are used, the response, 'Deo gratias' being
chanted in unison by selected members of the choir (Ex. 22):

Ex.22 Gregorian chant *Benedicamus Domino*

(Cantor) Be - ne - di-ca-mus Do - - - - - mi-no. ____
(Choir) De - o gra - - - - - ti-as. ____

The Notre Dame discanti, however, only use the melismatic portion of the soloist's section of the chant, e.g. that portion set to the word 'domino' in Ex. 22, and they are further distinguished from the organa in that the tenor also is written in modal rhythm. This means, of course, that the notes of the chant melody are sung very much faster than in organum, and in order perhaps to compensate for this and to make the length of the organum and discantus sections more equal, composers usually repeated the portion of the chant melody used in the latter. In the later Notre Dame pieces the discantus sections were called 'clausulae' (Latin, *clausula* = 'ending') because, as in Ex. 22, the part of the melody on which they are based usually comes at the end of a Gregorian chant.

The dominant characteristic of the Notre Dame composers was undoubtedly their ability to organize their material, for not only did they develop a system which gives the written notes both accent and metre, and divides their compositions into well-defined sections, but in their clausulae they frequently arranged the chant melody in the tenor so that it consists of a number of rhythmically identical patterns, and if the melody is repeated the pattern is usually altered in each repeat. This was not only the culmination of the Notre Dame School's pre-occupation with rhythm, but was also a very important innovation, because it eventually developed into the chief structural device of the fourteenth-century motet (see Chapter 5, p. 129). It also represents the highest intellectual achievement of the School, an achievement fully comparable with the new scholasticism and philosophy of men like Peter Abelard [1079-1142] and his pupil, John of Salisbury [c. 1115-80], and with the rise of independent thought fanned by the recently acquired knowledge of Arabian philosophy and science and, in Arabic translations, of the works of the great Greek philosopher, Aristotle [384-322 B.C.].

The two outstanding composers of the Notre Dame School are Léonin§ and Pérotin§. The former flourished from about 1150 to about 1180 and can be regarded as the bridge between the St. Martial School and the fully developed style of Pérotin. Thus the notation of several of Léonin's early organa shows modal rhythm in its infancy, for the grouping of ligatures is less regular, the rhythmic patterns change more frequently, and the general melodic line is more fluid than in his later pieces. His discanti, however, are rhythmically much clearer, due to the fact that both parts are written in modal rhythm, although even here the ligatures often give no indication of the note values—in fact, in both the organa and the discanti of Léonin and his contemporaries the rules of concord and discord are often as much a guide to the performer as the grouping of the ligatures. (The tempo of Notre Dame organa and discanti was almost certainly quicker than that of Exx. 19 and 20, because when there is little difference in rhythm and texture, between melismatic and syllabically underlaid compositions, as in this case, it is more natural to sing the latter at a slower pace than the former. During the Renaissance, however, the distinction between the two styles became more pronounced, rhythm and texture being simpler in syllabic pieces than in melismatic, and hence the latter was almost certainly sung more slowly—see Chapter 6) (Ex. 23* opposite).

In the replica of the original opening given in Ex. 23, the short vertical stroke which marks the end of an ordo can clearly be seen in the upper part; in the transcription this is shown by a rest or comma. The tenor notes of the organum section have been written as breves, this being the conventional way of showing that they have no fixed value. They are based on the chant given in Ex. 22. The slurs in the upper part indicate the ligatures in the original, and the notes printed small should be sung lightly. The organum section contains numerous instances of broken modal rhythm, and particularly striking are the rapid scale passages in bars 6, 7, and 43, which appropriately enough were called 'currentes' (Latin, *currere* = 'to run') and which show clearly that this kind of music was performed by soloists in whom, moreover, a certain degree of virtuosity was expected. These soloists were members of the choir who, because of their natural ability and special training, were chosen to perform the polyphonic settings of the chant. This applies to all mediaeval part-music from the St. Martial School onwards, and it should be remembered that to perform a Notre Dame organum or indeed almost any composition before 1600 with a body of more than about twenty singers and instrumentalists is as indefensible as playing a Mozart symphony on a modern full-sized orchestra.

* Transcribed from MS. Florence, Bibliotiça Medicea-Laurenziana, *plut. 29.I.* pp. 87ᵛᵒ, 88 (facsimile in W. Apel, *The Notation of Polyphonic Music : 900-1600,* 4th Ed., p. 247).

Ex·23 Organum *Benedicamus Domino*

In Leonin style (c.1160)

EX. 23 (CONTD.)

The discantus section of Ex. 23 is simpler and more consistent rhythmically than the organum section, but the chant notes in the tenor are not yet arranged in a definite, reiterated pattern. At bar 75, however, the chant is repeated and performed in shorter note values. The keen-eyed will notice that in bars 63 and 79 (the repeat) the tenor shows a local variation from the official version of the chant (Ex. 22), and that the last seven notes of the chant are missing from the end of the first statement (bar 74). Ex. 23 should be compared with that in *H.A.M.* (No. 29), which is in Léonin's later style, being more precise rhythmically and using a repeated pattern in the tenor of the last section (clausula).

Léonin's outstanding work is his *Magnus Liber Organi*, 'The Great Book of Organa' (i.e. organa generale), which consists of thirty-four pieces for the Canonical hours (see Chapter 1, p. 10) and fifty-nine for the Mass for the entire ecclesiastical year. Thus, for example, at First Vespers during Solemn Feasts, instead of singing the *Benedicamus Domino* chant in the traditional manner as shown in Ex. 22, a small choir (one to three voices per part and accompanied by suitable instruments) sang the polyphonic setting (organum and discantus) of the opening words, while the response ('Deo gratias') was chanted in unison by the select choir. This manner of performance also applied to Pérotin's organa and discanti (clausulae§), which, however, differ from Léonin's in their greater rhythmic precision and clarity of notation. Pérotin and his contemporaries in fact re-wrote some of the pieces in the *Magnus Liber Organi*, shortening them and making their rhythmic patterns more consistent, and also composing a number of clausulae which were intended as substitutes for Léonin's discanti. In these clausulae, of which there are a great many, the arrangement of the chant melody in the tenor is developed in three main ways from Léonin's somewhat tentative beginnings. (1) The melody is organized in a reiterated rhythmic pattern which fits the notes of the melody exactly and which is maintained through all its repeats (see Ex. 26); hence it is identical in principle and construction with the 'ground bass' of the seventeenth and eighteenth centuries. (2) The pattern is altered when the melody repeats, as in this tenor part, for instance (Ex. 24*).

* Transcribed from MS. Florence, ibid., p. 175 (facsimile in Apel, ibid., p. 255).

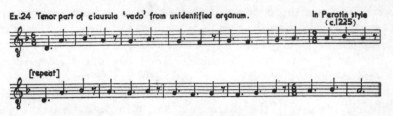

Ex.24 Tenor part of clausula 'vado' from unidentified organum.   In Perotin style
                                                                                    (c.1225)

[repeat]

(3) The pattern is maintained, but does not fit the melody exactly, and so when the latter is repeated it is given a different rhythmic guise, as in Ex. 25, where Arabic numerals show the repeats of the rhythmic pattern and Roman numerals the repeats of the melody (Ex. 25*):

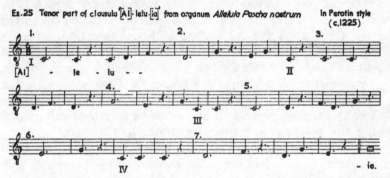

Ex.25 Tenor part of clausula ['Ai]- lelu-[ia]' from organum *Alleluia Pascha nostrum*   In Perotin style
                                                                                          (c.1225)

Here is a complete clausula of the Pérotin period which, being based on the same chant melody, was composed as a substitute for Léonin's discantus in Ex. 23. As in previous examples, slurs indicate the original ligatures and rests the ends of ordines, which in this case do not always tally between the two parts (Ex. 26† next page).

The thirteenth-century theorist known as Anonymous IV describes Léonin as "optimus organista" ("the greatest composer of organa") and Pérotin as "optimus discantor" ("the greatest composer of discanti [or clausulae]"); apart from this handsome compliment we know almost as little about Pérotin as about his predecessor, but it seems that he was at Notre Dame, possibly as a boy chorister, at about the same time as the choir of the Cathedral was completed in 1183, and he may have held the post of succentor or first bass in the choir

* Adapted from G. Reese, *Music in the Middle Ages*, pp. 301-2.
† Transcribed from MS. Florence, ibid., pp. 88ᵛᵒ, 89 (facsimile in Apel, ibid., p. 257).

from *c.* 1208 to 1238. Pérotin, however, was more than just a composer of clausulae, for he wrote organa as well, not only in two parts ('organa dupla') but in three and even four parts

Ex.26 Clausula from organum *Benedicamus Domino*   In Perotin style c.1225

('organa tripla' and 'quadrupla'§); in fact, his three organa quadrupla represent the peak of this particular type of composition. Undoubtedly he added much to the greater clarity of rhythm and grasp of musical structure, but his melodies, as we might expect, are inferior to Léonin's, whose organum sections in particular, with their predominantly stepwise motion, broad sweep, and largely unorganized rhythmic patterns, show the still powerful influence of Gregorian chant. Pérotin's melodies, on the other hand, employ leaps more often, are divided into short sections, and show a high degree of rhythmic organization. Both composers wrote melodically sequential passages—that is, passages in which a group of notes is repeated at a higher or lower pitch (usually the latter), keeping their exact rhythmic patterns and

general melodic shape, as, for instance, in bars 35-40 of Ex. 23.
This device was not new, for it had been used in a number of
Gregorian melodies, but not so frequently nor so extensively.
It is a most satisfying device, as there are few things the ear
enjoys more than recognizing a relationship with something
already heard. Melodic sequence, in fact, is the simplest form
of the two fundamentals of all music—unity and variety. The
balance between these two has not, of course, remained the
same in all periods. In Léonin's time variety predominated,
but with Pérotin the pendulum swung the other way, and it is
therefore no coincidence that, not content with unifying his
freely composed parts (duplum, triplum, and quadruplum) by
rhythmic means, he used an even more powerful device,
imitation, so called because a musical phrase in one voice is
later imitated in another, usually at the unison, fourth, fifth,
or their octave combinations above or below the pitch of the
original phrase. This device may have originated in England,
but occurs fairly often in the three- and four-part compositions
of Pérotin and his contemporaries; it is found in two forms.
The first can be shown diagrammatically thus:

| Triplum | Phrase A | Phrase B |
| Duplum | Phrase B | Phrase A |

and is known as 'stimmtausch', which simply means 'voice-
exchange'. It reappeared in the sixteenth century and was
called 'contrappunto doppio' or 'double counterpoint', but on
account of its difficulty if used extensively it occurs much less
often than ordinary straightforward imitation which became
common from the late fifteenth century onwards and which
has its roots in the second of the two ways mentioned, thus:

| Triplum | Phrase A | (Free part) |
| Duplum | (Free part) | Phrase A |

Sometimes there is more than one imitated phrase, just as in
stimmtausch there are sometimes more than two transposed
phrases—in fact, in one of Pérotin's organa quadrupla there is
a passage in which five phrases in the triplum part are imitated
a fifth lower by the duplum part. This is the beginning of what
we now call canon. Two examples of imitation will be found in
bars 19-25 and 52-4 (indicated by ⌐ ⌐) of the following organum
in Pérotin style. This fine example, with its dancing, changing

rhythms and its sequential passages (bars 36-9 and 70-7), the second of which provides a most satisfying climax, when compared with Ex. 23, will give some idea of the enormous progress in rhythmic organization that took place in the sixty years or so that separates the two pieces (see Fig. 1) (Ex. 27*):

Ex. 27 From the organum *Descendit de coelis*   In Perotin style (c.1225)

* Transcribed from MS. Wolfenbüttel Herzogliche Bibliothek, 1206, p. 7ᵛᵒ, 8 (facsimile in Apel, ibid., p. 233).

EX. 27 (CONTD.)

EX. 27 (CONTD.)

EX. 27 (CONTD.)

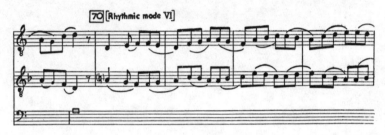

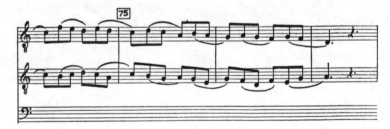

Fig. 1   Modal notation. The beginning of the organum
Descendit de coelis (see Ex. 27 p. 61).

One of the main difficulties in trying to find out how
mediaeval music should sound is the fact that as written down
it does not tell us exactly how it was performed. (This indeed
applies to nearly all music up to the middle of the eighteenth
century.) Admittedly by Pérotin's time notation was much less
ambiguous than previously, but there are two vital factors
which we know took place in performance, but which are
never shown in the MSS.—namely, improvisation and instrumentation. Improvisation meant that far from regarding the
written music as unalterable, a trained singer was sometimes
expected to add notes at various places, both to organa and
discanti. Just where or how he improvised we do not know, but
he might have 'filled in' a leap of a third or more with notes of
shorter value, or ornamented a long note with a trill or grace
note. Even the traditional chant melodies were embellished by
the addition of improvised parts in the style of the older
organum. To do this some of the choir stood round a lectern
or reading desk on which was placed a large MS. chant-book,
and while some sang the melody others improvised one or two
parts above it at the fifth or octave. This kind of performance
was later called 'discantus supra librum' or 'discant from the

book', and it was still practised in the fifteenth and even the sixteenth centuries, though in a somewhat modified form, as we shall see. The ability to improvise was thus as essential to a singer as the ability to sight-read, and the practice of ornamenting organa and discanti in this way continued long after the actual composing of them had ceased in the second half of the thirteenth century.

Instrumental accompaniment was an even more essential part of any performance than improvisation, and although composers never specified the exact number or kind of instruments, this was because they were less instrumentally conscious than later centuries, and were content to leave the choice and size of the 'orchestra' to the choirmaster, who in turn would select his players according to the particular occasion and also to the material and money he had at his disposal.

Of the instruments we know to have been used in church the most traditional was the organ, but the great organ, because of its unwieldiness and loudness, was almost certainly restricted to doubling those portions of the simpler chants (e.g. psalm-tunes) that were sung in unison. There were, however, two smaller types of organ called the positive and the portative which became popular in the twelfth century. Both operated on the same clumsy slider principle as the large organ, but because the wind pressure was considerably lower and the sliders were therefore easier to push and pull and because the sound was much less loud than on the great organ, they were suitable for playing or doubling the sustained notes in both Léonin's and Pérotin's organa. The positive was small enough to move about, but had to be set down before it could be played, as it needed one person to work the bellows and another to operate the sliders. The portative, however, as its name implies, was carried and played at the same time by only one performer, one hand or arm pumping wind and the other hand playing the notes. In the thirteenth century a keyboard was added to both these instruments which greatly increased the speed of performance, but more of this in the next chapter.

Of more importance, so far as part-music was concerned, were the bowed instruments. These became popular in the twelfth century, probably because they were admirably suited to accompanying the tripping rhythm and melodies of Léonin's and Pérotin's music, for they were capable of both a sustained ₒone and a flexible technique. The two chief bowed instruments were the vièle* and the rebec, both of Arabian origin. The vièle, the more important of the two, was generally played sitting down, the instrument being held in a more or less vertical position resting on the lap; usually it had five strings, the lowest of which provided a drone or pedal note, the melody being played on the upper four strings (see Plates I and IX). The rebec was smaller, and was placed under the chin, rather like the violin today; it had either three or five melody strings and produced a shriller tone (see Plate I). Allied to the vièle is the organistrum or hurdy-gurdy (called 'vielle' in the fifteenth century), which was very popular from the tenth century until the advent of the improved portative and positive organs in the thirteenth century. It was a curious instrument, for it consisted of two melody strings tuned either in unison or an octave apart which were simultaneously stopped when one of a number of rods with flat bridges attached was turned so that the bridge came into contact with the strings; in addition there were from one to three lower strings which sounded as a drone. All the strings were vibrated by a wheel made tacky with resin, which was rotated at the lower end of the instrument. The earliest organistrum needed two players, one to turn the wheel and one to manipulate the rods (see Plate I).

The simplest stringed instrument was the monochord, said to have been invented by Pythagoras in order to demonstrate his system of musical intervals. Whether this is true or not it was certainly used for teaching scales and tunes from his day to *c.* 1500, and although we have no record of its being bowed before the fourteenth century it must have been affected by the popularity of the vièle and rebec long before this.

Wind instruments formed the next most important group used in church, of which the chief was the flute family. This included both the transverse flute, the forerunner of the modern type, and the recorder, with its smaller and shriller cousin, the flageolet. All the members of this family were known in the East long before Christianity, but do not appear to have been played in church before the twelfth century, when, as with bowed instruments, the increasing liveliness of church music probably encouraged their use (see Plates I and VIII).

* This is sometimes spelt 'vielle', but it is less ambiguous if this term is reserved for the organistrum (see text).

Reed instruments also took part, especially the strident-sounding shawm with its double reed, offspring of the Greek aulos and ancestor of the oboe, having, like the latter, only one tube, not two as in the aulos (see Plate VII). Another wind instrument, which may have originated in Britain (eleventh century?) was the cornett, a small horn made of wood with its tube either straight or slightly bent in which a number of holes were pierced, enabling a greater range of notes to be played than in the horn proper. Its tone blended excellently with voices and it remained popular both in and out of church until *c.* 1750 (see Plate VI).

We saw in Chapter 1 how the Greek kithara was tolerated and even approved of by the early Church Fathers, and therefore it is not surprising that other plucked instruments were widely used in church, the two chief being the harp and the psaltery. The harp, which goes back to at least 3000 B.C., probably made its first European appearance in Scandinavia or even possibly in England round about the sixth century. Like the modern type, the strings—of varying number—were arranged vertically to the sounding-board, but were tuned diatonically, so that although they could play in any mode, they were incapable of transposition, for this involves one or more sharps or flats; not till the end of the sixteenth century were harps tuned chromatically with each string representing a semitone and transposition therefore possible (see Plates I and VIII). The psaltery, also of very ancient origin, had various shapes, but the most common was that of an inverted triangle with the top cut off, the strings, usually ten in number, lying horizontally above the sounding-board (see Plate I).

In addition to all the above instruments which produced notes of definite pitch, there were a number of percussion instruments. These included bells (see Plate I) and small drums of various shapes and sizes, such as the tabor, cymbals, and possibly tambourines.

Many of the instruments used in church, especially those that were bowed or blown, were introduced into Europe from the East by the returning Crusaders, but their widespread participation in the service cannot be explained only by their ability to play the part-music of the twelfth century; it must also have meant that the Church authorities regarded instruments in a very different light from that of the early Christian leaders. There were, of course, exceptions among the former, and of these Aelred, Abbot of Rievaulx in Yorkshire [1109?–1166], seems to have been especially severe on the use of instruments and indeed on the performance of part-music in general, particularly the way it was executed, although in the following translation by William Prynne [1600–1669] from Aelred's *Speculum Charitatis* ('The Mirror of Charity') allowance must be made for the translator's puritanical exaggeration: "Whence hath the Church so many Organs and Musical Instruments? To what purpose, I pray you, is that terrible blowing of Belloes, expressing rather the crakes of Thunder than the sweetness of a voyce? To what purpose serves that contraction and inflection of the voyce? This man sings a base, that a small meane [i.e. middle part], another a treble, a fourth divides and cuts asunder, as it were, certaine middle notes [i.e. improvising]. One while the voyce is strained, anon it is remitted, now it is dashed, and then againe it is inlarged with a lowder sound. Sometimes, which is a shame to speake, it is enforced into a horse's neighings, sometimes, the masculine vigour being laid aside, it is sharpened into the shrilness of a woman's voyce; now and then it is writhed and retorted with a certain artifical circumvolution. ... In the meantime, the common people standing by, trembling and astonished, admire the sound of the Organs, the noyse of the Cymballs and Musicall instruments, the harmony of the Pipes and Cornets."*

Another Englishman, the famous scholar John of Salisbury, also objected to the way vocal music was performed, remarking that if you heard "one of these enervating performances executed with all the devices of the art, you might think it a chorus of Sirens, but not of men, and you would be astonished at the singers facility, with which indeed neither that of the nightingale or parrot, nor of whatever else there may be that is more remarkable in this kind, can compare. For this facility is displayed in long ascents and descents, in the dividing or in the redoubling of notes, in the repetition of phrases, and the clashing of the voices, while, in all this, the high or even the highest notes of the scale are so mingled with the lower or lowest, that the ears are almost deprived of their power to distinguish."†

---

* Quoted from H. Davey, *History of English Music* (2nd Ed., 1921) pp. 16, 17.
† Quoted from H. E. Wooldridge, *Oxford History of Music*, I (2nd Ed., 1929), p. 290.

Despite these attacks and a few others like them, which incidentally may have been inspired by the incompetency of certain choirs or possibly their desire to show off, the Church as a whole did not object to the use of instruments nor to the new development in part-music provided these did not make a mockery of the service; in fact, it seems likely that the music of Léonin, Pérotin, and others, properly sung and accompanied by, say, a positive organ playing the tenor part, and vièles and harps doubling the upper part or parts, would have been regarded as a richer and worthier offering to the Almighty than if sung by voices alone. Indeed, to have been present at a celebration of High Mass on a feast day in Notre Dame must have provided a most profound experience both artistically and spiritually, with the fascinating blend of voices, organs, strings, wind, and percussion, and the immensely satisfying contrasts between the freely flowing Gregorian melodies, the wayward rhythm of the duplum part over the long tenor notes of a Léonin organum, and the throbbing waves of sound of a Pérotin clausula.

But Pérotin's achievement was no isolated phenomenon; the unity he brought through rhythmic organization, which reflected the attitude of the Notre Dame School as a whole, was inevitably part and parcel of the general artistic and intellectual outlook of the time. We have already mentioned the latter on p. 53, but the former was even more closely allied, for the Gothic style of architecture which arose at about the same time and in the same country that Léonin was active was also an expression, and the most outstanding one artistically, of the desire to unify (see Plate V). The oddly assorted pillars, the rounded and irregularly spaced arches, and almost haphazard ornamentation of the Romanesque style were replaced by regularly spaced and uniform columns made up of the clustered supports for the rib vaulting, which, like the arches, were pointed and so reached to a greater height than the rounded arch, allowing more light to enter the building, a practical consideration for northern countries, but one that did not affect the Romanesque architects working in their brilliant Mediterranean climate, with the result that Gothic architecture hardly affected Italy and Spain, the Romanesque style merging into the Renaissance during the fifteenth century. The greater height and constructional complexity of the nave imposed a severe strain on the outer walls, and in order to provide adequate support flying buttresses were invented. These consisted of massive tapering columns placed outside the church a few yards from the walls, but in line with the pillars inside which supported the nave; from these columns two half-arches 'flew' across the intervening space and strengthened the walls at the places where the maximum thrust from inside was exerted. The Gothic style was both more complex and yet more unified than Romanesque and represents a brilliant constructional and intellectual feat; moreover, its general character, in the twelfth century at any rate, was one of dignity and simplicity which was increased rather than diminished by the sculptured figures and stained-glass windows, for the figures were carved from the same stone as the portals, to ornament which was their chief function, and by being more formal than natural were able to blend with the main structure. The same was true of the stained-glass windows, and it did not matter if a shepherd, for instance, was depicted in a stiff and unnatural attitude, nor if he was surrounded by a multi-coloured flock of sheep, provided that the general design and colour scheme was satisfactory and in harmony with its surroundings when viewed from a distance. In gauging the colour effects, the Gothic artist used the technique of placing small pieces of, say, red and blue glass side by side in order that the eye, from some way away, would fuse them into a far richer colour than could be achieved by actually painting the glass purple, a technique rediscovered by the pointilliste painters some 700 years later.

Thus the clear-cut symmetry, simplicity, and unity of the early Gothic style with its ornamentation subordinated to the total effect, and the well-defined sections, incisive rhythms, simple melodies, and discreet instrumentation of Pérotin's music both show a distinct similarity in aim and achievement. Nevertheless, we must remember that his music—indeed, all part-music—constituted only a fraction of that performed in the church during the tenth to twelfth centuries, for it was obviously more difficult to sing than unison chanting or even extemporized organum, and was therefore only performed in the larger ecclesiastical establishments. Furthermore, the Church authorities as a body, and not only Aelred and John of Salisbury, may well have regarded it with less favour than the traditional method of performing the chant, because it not only obscured parts of the latter by either lengthening the notes so that the chant became unrecognizable or else chopping it up into short rhythmic patterns, but also because it was aesthetically inferior to the superbly wrought and wonderfully expressive Gregorian melodies, a view with which the present writer would agree, even though he finds much that is satisfying in Léonin's but more especially Pérotin's organa. Nor must we forget that the twelfth century produced a great many tropes and sequences together with a number of new melodies, and it was no accident that the organization of music into rhythmic patterns by the Notre Dame School took place at the same time as the introduction of regular metrical-accentual patterns into the sequence by Adam of St. Victor (see Chapter 1, p. 22). But although chant composition continued during the twelfth century, and indeed the thirteenth also, the melodies deteriorated in both quantity and quality, and it is to musicians outside the Church that we must look for the last spontaneous flowering of monophony.

PERFORMANCE

(See also pp. 54, 57, 65-70.)

The instruments mentioned below (and in the similar sections at the end of later chapters) are restricted to those likely to be available in amateur circles and which, if they are not direct descendants of, are roughly equivalent to the original ones; they are organ, violin, viola, 'cello, recorders, flute, oboe, bassoon, small drum, and triangle. The two last should not be used unless specifically mentioned in the details of performance given for each example. If the range of an instrument lies above that of a part as written, the notes should be, as they undoubtedly were in the Middle Ages, transposed up one or two octaves.

In accordance with mediaeval practice, no attempt is made at exact 'scoring', but details have been included in order to give some idea of the various ways in which the piece could have been performed originally.

The choice of instruments and the decision as to whether to double a voice by an instrument or to have two instruments playing the same part in unison or octaves should be dictated by four considerations:

(i) The fact that one of the main characteristics of mediaeval music is the differentiation of the parts through contrasts of timbre. Thus a two-part piece in which each part is of roughly the same range should not be sung by voices alone or played by two instruments of the same kind; in other words, if both parts are sung, then one or both of the voices should be doubled by an instrument; if the latter, then the instruments should have contrasting timbres.

(ii) The vertical sound of a piece must not be essentially altered. For instance, in Ex. 20 it would be wrong for a tenor to sing the upper part accompanied solely by a violin playing the lower part an octave higher, as this would result in the inversion of all the intervals, the less important fourth, for example, replacing the all-important fifth.

(iii) What instruments are at hand.

(iv) Individual taste.

Unless the contrary is specifically stated, there should not be more than three voices per part.

Ex. 18. Select choir with or without organ.

Ex. 19. *Upper part:* solo voice with or without instruments. *Lower part:* organ or 'cello with or without voices.

Ex. 20. Both of the parts should be sung, with instruments (except the organ) doubling one or both of them.

Ex. 22. Solo voice and select choir.

Ex. 23. *Upper part:* solo voice with or without instruments. *Lower part:* played by an organ (except in the discantus section) and/or 'cello with or without voices. A change of 'orchestration' in the discantus section is effective.

Ex. 26. Both parts should be sung by solo voices with instruments doubling one or both of them. (If an organ is used it should only play the lower part.)

Ex. 27. The triplum and duplum parts should be sung by solo voices with instruments doubling one or both of them. The tenor part should be played by an organ and/or 'cello with or without voices.

3

MUSIC OUTSIDE THE CHURCH:
SOLO SONG AND DANCE MUSIC

> Sweet sounds the viol
>   Shriller the flute,
> A lad and a maiden
>   Sing to the lute.
>
> He'll touch the harp for thee,
>   She'll sing the air,
> They will bring wine for thee,
>   Choice wine and rare.*

THESE verses come from a tenth-century Latin poem, *Iam, dulcis amica, venito* ('Now, O sweet beloved, come'), which is, in the words of its translator, "the most famous and perhaps the oldest of the earlier mediaeval love songs".† It was certainly set to music at least three times, but, like nearly all settings before the eleventh century, the notation is impossible to transcribe because it is written in staffless neumes and, just as in Gregorian chant, not until after Guido's improvements can we get any clear idea of the melodies to which many of the mediaeval Latin lyrics were sung.

Of course, popular music, both instrumental and vocal, must always have existed, but none of it has survived before the ninth century; indeed, it is remarkable that even as early as this anyone took the trouble to write it down, for such music has always relied on the handing down from generation to generation of its repertoire, as was the case, for example, with British folk-songs, most of which were not written down until the end of the nineteenth century, and only then because of the interest of a few professional musicians.

It is a common belief that many of the mediaeval churchmen were gay dogs and as fond of wine, women, and song as any other man. Unlike most common beliefs, this is true, and it is as

* Translated from the Latin by Helen Waddell, *Mediaeval Latin Lyrics* (4th Ed.), p. 145.
  † Ibid., p. 331.

well that it is, for if they who formed the bulk of the cultured, educated class had not been in love with the world as well as with their religion, literature (especially poetry) and to a lesser extent music would have been much the poorer; the only drawback is that as Latin was the accepted language in educated circles no songs in the vernacular were written down before the eleventh century.

The secular musicians of the tenth and eleventh centuries can be divided into two main groups: the educated group called 'goliards' which consisted of students, most of them young ecclesiastics who had not taken monastic or priestly vows, who wandered over Britain, France, and more especially Germany, and the largely uneducated group called 'jongleurs' in France, 'Gaukler' in Germany, and 'scops' and 'gleemen' in Britain.

The goliards,§ so called after a probably fictitious Bishop Golias, wrote in Latin and usually composed or arranged their own music. The subjects of their songs range from love songs, sometimes obscene, to spring songs, sometimes exquisite, from drinking songs, often coarse, to satirical songs, often bitter. These last, which were usually aimed at their religious superiors, eventually brought the wrath of the Church on their heads, and they were forbidden ecclesiastical protection and privileges.

The jongleurs and their confrères in Germany and Britain became increasingly active from the ninth century onwards. Unlike the goliards, they represent the continuation of the popular entertainers of earlier centuries, for both 'jongleur' and 'Gaukler' mean 'juggler'. Manual dexterity, however, was not the only accomplishment of these wandering vagabonds, and a competent jongleur danced, played several instruments, sang, performed tricks either himself or with trained animals, and was often an acrobat. Unlike the goliards, too, they sang what others had invented, and their songs were in the vernacular. Each year they attended 'refresher courses' during Lent (when they were forbidden to perform in public), and there they learned new songs and fresh tricks. Their scandalous behaviour exceeded even that of the goliards, and they were a constant thorn in the sides of both civil and ecclesiastical authority. A few of the more reputable ones, however, performed at society weddings and other aristocratic functions, and some even achieved the exalted position of being permanently attached to a feudal household. In Britain these resident musicians

were called 'scops' while their less fortunate (or talented?)
brethren—the gleemen—roamed the countryside. After the
Norman Conquest in 1066 both classes were called 'minstrels'.
We know less about these British entertainers than we do of
their Continental counterparts, but so far as musical performance is concerned it seems likely that their repertoire was
similar, consisting chiefly of the recital of heroic exploits. These
were called 'chansons de geste' or 'songs of deeds' and sometimes contained as many as 10,000 lines, all roughly identical in
metre and divided into sections of from twenty to fifty lines
each. Only one of the melodies has survived, which is unfortunate but not surprising, as the music must have been extremely
simple, easy to memorize, and therefore not worth writing
down. The solitary example probably gives us the clue to most
of the others, and it consists of a short phrase to which each
line of the poem was sung with 'ouvert' (open) and 'clos'
(closed) endings (see p. 81), the latter only being sung or
played at the end of a section of the poem. Whether the
jongleur accompanied himself while he sang or added free
(extemporized) instrumental preludes, interludes, and post-
ludes, or both, will probably never be known, but it may be
that there was no fixed manner of performance and that the
nature of the occasion and the singer's technical ability were
the deciding factors.

Both goliards and jongleurs continued to flourish after the
eleventh century, the former dying out in the early thirteenth
century, when the number of universities grew and students
became residential instead of wandering around Europe from
one famous teacher to another. A number of goliard songs
were called 'conducti', though exactly why is not clear. The
name was probably first applied to tropes sung during processions when the priest was 'conducted' from one part of the
church to another, but by the eleventh century this type of
song embraced both secular and sacred subjects (though very
few found a place in the liturgy) and conducti exist which
express grief for the death of an archbishop, praise at the
coronation of a king, a stern warning on the corrupt morals of
ecclesiastical or courtly dignitaries, jubilation over a famous
victory, political criticism, and even the delights of love. The
conductus in fact can be regarded as an expansion of the hymn,
which, as we saw in Chapter 1, had been used for moral and

even political purposes during the early years of the Christian Church, particularly as a weapon with which to combat heresies (see Chapter 1, p. 7). Like many of the hymns, conductus poems are in Latin and are metrical, and the music was nearly always newly composed.

The jongleurs, before they were organized into guilds in the fourteenth century and therefore became 'respectable', received a new lease of life from their association with the first great flowering of secular art—the songs of the troubadours§ from Provence and their northern imitators, the trouvères.§

Up to the end of the eleventh century music outside the Church was practised first of all by musicians from the lower classes (the jongleurs, etc.) and later by middle-class poet-composers (the goliards), but from *c.* 1080 to *c.* 1300 the aristocracy entered the field, and instead of devoting their time exclusively to hunting, fighting, and drinking they began to patronize the arts and letters; indeed, many of them went further and actually composed songs and even the music to which they were sung, but as learning and even the ability to write was not an essential part of a knight's education, some of the melodies were probably invented or adapted from existing ones by the more educated jongleurs, who may even have written down the poems which their noble masters made up in their heads. It is sometimes stated that all troubadours and trouvères were of high birth. This is not true, as some of the most famous were of very humble and, in at least one case, unknown parentage. The common factor running through this secular art was not so much the noble rank of the composers, although a great many of them were in fact out of the 'top drawer', particularly in the early years, but the refined way in which the sentiments of the poem (almost always about love) were expressed. Thus love to the troubadour and trouvère was a more disembodied emotion than it was to the goliard; woman was placed on a pedestal, largely due no doubt to the devotional enthusiasm accorded to the Virgin Mary, which reached its height in the early twelfth century, and hence a love song did not usually express the real feelings of the singer, but was an imaginative, artistic, and popular means of winning recognition. The difference in approach between the eager, impetuous, and passionate appeal contained in the last two verses of the goliard love song mentioned on p. 74 and given below, and the delicate, restrained, and tender lines of the anonymous trouvère poem which follows it are typical.

> Dearest, delay not,
> Ours love to learn,
> I live not without thee,
> Love's hour is come.
>
> What boots delay, Love,
> Since love must be?
> Make no more stay, Love,
> I wait for thee.*
>
> *Gentle heart could you love true,*
> *Heart to whom my love I've tendered?*
> Night and day I think of you.
> *Gentle heart could you love true?*
> Live I cannot without you,
> To your beauty I've surrendered.
> *Gentle heart could you love true,*
> *Heart to whom my love I've tendered?*†

Another difference between the goliard and the troubadour and trouvère poems is that those of the latter are usually constructed on one of several plans, particularly those of the trouvères. This is not surprising when we remember that the trouvères arose at about the same time and in the same part of France as the Notre Dame School, whose chief characteristic was, as we have seen, the ability to organize their material. Thus while the rhythm of the earlier troubadour melodies, like the syllabic Gregorian chants, almost certainly follows that of the texts or, if the song is fairly melismatic, was sung in a free manner, most of the trouvère songs and, as a result, the later troubadour songs as well were not only sung in modal rhythm, but were also cast into a number of moulds or forms. Admittedly the notation of many of these later songs does not definitely imply modal rhythm, for they are mainly syllabic and thus lack the well-organized ligature groupings of Pérotin and his contemporaries, but modal rhythm was in the air and secular composers could hardly have escaped its influence.

We are on much safer ground, however, when we come to the other intellectual aspect of troubadour and trouvère

---

* Helen Waddell, ibid., p. 147.
† G. Reese, *Music in the Middle Ages*, p. 222.

composition—namely, form—and as we have not the space to discuss in detail all the different kinds, we shall limit ourselves to the more important—the 'rotrouenge', the 'lai', the 'ballade', the 'virelai', and the 'rondeau', of which the last three became the chief forms of secular music in the fourteenth and fifteenth centuries.

The rotrouenge, possibly so called from the Latin *retroientia*, or 'repetition', consists of two melodic phrases, the first of which is repeated a number of times, while the second is either sung once to the refrain (chorus), which is repeated at the end of each verse and which was usually sung by the audience, or else twice to a line of the verse plus the refrain. The most convenient way of showing this is alphabetically, small italicized letters representing the lines sung by the soloist and capital italicized letters representing the refrain. Thus the rotrouenge is either *a* (repeated) *B*, or *a* (repeated) *bB*. The musical form, on the other hand, is usually shown by roman capital letters, and in this case is either A (repeated) B, or A (repeated) BB. Here is a short and most attractive example of the latter type (*a a b B*) (only verses 1, 4, and 5 are given, and the refrain—here and elsewhere—is underlined) (Ex. 28*):

Ex. 28 Rotrouenge · *A la fontenele*

Anon (Trouvère)

IV

Dites moi, Marote, seroiz vos m'amie?
A bele cotele ne faudroiz vos mie.
Et chainse et ride et peliçon avrez, se je ai vostre amor.

Merci, merci (etc.).

* From F. Gennrich, *Die altfranzösiche Rotrouenge*, p. 60 (see also G. Reese, ibid., p. 220).

Tell me, O Marote, wilt love me alone, dear?
I a robe will give you for thy very own, dear,
A skirt, a furry cloak as well, and gold if I but have your love.

Have pity, pity (etc.).

<hr>

V

Sire chevalier, ce ne di ge mie
C'onques a nul jor, fusse vostre amie;
Ainz ai a tel doné m'amor dont mi parent avront anor.

Merci, merci (etc.).

<hr>

Knight, that you could win me I am not denying,
Nor that I might some day to your arms come flying,
But I do dearly love a man my father holds in high esteem.

Have pity, pity (etc.).

<hr>

The melody of this song is in the Mixolydian mode, and although the modes exerted a strong influence on troubadour and trouvère melodies, many of the latter show a distinct and growing tendency towards our major and minor keys.

The lai has essentially the same structure as the sequence (see Chapter 1, pp. 21-2), from which it undoubtedly derived, for it is made up of a number of verses which differ from each other in the length of their lines. Unlike the sequence, which always has two lines to a verse, the lai verses often have three or four lines each and even on occasion as many as eight. Thus the first four verses of a lai might be *aa, bbbb, cc, ddd*. As the verses differ in construction, so does the tune for each verse, although some kind of unity is often preserved by the repetition of melodic fragments in each verse setting (see *H.A.M.*, 19, i).

The French word *ballade*, like 'ballet', 'ballad', and 'ballata', (see Chapter 5, p. 167), derives from the Latin verb *ballare* (='to dance'), and the first ballades were undoubtedly dance songs. As early as the thirteenth century, however, they lost their association with the dance and as a result became more complex. The simplest and probably the earliest type has the form *a a b*, i.e. with no refrain, but the commoner and probably later types do have a refrain, for this device was and still is a very popular one, not only because the ear enjoys repetition, but also because an audience usually welcomes an opportunity to join in. The most popular of the commoner types of ballade§ has the poetic form *ab ab cd E*, the musical form of which can be

simplified to A A B, in which A = *ab* and B = *cd E*. The following
song by the troubadour Andrieu contredit d'Arras [*c.* 1180-
1248] is an example, and a remarkably fine one (Ex. 29):

One feature of the ballade, clearly shown in the above
example, is the use of ouvert and clos cadences for the first
section, the 'open' cadence ending on any note but the final of
the mode, while the 'closed' cadence rounds off the section by
ending on the final, the effect being the same as our imperfect
and perfect cadences.

Although the most common form of the ballade is *ab ab cd E*
there are in fact two other but infrequently used types, both of
which begin and end with a refrain, a characteristic of the
virelai§ also, with its form *A bb a A* or *AB cc ab AB*, in which the
final refrain of a verse serves as the first refrain of the next

verse, thus making the poem continuous. The name probably derives from *virer*, 'to turn', and 'lai', in the sense that it is a lai with verses of four lines and musical form B B A A with the A phrase 'turned' back to the beginning, as in this charming example (Ex. 30*):

Ex.30 Virelai - *E, dame jolie*   Anon.(Trouvère)

Although the popular instrumental rondo of the seventeenth and eighteenth centuries with its A B A C A D ... A structure has something in common with the mediaeval rondeau§ it is very unlikely that there is any connexion between the two. The simplest and earliest type of rondeau has the form *a A ab AB*, but the fondness for refrains which we noted in connexion with the ballade led to a later and commoner variety in which the complete refrain was sung at the beginning as well as at the

* Adapted from F. Gennrich, *Rondeaux, Virelais und Balladen*, Vol. I, p. 129.

end—*AB a A ab AB*. This is the form of the poem quoted on p. 78 and of the following very modern-sounding example (Ex.31*):

Ex.31 Rondeau - *Diex d'Amours*   Anon. (Trouvère)

The forms of troubadour and trouvère song nearly all developed from ecclesiastical chant—in particular, the litany, the sequence, and the hymn—but the three most popular and lasting forms, the ballade, virelai, and rondeau, probably have their roots in an earlier dance-song which was purely secular and owed nothing to the Church. A number of the melodies, however, are clearly adapted from chants and are among the earliest examples of *contrafacta*—that is, songs in which the original sacred words are replaced by secular ones, or vice versa.

Although most of the mediaeval lyrics are concerned with love, they are by no means restricted to the worshipping from afar approach; thus there are 'albas',§ or 'dawn songs', in which a faithful friend stands watch for two lovers and warns them of the approach of day, 'chansons de toile',§ or 'spinning songs', in which an unhappy wife complains of her husband or a maiden pines for her absent sweetheart, and 'pastourelles', in which a knight woos a virtuous shepherdess who sometimes—as in Ex. 28—preserves her virtue! There are also songs which deal with other topics, such as mourning songs, satirical songs, and, more important, the 'sirventes', or 'songs of service', which often have a political or moral bias and are sometimes very outspoken in their comments on a particular nobleman (see Ex. 33).

* Adapted from F. Gennrich, ibid., Vol. I, p. 24.

One of the annoying things about mediaeval church music is the shroud of anonymity which covers nearly all its composers, but this is fortunately not the case with the troubadours and trouvères, as a great many names have come down to us. These are usually grouped into three periods: *c.* 1080–*c.* 1150, *c.* 1150– *c.* 1250, *c.* 1250–*c.* 1300, the trouvères being in the ascendant during the last two periods and the troubadours up to the early thirteenth century, although the latter might have sustained the high quality and spontaneity of their songs right through this century if it had not been for the crippling blow which the Church, in her zeal to exterminate heretics, dealt Provence during the twenty years' massacre and destruction known as the Albigensian Crusade (1209-29). Among the more important of these poet-musicians were Count Guillaume of Aquitaine and Poitiers [1070-1127], the earliest troubadour we know, Marcabru§ [d. *c.* 1147], a commoner and, oddly enough, a woman-hater, Bernart de Ventadorn§ [d. 1195], also a commoner and one of the greatest troubadour poets, Guiraut de Bornelh§ [d. *c.* 1220], who was called 'Master of the Troubadours' by his contemporaries, Guiraut Riquier§ [d. 1292], the last but by no means least of the troubadours, Blondel de Nesles [*c.* 1150-1200], the first of the trouvères, but who did *not* discover the dungeon into which his master Richard Cœur-de-Lion had been thrown by singing a song composed by the two of them, nor did he rescue him, Colin Muset§ [early thirteenth century], one of the educated jongleurs whose songs entitled him to be called a trouvère, Thibaut IV, King of Navarre§ [1201-1253], an unscrupulous monarch, but an inspired composer of love songs, Adam de la Halle§ [*c.* 1230- *c.* 1288], another commoner and possibly the last of the trouvères, but more renowned and important for his part-music than for his solo songs (see Chapter 4, p. 117); he also either composed, or borrowed from folk-songs, or both, the music for *Li Gieus* [=*Le Jeu*] *de Robin et Marion,*§ a pastoral play with songs inserted in the dialogue. Only the songs have survived, but Adam can lay claim to have compiled the first secular opera. We could add other names of troubadours and trouvères, but to extend the list would not add to the delight which can be found in this often exquisite if sometimes stilted poetry and the charming, even ravishing melodies to which it is set.

It was natural enough for the Provençal troubadour movement to spread into northern France, and it was almost as natural for it to cross the frontier into Italy, but the effects were vastly different, for so far as we know French influence south of the Alps was confined to the poetic forms, not the music. Italian secular music, in fact, like secular learning, flourished much later than in other countries and for the same reason—the power and proximity of Rome. But singing was not confined to the liturgy only, and from at least the time of St. Francis of Assisi [1182-1226], whose famous *Hymn to the Sun* was certainly set to music now unfortunately lost, a number of songs with religious texts were composed, particularly during the late thirteenth and fourteenth centuries. During this period, as a result of political and religious upheavals and their attendant bloodshed, and of widespread outbreaks of the plague, bands of wandering penitents were formed who, as they journeyed about northern Italy, chastised themselves for their sins and sang hymns of praise called 'laude spirituali'.§ The form of many of these laude closely resembles the French virelai, and they also show the same tendency towards major and minor tonality, but the melodies, because they were sung by a group, and usually a marching group at that, are simpler and probably in binary rhythm. This lauda, for example, would be most exhilarating to march to (Ex. 32*):

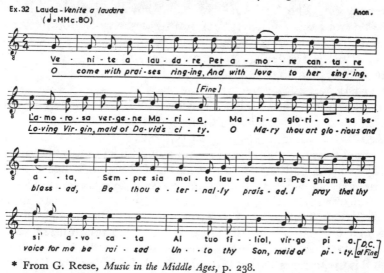

Ex. 32 Lauda - *Venite a laudare*
(♩ = MM c.80)

Ve · ni · te a lau · da · re, Per a · mo · re can · ta · re
O come with prai · ses ring · ing, And with love to her sing · ing.

L'a · mo · ro · sa ver · ge · ne Ma · ri · a, Ma · ri · a glo · ri · o · sa be·
Lo · ving Vir · gin, maid of Da · vid's ci · ty. O Ma · ry thou art glo · rious and

a · · ta, Sem · pre sia mol · to lau · da · ta: Pre · ghiam ke ne
bless · ed, Be thou e · ter · nal · ly prais · ed. I pray that thy

si' a · vo · ca · ta Al tuo fi · · liol, vir · go pi · a. [D.C.]
voice for me be rai · sed Un · · to thy Son, maid of pi · · ty. [al Fine]

* From G. Reese, *Music in the Middle Ages*, p. 238.

The penitential movement in Italy, with its practice of self-chastisement or flagellation, became almost a mania in the fourteenth century and invoked strong Papal action, as a result of which it had almost entirely disappeared by the end of the century; but the singing of devotional songs outside the church continued in popularity and prepared the way for the sixteenth-century oratorio. Before the authorities had banned the movement, however, it had caught on in Germany, where it was particularly rife during the terrible plagues of 1348 and later, known as the Black Death. These German penitential songs were called 'Geisslerlieder'§ or 'flagellation songs', and although the movement was banned at the same time as the Italian it persisted longer owing to the greater remoteness of Rome and the strong morbid streak in the German character.

German songs of course had existed long before the Geisslerlieder, but not until the latter half of the twelfth century did a definite group of song composers arise; these were the Minnesinger,§ or 'singers of chivalrous love', and it was the art of the troubadours that was their main inspiration, for in 1156 Frederick Barbarossa, or 'Redbeard' [1123-1190], Emperor of the Holy Roman Empire and leader of the Third Crusade, married Beatrix of Burgundy, who took with her to Germany a troubadour named Guiot of Provence, and it was almost certainly their influence that initiated the Minnesänger movement. The German composers, however, most of whom came from the south (Austria), did not slavishly imitate their French models, even though their best period, *c.* 1190-*c.* 1250, saw French influence at its strongest. The main reason for their independence was the difference between French and German verse, particularly the fact that the former was measured by the number of syllables in the line, while the latter was measured by the number of accents, which meant that the number of unaccented syllables could vary from line to line; thus the melodies were sung in either binary or ternary rhythm, depending on the position of the poetic accents, or else in free rhythm as in the more melismatic troubadour songs.

The forms used by the Minnesinger are less easily classifiable than their French counterparts, but apart from the 'leich', which corresponds to the French lai, the main musical one, capable of many variations within itself, is called 'bar' form and is the same as that of the ballade—A A B, the second section sometimes containing modified or complete repeats of the first section (see Ex. 33). The poetic types, on the other hand, are

Ex. 33 Minnelied·*Der kuninc Rodolp mynnet got*   "Der Unvürzaghete"
(♩ = MM c 60)

Der | ku - ninc Ro - dolp | myn - net got und | ist an tru - wen
Der | ku - ninc Ro - dolp | rich - tet wol und | haz - zet val - sche
King | Ru - dolph loves Al - - migh - ty God his | faith'- ful - ness ne'er
King | Ru - dolph judg - es right - eous - ly and | hat - eth all false

ste - te, Der | ku - ninc Ro - dolp hat sich ma - ni - gen scan - den wol vür - sa - get.
re - te, Der | ku - ninc Ro - dolp ist ein heit an — tu - gen - den un - vür - tza - get.
break - ing; King | Ru - dolph has re - sist - ed well ma - ny a de - vi - lish temp - ta - tion.
speak - ing; King | Ru - dolph's brave and vir - tuous deeds de - - serve our ad - mi - - ra - tion.

Der | ku - ninc Ro - dolp e - ret got und al - le wer - de vrou - wen, Der
King | Ru - dolph ho - nours God and ev - 'ry maid of no - ble bear - ing; King

ku - ninc Ro - dolp let sich dick' in — ho - en e - ren scou - wen, Ich
Ru - dolph oft re - - veals him - self in — ac - tions fine and dur - - ing. I

gan ym wol, daz ym nach sy - ner mil - te heil ge - - schiht, — Der
wish in mea - sure of his wealth that he may get his — due, — For

mei - ster syn - gen, gi - gen, sa - gen daz hort her gern und git yn drum - me nicht.
when the min - strels play or sing, he — glad - ly hears, but gives them not a sou!

direct imitations of French models, and although love is still the predominant topic it is treated in an even more idealized and less personal way, the mystical trait in the German character finding its main outlet in songs of praise to the Virgin Mary, the ideal woman, thus transmuting the earthly passion of the earlier goliard poems. Epic songs and songs of a political or moral nature were also popular, the latter being the equivalent of the sirventes, and the following example by 'The Dauntless One' (whoever he may have been) has a decided sting in its tail. It also shows one of the more complex variations of bar form—a^1a^2 a^1a^2 b^1b^2 c, where $a^2=a^1$, but with a clos instead of an ouvert ending, and b^2 is derived from b^1 and a^1 (Ex. 33,* previous page).

Although the melody of the above example is clearly in the major mode, this is much rarer than in troubadour and trouvère songs, for Minnelied is not only more modal, but actually avoids the one mode, the Mixolydian, which of all the ecclesiastical modes comes closest to our major scale.

Among the more important Minnesinger there is one who has become widely known through the opera by Wagner which bears his name, Tannhauser§ [fl. mid-thirteenth century], who actually did take part in a Tournament of Song in 1207 together with another Minnesinger, Wolfram von Eschenbach [fl. *c.* 1200], the author of an epic poem called *Parzival* which Wagner used as the basis of his own opera of that name. Other Minnesinger include Neidhart von Reuenthal§ [*c.* 1180-*c.* 1240], Rumelant [fl. mid-thirteenth century], and Heinrich von Meissen [d. 1318], nicknamed Frauenlob§ because in a contest with another Minnesinger he strongly advocated the use of *Frau* (lady) instead of the more usual *Weib* (woman) when referring to the fair sex. With Frauenlob and his successors, such as Hugo von Montfort [1357–1423], the natural spontaneity of the movement diminished, although it must be remembered that much of their music which has come down to us was probably edited by the Meistersinger in the fifteenth and sixteenth centuries in order to conform to their rules; but more about them in Chapter 6. Undoubtedly the most outstanding Minnesinger is Walther von der Vogelweide§ [d. *c.* 1230], the model song composer for young David in Wagner's opera, *Die Meistersinger*. Born into the lower ranks of the nobility, Walther spent many years as a minstrel, singing songs of which he composed both words and music, and though most of the latter is fragmentary, enough remains to justify the very high regard of his contemporaries, and even to claim that artistically they are unequalled,¶ let alone surpassed, by any German compositions before the late fifteenth century. Walther's ability to write his songs was by no means general among his fellow Minnesinger, for most of them had to dictate both poems and melodies to professional scribes in much the same way as some 'composers' of popular tunes do today.

---

* Adapted from F. L. Saran, *Die Jenaer Liederhandschrift*, Vol. II, p. 26.

Here is part of what is probably Walther's finest song, a Crusading song in which he prays for the deliverance of Jerusalem and ends with an exhortation to all men (Ex. 34*):

Ex. 34 Minnelied - *Vil süeze waere minne* ('Walther's *Kreuzlied*') Walther von der Vogelweide

* Adapted from C. Bükler, *Untersuchungen zu den Melodien Walthers von der Vogelweide*, p. 79. (There are sixty more lines.)

So far we have traced the influence of the troubadour movement into northern France, eastwards into Italy, and north-eastwards into Germany. Now we will turn south into Spain, a country closely bound to France by cultural and political ties and where the visits of several troubadours, among them Guiraut de Bornelh and Guiraut Riquier, were mainly responsible for the rise of a native school of composers who wrote a large number of songs called 'cantigas',§ of which over 400 have survived. This number would certainly have been less had it not been for the enthusiasm of King Alfonso the Wise [reigned 1252–1284], who was responsible for their collection and who probably contributed some himself. Most of the cantigas, like the Italian laude, are religious but non-liturgical, being chiefly concerned with the miracles of the Virgin Mary, and this avoidance of the purely secular is a feature of Spanish music which persisted for several centuries, as we shall see. To be sure, there must have been popular songs and dances which owed nothing to religion both before and during the troubadour influence in the thirteenth century, but as usual they were either not written down or have since been lost.

The most common form of the cantigas is the same as the virelai, as in this delightful example. (Unfortunately, space does not permit the full story of the miracle to be told) (Ex. 35*).

Artistic movements, like armies, have always found it difficult to gain a foothold in Britain, and when, in 1152, Eleanor of Aquitaine married her countryman, Henry of Anjou, who later became Henry II of England [reigned 1154–1189], she was largely unsuccessful in her attempts to introduce troubadour song to the English Court, even though it is almost certain that the famous Bernart de Ventadorn himself paid a visit. Compared to the other European countries already mentioned, very few minstrel songs of the period have come down to us, mainly because the only language fit for literature, and therefore written by educated people, was the Norman-French of the trouvères, until the late thirteenth century, when it was gradually replaced by English (including Scots). Most of the songs that have survived are settings of religious texts in Latin, such as hymns to the Virgin or poems commemorating local saints like Thomas à Becket, whose murder was connived

* Transcribed from *Bulletin Hispanique*, Vol. XIII, Plate 10 (see also *The New Oxford History of Music*, Vol. II, p. 262).

at by Henry in 1170. Even the few purely secular songs in the vernacular often contain a moral (e.g. *Worldes blis*,§ *H.A.M.*,

Ex.35 Cantiga–*Maravillosos et piadosos*   Anon.
(♩.–MM c.60)

23B), but others express a more worldy sentiment, such as the plaintive longing of a lover for his mistress. The following charming example must have been typical of many others now unfortunately lost (Ex. 36* overleaf).

But the gay, springlike mood of mediaeval Britain was more truly reflected in her part-music (as we shall see in the next chapter) and her dances, for one has only to hum through Ex. 40c in *H.A.M.* to be struck by the vitality and freshness of this astonishingly modern-sounding piece with its fascinating three-part ending. The general name for mediaeval dances was 'estampie',§ and as they consist of a varying number of phrases each repeated twice (with ouvert and clos endings) they probably derived from the ecclesiastical sequence. (*H.A.M.*, 40B is a most attractive example.)

The instruments which played this dance music and which

* Adapted from J. Saltmarsh, 'Two Mediaeval Love Songs set to Music', *The Antiquaries Journal*, Vol. XV.

took part in the performances of solo song were many and varied, including all those mentioned in Chapter 2 except the great organ. The portative, however, and to a lesser degree the

Ex.36 *Bryd one brere*   Anon.
(♩·=MM c.80)

1. Bird on a   bri - - ar,   bird, bird on a   bri - ar,   Love's in   my   heart, 'tis
2. I   am so   blithe, O   thou bright bird on   bri - ar,   When I   see ____   that
3. Might she be   mine still to   hold   and to   have, ____   Stead - fast   of ____   love,

love   that   I   crave.   Blithe - ful   bird   up - on   me   have
maid   in   the   hall.   She ____   is   white   of   limb, love - ly,
love - ly   and   true.   Of ____   my   sor - row   she might me

mer - - cy,   Or   build, love, build   thou   me ____   my   grave.
true, ____   She ____   is   fair   and   flow'r ____   of   all.
save; ____   Joy ____   and   bliss   were   e'er   to   me   new.

positive, became exceedingly popular after the application of the keyboard in the early thirteenth century. This made a much greater speed of performance possible, and it is likely that the invention arose as a result of the increasing complexity of the upper parts in Pérotin's music and that of later composers. At first the sliders were replaced by pins, each with a button on the end which, when depressed by a finger, pushed open a valve and so admitted wind to the pipes. When the finger was lifted a spring automatically closed the valve. Soon afterwards the button was replaced by a wooden strip or key, hinged at one end, which when depressed operated the pin and valve as before. The great advantage of the key compared to the slider was that it was far less clumsy and therefore could be operated more quickly, and it was superior to the button in that it gave a larger surface for the finger to move on (see Plates X-XII).

The keyboard was obviously such a wonderful discovery, or rather rediscovery, that it cannot have been long before it was applied to a stringed instrument, and the one affected was the organistrum, which by the early thirteenth century had developed in two ways from that described in Chapter 2, p. 67. Firstly, it had become small enough for one player to turn the wheel and manipulate the bridges (Plate XII), and, secondly, the bridges had been replaced by sliding pieces of wood, each with two upright bits of wood (tangents.). When the sliders were pushed in the two tangents pressed against the two melody strings and 'stopped' them. It was soon discovered that if the sliders were pushed with sufficient force the impact of the tangents alone would cause the strings to sound—in other words, there was no need to excite the strings by means of the rosinned wheel. From this it was but a short step to constructing a tangent which would hit the string from below when a key was depressed. But this was only capable of playing a series of single notes, because there was only one string. When a number of strings were used the clavichord was born, but up till *c.* 1700 most of the strings still had more than one tangent and were thus called 'fretted' clavichords (see Chapter 6). The sound of this instrument was much softer and sweeter than the organistrum, and hence was only suitable (as it always has been) for intimate occasions. Its use in a church service would be quite out of the question.

Other instruments which so far as we know were used almost entirely outside the church were the lute, guitar, bagpipes, panpipes, horns, trumpets, and a few percussion instruments, such as castanets and triangles. The lute and guitar were plucked stringed instruments, the main difference between them lying in the shape of the body, the lute resembling a pear cut in half, while the guitar had a flat back and incurved ribs like the modern type, or the ukelele. The bagpipe, although it was known in the East before Christianity, achieved greater importance in Europe and has an unbroken history from Roman times to the present day. It was especially popular in the Middle Ages, and in fact it has been suggested that the sustained-tone organum of the twelfth and early thirteenth centuries was influenced by the instrument's characteristic drone. Panpipes too are still used today, though either as a toy or else by choir conductors or string players who have no piano handy. They have always consisted of a number of pipes bound together, each of different length and therefore of different pitch (see Plate I). The horn took its name from the material of which it was usually made, although wood and occasionally metal were sometimes used. Its chief function was in hunting and for signalling (see Plate IX). The same applies to the trumpet, and although both were known in various shapes and sizes in the East the trumpet appeared in Europe long before the horn, largely owing to its martial character, which the Romans fully exploited. Neither instrument could play more than two or three notes.

The songs of the troubadours and their imitators all over Europe were not only "the first great flowering of secular art", but also the last spontaneous outburst of monophony, the beauty, variety, and perfection of which has only recently begun to be appreciated, and it is high time that a selection of these songs with suitable translations was published separately as well as included in future editions of popular song-collections.

Up to the end of the thirteenth century all part-music was composed for the church and all secular music was monophonic, but from *c.* 1200 onwards part-music was increasingly used for both sacred and secular purposes, while monophony declined. Moreover, the style of part-music in the thirteenth century was universal—in other words, there was no musical difference between a part-composition written for a saint's day, a secular song, and an instrumental dance for portative organ, vièle, and recorder. Of this style Pérotin was the founder.

PERFORMANCE

(See also pp. 76, 78.)

The songs of this period were almost certainly accompanied, usually by a plucked instrument, when originally sung, but as the modern equivalents (harp, lute, guitar) are not generally available they may be sung by a solo voice with a violin, viola, recorder, flute, or oboe doubling the refrain, when there is one. In Ex. 32 the refrain might well have been sung by a number of voices with the addition of some percussive instrument, such as a small drum or triangle.

4

THE ALL–EMBRACING STYLE OF THE
THIRTEENTH CENTURY

"I<small>T</small> may be granted that Mozart's religious feeling comes out most fully in his motets and they, together with the best of such pieces by other composers, may fittingly enough find a place in any but the most solemn services. But as for the Masses of Haydn, Mozart and Beethoven, I must confess my utter inability to understand how anyone immersed in prayer can listen to them, or listening to them, pray.... Haydn and Mozart wrote to please their patrons; Beethoven, with his 'Man, help thyself' and 'The starry heavens above us the moral law within us' was many a long league away from the old Catholic feeling. All three wrote first and foremost as modern composers, using every device they knew to add to the purely musical interest of their work. Sincere they were, but their sincerity was another thing from the profound naïve sincerity of the earlier men.

"The older music rolls along without a suggestion of display, lovely melody winding round lovely melody, and all combining to form a broad, sweeping, harmonious mass of tone that carries the spirit resistlessly with it. This is the true devotional music."*

There always have been and there probably always will be people whose attitude to church music makes them think, speak, or write in a manner similar to the above. It is the same kind of outlook that believes laughter in church to be irreverent and that to dress in one's best suit promotes piety. Such people lack the imagination to see that what is offensive to them may be quite acceptable to others, or that what is intolerable now may well have been completely satisfying in the past. On the other hand, there is a very common belief that at certain times in the past church music has been written which represents the ideal. The Catholic Church, for instance, states categorically

* From the *Morning Post*, quoted in R. Terry's *Catholic Church Music*, 1907, p. 50.

that Gregorian chant, and to a slightly lesser extent the masses and motets of Palestrina in the sixteenth century, are to be regarded as the highest attainments in this sphere, and that the farther more recent compositions stray from the atmosphere of these works the less suitable are they for the liturgy. The Catholic Church is not alone in this respect, for several other religious bodies have, at various periods in history, severely restricted the nature and use of church music. But what is important surely is not only what I personally feel to be a devout piece of music, which appeals to me both religiously and artistically, but also that I should tolerate and try to understand music which, while striking no chord in me, clearly means or has meant a great deal to others. In other words, any artistic creation is acceptable to God provided its creator has given of his best. What should not be tolerated is work that is slipshod or that is, with a tongue-in-the-cheek attitude, deliberately written in a style that is popularly regarded as suitable for church, but which is foreign to the creator's own. You may prefer the famous *Missa Papae Marcelli* of Palestrina to the *Missa Solemnis* of Beethoven, but that is no reason for saying that one is more religious than the other. You may find the use of a large orchestra in church objectionable, but to Beethoven this was the only way by which he could fully express all he had to say.

It is frequently forgotten when holding up Palestrina as a paragon composer of church music that not only was there very little difference in style between his sacred and secular work, but that he actually based some of his masses on secular pieces either by himself or others, even after this procedure had been condemned by ecclesiastical authority, and that in the *Missa Papae Marcelli*, which is usually regarded as a model church composition, he begins three of the movements with the first phrase of an extremely well-known French song. In so doing he was merely conforming, albeit unconsciously, to a tradition which stretched back to the early days of Christian chant (see Chapter 1, p. 5).

The differences between sacred and secular styles in the thirteenth century were far fewer, however, than in the sixteenth century—in fact, as the century progressed the musical distinction between the two completely disappeared. Round about 1200 there were three styles, organum, clausula, and conductus; the first two, which we have already described in Chapter 2, were used exclusively in the liturgy, but the third style was frequently used for secular texts, and even when sung in church was not so intimately connected with the liturgy as were organum and clausula.

The thirteenth-century conductus§ was so called because it had three features in common with the Latin songs of the same name mentioned in Chapter 3; these are metrical texts in Latin, syllabic underlay of the music, and the fact that, generally speaking, all the parts are newly composed. All these features distinguish the conductus from organum and clausula, in which the words are almost invariably in prose, with many notes to a syllable, and the tenor part is borrowed.

A further difference is that none of the parts in a conductus are arranged in repeated rhythmic patterns, and they all move together in the same rhythm, i.e. contrapuntally like a clausula, but unlike the polyphonic organum. It was also the first kind of part-music in which a composer could give completely free rein to his melodic invention. Sometimes, however, a composer would incorporate part of an existing clausula, with its rhythmically organized Gregorian tenor, into a conductus, probably because a word or even a syllable of his secular poem reminded him of part of a clausula set to the same word or syllable which he or someone else had already composed. This procedure is the reverse of that practised by Palestrina, for example (see above), but because something intimately connected with the liturgy was torn from its context and used in a secular work it too may well have caused a frown in high places.

The conductus was extremely popular from the time of Pérotin to about 1250, and it covered a similar range of subjects as those mentioned in Chapter 3. Here, for example, is a very fine one, possibly composed by Léonin, in which the poem expresses both grief and indignation at the murder of Thomas à Becket on 29th December 1170 (Ex. 37* overleaf).

Léonin (if it was he) was not the first to write in this style, for *Mira Lege* from the St. Martial School (Ex. 20) was, as we noted in Chapter 2, a forerunner of conductus style. The origin of this kind of composition, however, probably came from Britain or Scandinavia, for all British compositions of the late twelfth and early thirteenth centuries are less polyphonic and more

* Adapted from H. Gleason, *Examples of Music before 1400*, p. 43.

contrapuntal than those of the contemporary Notre Dame
School, and, as we shall see, this preference for the more
sonorous and full-blooded effect of all parts moving together
was a characteristic of British music for some time to come.
Another pointer in the same direction is the fact that thirds and
sixths were used to a far greater extent in Britain than on the
Continent, and these 'imperfect' concords were then, as
they are today, richer in sound than the fourth, fifth, or
octave.

Ex.37 Conductus-*Novus miles sequitur*   Leonin(?)
(♩ = ♩ = MM c.60)

No - vus mi - les se - qui - tur___ Vi - am no - vi re - gis.
Fol - lows now a sol - dier new___ In the path - way roy - al.

Bo - nus pa - stor pa - ti - tur___ Pro sa - lu - te gre - gis.
For his flock a shep - herd true___ Dies, for he was loy - al.

Tho - mas a - gni san - gui - ne La - vat sto - le ge - mi - ne
In the lamb's blood spilt for men, Tho - mas wash - es white a - gain

Pur - pu - ram ru - ben - - - tem. Res est sa - tis e - vi - dens
Pur - ple robe, once go - ry. Thus 'tis clear to all men's sight

Quod il - lus - trat oc - ci - dens To - tum o - ri - en - tem.
Why his fall il - lu - mines bright The One, ris'n in glo - ry.

The evidence that British music was different from Continental and that this difference was due mainly to the preference for the 'imperfect' concords, especially thirds, is fourfold. Firstly, an excerpt from a manuscript, *Descriptio Kambriae*, by a certain Gerald de Barri or, to give him his more usual Latinized name, Giraldus Cambrensis [*c.* 1147–1220], in which he describes his travels in Wales. The excerpt in question states that improvised singing in a number of different parts was a frequent practice with Welshmen, and that the same kind of singing, but in two parts only, was also heard in northern England. He stresses the fact that this kind of two-part singing was not general in Great Britain and suggests that it came from the Danes and Norwegians, who had frequently invaded our northern coasts. Gerald was a cultured, widely-travelled man who came from an aristocratic family and was well known in scholarly circles both abroad and at home; thus the singing he describes must have been markedly different from that on the Continent for him to single it out for special mention. Secondly, the thirteenth-century theorist known as Anonymous IV, who was probably an Englishman, states that major and minor thirds were esteemed the best consonances in the West of England, which would include Wales. Thirdly, the few examples of late twelfth- and thirteenth-century British part-music§ that have come down to us show a greater use of thirds and sixths than contemporary Continental pieces. And, fourthly, there exists a twelfth-century hymn, probably written in the Orkneys, which is almost entirely a succession of thirds§ (see *H.A.M.*, 25C). The Orkneys were a Norwegian possession from the ninth to the fifteenth centuries, and if Gerald's suggestion is correct then the singing he describes was almost certainly similar to that notated in this hymn.

The next example (Ex. 38,* p. 100) should be compared with Ex. 37.

This stirring, possibly processional, song, with its repeated first and last phrases in the lower part, is noteworthy not only because of the number of thirds it contains, but also because of its word-painting—that is, the composer has portrayed the sense of the words in his music. Thus in the third phrase, the line "Now are rich men trodden down" ("Dives nunc deprimitur"), both parts descend, and at the end of the piece the voices

* Adapted from A. Einstein, *A Short History of Music* (5th Ed.), p. 206.

have a whole 'flight' of notes on the word 'winging' ('fugatur'). Admittedly it was quite common (but entirely optional) to end a conductus with what was then called a 'cauda' ('tail'), but the fact that the poem ends with this word (perhaps a deliberate choice by the poet if he had a musical setting in mind) must clearly have influenced the composer.

ex. 38 Conductus *Redit aetas aurea*   Anon. (1189?)

EX. 38 (CONTD.)

Redit aetas aurea was composed for and probably sung at the Coronation of Richard I (the Lion-hearted) in 1189, and its English origin is therefore certain. What is not so certain (and this applies to all conducti) is the way it should be transcribed, for the music, with its syllabic underlay and metrical verse, is not notated in modal rhythm, and hence gives the modern editor less help than in the case of organa. Despite this rhythmically vague notation, however, most scholars now agree that all conducti were in fact performed in one of the rhythmic modes, though the choice of which one is often difficult to decide.

Although the conductus was only popular during the first half of the thirteenth century on the Continent, it persisted in Britain in various modified forms up to *c.* 1450. The earliest of these modified forms was called 'gymel'§ (but the name was not used before the fifteenth century), which is an Anglicized abbreviation of the Latin 'cantus gemellus', or 'twin song', and its two parts move mostly in a succession of thirds and sixths. Later, in keeping with the British love of sonority, a third part was sometimes added, with the result that nearly every 'chord' contains a third or a sixth as compared to the fourths and fifths of Continental compositions (Ex. 39*).

* Transcribed from *Early English Harmony* (ed. Wooldridge), Vol. I, Plate 36.

Ex.39   Gymel style - *Salve virgo virginum*

Anon. Late 13th cent.

(♩ = ♩· = MM c.80)

There is little doubt that in the above hymn to the Virgin Mary the two lower voices are the original gymel, for they move almost entirely in thirds, but the topmost voice adds considerably to the sonority of the piece by frequently singing the fifth above the lowest note, and as a result nearly half the chords are full major or minor triads (i.e. chords consisting of the root, third, and fifth). In the original the words are placed beneath the lowest voice only, but they were meant to be sung by any or all of the parts.

Although the rich effect of the gymel sounds surprisingly modern to our harmonically-conditioned ears, and although the melodies are often charmingly fresh and simple, it is most probable that to a thirteenth-century Frenchman such music was out of date and not nearly so expressive, artistic, or subtle as the motet,§ which, from about 1225, was all the rage in France, its popularity being the main reason for the decline of the conductus.

The origin of the motet can be traced back to a few organa of the St. Martial School in which the two parts sing different words (see Ex. 19), a different text from the tenor being added to the florid upper part, probably as an aid to the singer (compare the origin of the sequence in Chapter 1, p. 21). That this idea was not adopted at first by the Notre Dame School§ may have been due to ecclesiastical objections that the words of the chant in the tenor would be obscured by the simultaneous rendering of a completely different text in the upper voice. In the early years of the thirteenth century, however, the idea was applied to the conductus which, being in the main a secular type, could not possibly have offended the authorities on religious grounds. The result was a class of composition now called 'conductus motet':§ conductus because none of the voices uses a borrowed melody and all move together in the same rhythm, motet because the upper part or parts have different words from the tenor.

The singing of two or more texts at the same time (polytextuality) was clearly popular with the Notre Dame and later composers, for, disregarding the admonishments of the clergy, they added different texts to the upper part or parts of some of their clausulae, thus producing the motet proper. The chant melodies in the tenor part of most clausulae are, as we saw in Chapter 2, arranged in repeated rhythmic patterns, and this feature is one of the main characteristics of most thirteenth-

century motets, the other and more important being polytextuality. The name 'motet' comes from the Latin *motetus*,
which in its turn was derived from the French word *mot*
(='word'), and the part immediately above the tenor, which
in organa was called duplum, was now called 'motetus' because
new 'words' were added to it, and the name was soon applied
to all compositions of this type.

Because the clausulae were an integral part of the liturgy, so
were those motets in which new words were simply added to
the upper voice or voices of the former. It was not long, however,
before the motet became an independent type of composition,
but it was still used liturgically, for it was still based on a
Gregorian melody in the tenor while the words of the upper part
or parts were poetic paraphrases of those of the chant. For
instance, in Ex. 40 the tenor is taken from the Gradual sung
during the Feast of the Assumption of the Blessed Virgin Mary
which begins 'Propter veritatem', the notes in the tenor being
those that are sung to the word 'veritatem' in the original
chant. The words of the two upper parts are poems in honour
of the Virgin—in fact, the fifth line in the motetus part, "And
he didst raise thee up this day" ("Qui te assumpsit hodie"),
refers specifically to the Assumption; thus the whole composition
is a wonderfully subtle and expressive hymn of praise to Our
Lady (Ex. 40*):

This is a more than usually interesting motet because,
although the twice-stated tenor melody, unlike most, is not
arranged in repeated rhythmic patterns, the two upper parts
have very definite structures which have been shown by letters,
the motetus being *ab bb ab ab* while the triplum is *AB CC
AB AB*, which is identical with the troubadour and trouvère
virelai (see Chapter 3, p. 81). Furthermore, the melody of the
motetus has been lifted bodily from a troubadour song.

Although the actual intrusion of secular songs or song-forms
into the liturgical motet is not very common, there is no doubt
that the lyricism of the former considerably influenced the
latter and contributed greatly to a musical style which made no
distinction between sacred and secular; thus the only difference
between a motet or conductus which portrays the joys of the
blessed in Paradise and one which paints the delights of wine,
women, and song in Paris (as in Ex. 41,† pp. 106-7) is the words.

---

* From Y. Rokseth, *Motets du XIIIᵉ Siècle*, p. 10.   † Adapted from *H.A.M.*, 33ʙ.

Ex.41 Motet - *On parole - A Paris - Frèse nouvele*   Anon. 13th.cent.

EX. 41 (CONTD.)

De bon cler vin et de cha - - pons, Et d'est - re a - veue bons com -
With ca - pons fat and beau - jo - - lais, And with good com - pa - ny

-gnons, Sens sou - ti - - - - e, grant
great. Spark-ling wit and joy

fran - - - - - ce! Frè - - - - se nou - -
-ber - - - - - ries! Fresh fine straw - -

-pai -gnons, Liés et joi - - ans, Chan-tans, truf - -fans et a - mo - rous,
al - way, So blithe and gay, sing-ing, cheat - -ing and a - mo - rous;

bau - - - dour, Bíaus joi-aus da - - mes d'ou - - nour,
is there, And ma-ny fine la - dies fair;

- ve - - - le! Mue-re fran - - ce, mue-re, mue-re fran - -
-ber - - - ries! Black-ber-ries, come buy my wild black - ber - - -

Et d'a - - voir, quant c'on a mes-tier, Pour so - la - -
And to have, when we need so -lace, The fair of

Et si truev' on bien en - - - - - tre - deus
And some good times there are one finds when

- ce! Frè - - se nou - - ve - - - le
-ries! Fresh fine straw - ber - - - ries

- cier Be - les da - mes a de - vis: Et tout ce truev'on a Pa - - ris.
face, Those la - dies ex - -ceed-ing kind: And all this in Pa - - ris you find.

De men - re feur - pour ho - mes de -, - si - - teus.
Food and drink can be shared by all poor men,

Mue - re fran - - - ce, mue - re, mue-re fran - - - - ce!]
Black-ber-ries, come buy my wild black - ber - - - - ries!

The thirteenth-century motet has often been regarded as the most difficult type of composition to understand and appreciate in the whole history of western music before the twentieth century, not only because of the simultaneous performance of two or more different texts, sometimes in two different languages, e.g. French and Latin, but also because the actual sound of the music is bare, even harsh, when compared to the more sonorous, smoothly-flowing conductus.

The whole point of polytextuality, to begin with at any rate, was to enrich the chant by adding fresh words, usually in verse, which enshrined and expanded the meaning or purpose contained in the chant itself, as in Ex. 40; thus the authors of these added texts were stimulated by the same desire as that which prompted the writers of tropes and sequences. As for the largely incomprehensible jumble of words which inevitably results during a performance, two points should be borne in mind. Firstly, that this music, and in fact practically all music up to about 1600, was not intended for the general public; this applies to the liturgical as well as to the purely secular motet. In the former it was—and still is in cathedrals and monasteries —the act of worship expressed through the service that mattered, not the presence or absence of a congregation, and to the choirmen themselves and even to the officiating clergy the subtle technique in which two or three different texts simultaneously express the same sentiments would be fully intelligible and eminently satisfying. The same applies to the secular motet, which was always written for and performed by the cultured *élite* of society. The second point to remember is that the singing of different words at the same time has been a favourite and most dramatic operatic device from Mozart to the present day; in fact, operatic ensembles frequently go further than the average thirteenth-century motet because they express several different and often completely opposed sentiments, but as the audience knows roughly what these sentiments are from the previous action of the drama, it simply abandons itself to the total impression. Similarly in the thirteenth century; but it is also quite likely that when performing a motet like Ex. 40 or 41, particularly for the first time, only the tenor part was sung or played to begin with, then the tenor and motetus parts together, and finally the whole composition, with instruments either playing the unsung parts or else doubling the voices.

The manner of performance suggested above describes exactly the method by which a composer wrote a motet, for he first of all selected a melodic fragment, either from a chant or a secular song, and, having arranged the notes in repeated rhythmic patterns and decided on the number of repeats of the melody, he used this as his tenor, the basis of his composition. (The tenor of Ex. 41 may have been newly composed; if so, it was exceptional. On the other hand, it may have been a popular street-cry of the times.) Next he added the motetus, and finally the triplum. This is known as 'successive composition', and is clearly shown in Ex. 40, where both the upper parts are very attractive melodies, and if one were omitted the piece as a whole would not suffer greatly—in fact, to many ears it would gain, for it is between the upper parts that the most licence was allowed and the greatest dissonance occurs; in other words, provided that each upper part was concordant with the tenor at the beginning of every group of three 'beats', it did not matter what happened between the upper parts themselves. The concords were the unison, fifth, and their octaves (though some theorists included the major and minor thirds as well), and although a discord in the form of an accented passing note was permitted on the first 'beat', it had to resolve on to a concord. Thus the whole conception of polyphonic composition was very different from the normal one of today, which considers the sound of *all* the parts, both vertically as chords and horizontally as melodies. The thirteenth-century composer, indeed, enjoyed greater freedom than any composer between the fourteenth and twentieth centuries. Consecutive unisons, fifths, and octaves between the tenor and any other part were allowed because they were liked, while consecutive fourths, seconds, and sevenths between the upper parts were probably regarded as spicy discords which were subordinate to, while at the same time offsetting, the fundamental concords with the tenor.

So far we have only dealt with the purely liturgical and wholly secular motet. But there was another kind which seems positively blasphemous at first, for it combined both sacred and secular texts—for instance, a hymn to the Virgin Mary and a poem in which a lover yearns for his sweetheart (*H.A.M.*, 32B). Occasionally the two texts had nothing in common, but usually, as in the above instance, they were linked in the sense that they expressed much the same sentiments, only on different planes. This blending of sacred and secular was not peculiar to musicians, for once again we find an exact parallel in the architecture of the period, or, rather, the sculpture that formed an integral part of the magnificent Gothic cathedrals which reached their greatest perfection in France during the thirteenth century. As we saw in Chapter 2, the rigid, un-naturally-posed figures of the twelfth century were subordinated to the column they ornamented or to the design as a whole, but in the thirteenth century not only did decoration become increasingly rich and more widely used, but it also became more naturalistic. Figures became human, with smiling faces, tilted heads, expressive hands, and their clothing arranged in natural folds. The austere symbolic dignity of the earlier portrayals of Mary and the infant Jesus now gave way to the everyday picture of mother and child; humanity reflected divinity. Although the subject-matter, general treatment, and placing of the main pieces of sculpture were dictated by the Church, the less important or conspicuous places were appar-ently left to the carvers in wood and stone to do what they liked with, and it is in these places that one sees most clearly the increasing naturalism of the century. Animals, plants, mytho-logical monsters, and fantastic—even grotesque—figures, half man, half beast, can be found tucked away in corners or high overhead, both inside and outside the cathedral.

Thus the thirteenth-century craftsmen and composers alike saw nothing incongruous or irreverent in associating things secular with things sacred, and both sculpture and motet represented what might well be called the 'art of analogy', in which the experiences and wonder of this world were used to help understand and partially reflect the glory of God; and it was no coincidence that this conception of the relationship between divinity and humanity was one of the main themes running through the works and teaching of the Church's most brilliant and saintly scholar, Thomas Aquinas.

The changes in the motet during the thirteenth century were not limited only to the use of the vernacular (French) or to the borrowings from earlier secular songs, for a casual comparison between Exx. 40 and 41 will show that the triplum part has become much more animated compared to the other parts during the twenty-five years or so which separates the two pieces—in other words, the tendency throughout the century was towards greater rhythmic independence of the parts.

The difference between the number of notes in the upper voices and in the tenor led to a new way of arranging the parts, for it was clearly wasteful to continue writing in score when the tenor had so few notes compared to the others, and parchment was very expensive. The most economical method was to write the parts separately and so use up as much of the page as possible, like this:

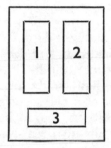

Where 1 is the triplum part, 2 the motetus, and 3 the tenor. If the motet was too long for a single page it was usually spread over two pages in this manner:

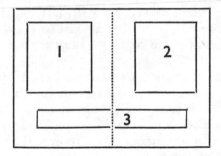

This separating of the parts on one or two pages (usually called 'choir-book' arrangement today or, in the fifteenth and sixteenth centuries, 'cantus collateralis', i.e. 'song [written] side by side' (see Chapter 6)—was used from about 1225 to about 1600 for practically all manuscript music except that written in conductus style, which was always written in score because all the voices have roughly the same number of notes.

The rhythmic independence of the parts in the motet is usually compensated by the repeated patterns in the tenor which give a basic rhythmic unity to the whole piece, and the more frequent but still fairly rare use of voice-exchange, an extreme example being the motet *Alle-psallite cum-luya*§ (*H.A.M.*, 33A), in which the two upper voices swop every phrase except the last. (The text, incidentally, is rather curious in that it consists of three tropes of the word 'Alleluya'.)

A more complex form of voice-exchange is the British ron dellus',§ in which all three voices exchange phrases, but the most famous and remarkable piece of imitative writing is the so-called Reading Rota, *Sumer is icumen in*,§ which probably dates from the middle of the century. This six-part double canon is so well known that we shall not describe it in detail, but simply point out that technically it was far more ambitious than anything on the Continent until the fifteenth century, and that it cannot have been a flash in the pan, but must have been preceded by a number of other such pieces, which alas have not survived. It is ambitious, too, in its use of six voices, and this supports what has already been said about the British love of sonority.

The increasing animation of the upper voices, particularly the triplum, developed rapidly during the last half of the century, and reached its peak in the motets of a certain Petrus de Cruce§ (or Pierre de la Croix) [fl. latter half of thirteenth century], and as he played a vital part in altering the way in which music was written down we must first of all see what it was that he altered.

Up to about 1225 all part-music, with one exception, was written down in much the same way as that described in Chapter 2—that is to say, in groups of notes called 'ligatures' in which the alternations of long and short notes depend entirely on the arrangement of the ligatures. The exception was the conductus, in which ligatures could not be regularly used, because each syllable of the text corresponds roughly to one note. The same became true of the motet, and composers found it necessary to make clear to the singers which notes were long and which short; they therefore made two of the note shapes already in use in ligatures independent; these were the 'longa' (the 'virga' of Gregorian chant) and the 'brevis' (the 'punctum' of Gregorian chant). Later on (*c.* 1250), because composers wanted to write more flexible and expressive melodies, a shorter note value came into use, the 'semibrevis', with the shape ♦, also borrowed from Gregorian chant, but this (unlike the long and breve) had no independent existence and was regarded simply as a breve broken up, and hence could only be used in groups of two or three per breve unit. All these changes spelt the death of the old ligature groupings, and round about 1260 a theorist called Franco of Cologne [fl. *c.* 1250-after 1280] introduced a new notation in an admirable set of rules which he expounded in his *Ars Cantus Mensurabilis* ('The Art of Measured Song').

Franco's rules can be summarized as follows:

1. As in the older notation, the number three is the only perfect one.
2. There are four note shapes, the duplex longa, longa, brevis, and semibrevis, of which only the first three may be used singly.
3. The standard note value (tactus) is now the perfect breve, not the perfect long.
4. The double long has only one value, while the other three may each have two values, and these are reckoned by the perfect breve, thus (modern equivalents are placed in brackets):

(N.B.—Discounting the double long, only the perfect long and the perfect breve may be used singly, for an imperfect long must be followed or preceded by a perfect breve, and an altered breve must be preceded by a perfect breve.)

The values of the long (*L*), breve (*B*), and semibreve (*S*) depend on their position, e.g. (in modern notation and with bar lines):

5. The *shape* of a ligature, not its position in a number of other ligatures, determines invariably the values of the notes

it contains, so that now the ligature ◼◼, for example, always means two perfect breves (♩♩), whereas before it could mean either *L B* (♩ ♪) or *L B* (♪ ♩), depending on whether it was written in the first or second rhythmic modes.

6. The vertical lines of haphazard length which marked off the ordines in the earlier notation and which stood for rests of varying duration are now replaced by lines of definite length which represent different rests (see Fig. 2).

While much of Franco's *Ars Cantus Mensurabilis*, like most theoretical works, simply summarizes previous practice, some of his rules are new and were clearly formulated in order to achieve a greater degree of consistency in notation—for example, his exact evaluations of ligatures and his rigid ternary division of the breve. As regards the latter, we have already seen that duple time almost certainly existed in the twelfth and thirteenth centuries in both monophony and part-music (see Chapter 2, pp. 49-50, and Chapter 3, pp. 85-86), and in fact there are a few pre-Franconian pieces that admit of no other interpretation; moreover, the very word '*semi*breve' must surely have meant that originally the breve was 'halved'.

Although the advantages of Franco's system outweighed its disadvantages—it remained the basis of all notation up to the end of the sixteenth century—it was continually expanded or pruned by later composers and theorists. To begin with, composers found that they needed a note smaller than the semibreve in order to be able to write more lively and quicker-moving melodies, particularly in the triplum part of their motets. To us the obvious solution would have been to invent a different note shape, but the idea of creating something completely new was largely foreign to the thirteenth-century mind; thus in the motet the most important part—the tenor—was borrowed, the upper voices were mostly made up of well-established melodic fragments, and even the note shapes themselves, the long, breve, and semibreve, had existed previously in Gregorian chant. What happened then was that round about 1280 certain composers, of whom Petrus de Cruce seems to have been the first and most important, continued to use the shape of the semibreve, but gave it values ranging from two-thirds of a breve (as with Franco) to one-seventh of a breve, and in order to show how many semibreves were meant to be sung in the time of a breve they marked off the groups by placing a long, or a breve, or a long or breve rest, or a ligature, or a dot at the beginning and end of each group. The dot in fact served much the same purpose as our modern bar-line, and although to our way of thinking it represents a real step forward in helping to make the notation clearer, in actual fact it did not remain in use for very long, for reasons which will become plain in the next chapter.

Another disadvantage of Franco's system was that it did not admit what we should call duple time, but only triple—in other words, a perfect long or breve could not be divided into two equal parts, but although duple time did not come into its own until the fourteenth century, Petronian notation (i.e. that used by Petrus de Cruce) prepared the way by, for example, making four semibreves equal a perfect breve, and the division of the latter into five or seven parts heralded the fall from power of the number three (*H.A.M.*, 34, 35; see Fig. 2*).

FIG. 2   Petronian notation. The last part of the motetus (left hand column) and duplum, and the complete tenor (bottom stave of both columns, right to left) from the motet *Garrit gallus—In nova fert. Le Roman de Fauvel.* (See Chapter 5.) Note the semibreve groupings by means of dots, rests, etc., and the semibreves with downward tails, e.g. motetus stave 1, 3rd note, stave 2, 5th note. The white ligatures in the tenor are red in the original. (See Ex. 51.)

* Facsimile in W. Apel, *The Notation of Polyphonic Music, 900-1600*, 4th Ed., p. 331.

Petrus de Cruce and his fellow composers wrote both sacred and secular motets, but the number of the latter was beginning to outstrip the former as the preference for secular song became stronger—a preference which reached its peak in the next century. Alongside this trend and to some extent linked with it was the growing independence of the composer, who, having established a musical style capable of enriching the liturgy on the one hand and courtly entertainments on the other, increasingly favoured the latter because. it gave him more scope for experiments and was not subject to such dictatorial authority. His treatment of the words he set shows another side to his independence, for the subtlety and expressive qualities of his music began to assume greater importance than they had previously, and many late-thirteenth-century motets disregard the natural accents of the text in a most flagrant manner, largely owing to the rapid groups of semibreves syllabically underlaid. The result is sometimes grotesque, but then so are many of the gargoyles on Gothic cathedrals. Admittedly we do not know the exact speed at which Petrus de Cruce's motets (or any other mediaeval music) were performed, but because the breve was now the unit of time this did not mean that it was twice or thrice as quick as the long in the time of Pérotin. In fact there are good grounds for believing that the unit of time, no matter what its note value, has remained fairly constant right through history for what we might call standard pieces, and is roughly equal to the human heart-beat, i.e. between M.M. 70 and 80. (By standard pieces is meant those that require no pronounced subjective interpretation, such as the average hymn-tune. For further discussion on this point, see Chapter 6.) Of course, the speed of the time unit has not always remained the same because there must always be an interim period during the changeover from one time unit to another, and the introduction of shorter note values also had its effect. Thus, Pérotin's time unit, the long, would be about M.M. 80 (the breve therefore being about M.M. 240), but with Franco the changeover to the breve time unit had only just begun and the long was still an important note, with the result that the breve was neither as fast as it was in Pérotin's music nor as slow as it should have been, so to speak, i.e. M.M. 80; it was probably about M.M. 130. Petrus de Cruce's groups of semibreves, however, must have slowed the breve down considerably,

PERFORMANCE

also pp. 108, 116-18.)

37. This may be sung with instruments or played by instruments alone.

38. As for Ex. 37.

39. As for Ex. 37.

40. As for Ex. 37, except that the lowest part is better played than sung.

41. As for Ex. 37.

and in his music it must have been about M.M. 55. We shall see in the next chapter that the breve became slower still because the semibreve became the new time unit.

The increasing animation of the motet during the thirteenth century and the growing delight in music for its own sake are perhaps most clearly shown in the curious—even bizarre—type of composition called 'hocket' (French, *hoquet* = 'hiccup'). In its simplest form this is a two-part piece in which each note of the tenor melody is repeated in the other part (called 'hoquetus'), with the voices singing and resting alternately (Ex. 42).

Ex.42

The number of actual hocket compositions are few, but it became a popular means of ornamenting part-music, particularly motets (*H.A.M.*, 35, bars 8, 9, 17, 18, etc.), and while we know that this device was used in primitive music, no European examples earlier than the thirteenth century have come down to us, although Aclred (see Chapter 2, p. 69) describes what is presumably hocketing in his *Speculum Charitatis*: "Sometimes thou may'st see a man with an open mouth, not to sing but, as it were to breathe out his last gaspe, by shutting in his breathe, and by a certaine ridiculous interception of his voyce, as it were to threaten silence, and now againe to imitate the agonies of a dying man, or the extasies of such as suffer."[*]

It was almost inevitable, considering the growing popularity of part-music during the thirteenth century, that some of the more educated trouvères would compose pieces in which the forms of the solo song, especially the rondeau, virelai, and ballade, are set polyphonically. This fusing of the old with the new produced an art form which reached its peak in the fourteenth century, but it had already caught on in the thirteenth, particularly with Adam de la Halle§ (see Chapter 3, p. 84), and Jehannot de l'Escurel§ [d. 1303]. Most of these pieces are based on a previously composed solo song, and in

[*] Prynne's translation, quoted from Davey, ibid., p. 17.

this, i.e. the use of an existing melody, they resemble the motet, but unlike the latter all the parts have the same words, and the borrowed melody is not always in the tenor, being sometimes placed in the middle part. When this happens the tenor becomes a kind of bass—in other words, its prime function is to support the upper voices. This new conception of the tenor had far-reaching results, because for the first time it was not invariably regarded as the most important part, and in writing a composition of this type a composer might first of all borrow a trouvère rondeau, say, ornament it a little perhaps, add a tenor below it, and finally write a third part above it, a method of composing quite different from that of the motet and conductus, both of which started with the tenor and added the upper parts afterwards.

Of all the types and forms of thirteenth-century music the motet is undoubtedly the most important, for, apart from being more subtle, refined, and expressive, its characteristics reflect more faithfully the artistic attitude of the times, although the conductus too shared in its impartial use on either sacred or secular occasions. It is easy enough to say this, but it is much more to the point that we should be convinced of the motet's superiority through actual performance, and in this connection a few practical tips may be useful. Sing the original words if your knowledge of mediaeval Latin or French is good enough for you to understand what you are singing; if not, then get someone to provide a translation which will fit the music and which keeps more to the spirit of the original than to the letter. Sing the parts one at a time in order to get their flavour, and then sing the two lowest parts together (tenor and motetus), and finally all three, as suggested on p. 108. In an age which takes to Debussy as our forbears took to Brahms it should not be long before this music makes its appeal. As regards actual performance, the same conditions hold as in the thirteenth century—in other words, any combination of voices or suitable instruments was permitted by the composer, but whereas the motet tenors were probably more often played by instruments only, the upper parts were performed by voices and instruments either together or separately, and this applies to all the parts of a conductus. Once again it must be remembered that the number of those taking part was small. The instruments were those already mentioned in Chapters 2 and 3.

The thirteenth century was an ast... Gothic cathedral reached its highest p... beauty; men were becoming intellectu... while the Church's authority was still... individuals such as Thomas Aquinas w... philosophy, particularly that of Arist... doctrine, in spite of the fact that in 1215 the... Aristotle's works; in science the solitary vo... [c. 1214-1292] rejected the attitude which... popular opinion, and outside authority abo... verified theories, and so pointed the way... scientific methods; the end of the century s... unsurpassed lyric poetry of Dante [1265-132... influenced by the troubadour, Arnaut Danie... which culminated in the *Divine Comedy* written... twelve years of his life. In the world at large Co... the capital of the Eastern Roman Empire, was t... the Fourth Crusade (1202-4), but was regained by... in 1261, largely because the Church found it i... difficult to raise sufficient enthusiasm for the later... the power of the Church in fact was waning, and in... Edward I was beginning to draw his country aw... complete subjugation to the Pope. In no single a... however, whether spiritual, intellectual, political, or a... did such enormous changes take place or was there so g... variety of expression as in music: monophony and polyph... Gregorian chant, organum, and clausula, trouvère song... conductus, motet and secular part-song, liturgical music... music for every aristocratic occasion, the beginnings... independence from the Gregorian tenor melodies, especially... the polyphonic rondeau, virelai, and ballade (cantilenae), th... increasing flexibility of rhythm and melody and with it the... rapid development of notation, from Pérotin's lack of differ-entiated shapes to Franco's classification of note values and their extension by Petrus de Cruce, the widespread use of instruments and the epoch-making re-discovery of the keyboard. As one writer has said: "The thirteenth century is one of the greatest in music history, being comparable with the sixteenth, eighteenth, and nineteenth."*

* G. Reese, *Music in the Middle Ages*, p. 329.

(See...
Ex.
Ex.
Ex.
Ex.
E...

THE NEW ART

The pope sits on his holy chair, which stood
For rock of Peter once, but now is wood.
He looks at Fauvel there in his presence,
To whom the assembled make great reverence,
And groom him constantly from morn till night.
The pope then stretches out his hand so white,
And by the bridle through his palace rooms
He gently leads him, blaming not the grooms.
And now, while softly rubbing Fauvel's head,
He says, 'A lovely beast, he must be fed.'
The cardinals, who wish to please anew,
Reply, 'O holy Father, thou speak'st true.'*

THIS quotation comes from a very famous French poem
called *Le Roman de Fauvel*§ ('The Fable of Fauvel') written in
1310 and 1314 by a certain Gervais de Bus. Its main purpose
was a violent attack on the Church, and although the above
passage may seem harmless enough at first sight, its sting will be
fully appreciated when it is realized that 'wood' was symbolical
of 'inconstancy' and that Fauvel was a fictitious horse or ass,
the name being derived from the initial letters of the following
vices: *Flatérie, Avarice, Vilanie* (depravity—'u' and 'v' were
interchangeable in the Middle Ages), *Variété* (fickleness)
Envie, and *Lascheté* (cowardice), so that when anybody groomed,
caressed, or praised Fauvel they were in fact revelling in
wickedness. Such a criticism would hardly have been possible
in earlier centuries, and *Le Roman de Fauvel* indicates in a
striking manner the disrespect with which the Church was
regarded during the fourteenth century by a great many
intelligent and cultured people.

The reason for this was not only due to the waxing interest in
pagan philosophy and science, but also to the waning authority
and saintliness of the Church herself. The trouble started near
the end of the eleventh century, when a succession of popes

* Freely translated from lines 105-16.

began to claim complete supremacy in the realm of Church *and* State—in other words, to insist that emperors and kings must bow to Papal rule. To enforce their claim, armies were either hired or offered indulgences—which to the mediaeval peasants meant free tickets to Heaven—and the amount of blood that the Church shed as a result, coupled with the widespread torture and death inflicted on those she regarded as heretics (e.g. the Albigensian Crusade) and the shocking corruption of most of her clergy, caused her prestige to sink rapidly until the crowning scandal of the Great Schism (1378-1417) was reached during which two Popes, one at Avignon (France) and one in Rome, simultaneously claimed to be God's highest representative on earth and used all the religious, political, and financial means at their disposal to obtain support for their respective claims. To make matters worse, all this happened while the so-called Hundred Years' War (1339-1453) was ravaging France (the battles of Crécy, 1346, and Agincourt, 1415), and it followed shortly after the virulent plague known as the Black Death had swept over Europe from the East, killing about 25 million people, including over half the population of Britain. At the very time when the Church should have been a source of hope and inspiration, she was found lacking; small wonder, therefore, that her hitherto unassailable position began to crumble and the seeds of religious revolt and secular power began to germinate; small wonder also that composers, following the general trend of the times, found a greater incentive and satisfaction in writing for the royal courts and the aristocracy which thronged them, where new ideas and experiments were encouraged and no clerical authority hampered their creative faculty, than for a Church discredited by corruption and split by rival factions and which actively discouraged the new developments in music.

We have already quoted the criticisms on church music by Aelred and John of Salisbury, but the climax came when John XXII, an Avignon Pope from 1316-34, issued a decree in 1324-5 which contains the following sentences: "Certain disciples of the new school, much occupying themselves with the measured dividing of time, display their method in notes which are new to us, preferring to devise ways of their own rather than to continue singing in the old manner; the music, therefore, of the divine offices is now performed with semibreves and in his music it must have been about M.M. 55. We shall see in the next chapter that the breve became slower still because the semibreve became the new time unit.

The increasing animation of the motet during the thirteenth century and the growing delight in music for its own sake are perhaps most clearly shown in the curious—even bizarre—type of composition called 'hocket' (French, *hoquet*='hiccup'). In its simplest form this is a two-part piece in which each note of the tenor melody is repeated in the other part (called 'hoquetus'), with the voices singing and resting alternately (Ex. 42).

The number of actual hocket compositions are few, but it became a popular means of ornamenting part-music, particularly motets (*H.A.M.*, 35, bars 8, 9, 17, 18, etc.), and while we know that this device was used in primitive music, no European examples earlier than the thirteenth century have come down to us, although Aelred (see Chapter 2, p. 69) describes what is presumably hocketing in his *Speculum Charitatis*: "Sometimes thou may'st see a man with an open mouth, not to sing but, as it were to breathe out his last gaspe, by shutting in his breathe, and by a certaine ridiculous interception of his voyce, as it were to threaten silence, and now againe to imitate the agonies of a dying man, or the extasies of such as suffer."*

It was almost inevitable, considering the growing popularity of part-music during the thirteenth century, that some of the more educated trouvères would compose pieces in which the forms of the solo song, especially the rondeau, virelai, and ballade, are set polyphonically. This fusing of the old with the new produced an art form which reached its peak in the fourteenth century, but it had already caught on in the thirteenth, particularly with Adam de la Halle§ (see Chapter 3, p. 84), and Jehannot de l'Escurel§ [d. 1303]. Most of these pieces are based on a previously composed solo song, and in

---

* Prynne's translation, quoted from Davey, ibid., p. 17.

this, i.e. the use of an existing melody, they resemble the motet, but unlike the latter all the parts have the same words, and the borrowed melody is not always in the tenor, being sometimes placed in the middle part. When this happens the tenor becomes a kind of bass—in other words, its prime function is to support the upper voices. This new conception of the tenor had far-reaching results, because for the first time it was not invariably regarded as the most important part, and in writing a composition of this type a composer might first of all borrow a trouvère rondeau, say, ornament it a little perhaps, add a tenor below it, and finally write a third part above it, a method of composing quite different from that of the motet and conductus, both of which started with the tenor and added the upper parts afterwards.

Of all the types and forms of thirteenth-century music the motet is undoubtedly the most important, for, apart from being more subtle, refined, and expressive, its characteristics reflect more faithfully the artistic attitude of the times, although the conductus too shared in its impartial use on either sacred or secular occasions. It is easy enough to say this, but it is much more to the point that we should be convinced of the motet's superiority through actual performance, and in this connection a few practical tips may be useful. Sing the original words if your knowledge of mediaeval Latin or French is good enough for you to understand what you are singing; if not, then get someone to provide a translation which will fit the music and which keeps more to the spirit of the original than to the letter. Sing the parts one at a time in order to get their flavour, and then sing the two lowest parts together (tenor and motetus), and finally all three, as suggested on p. 108. In an age which takes to Debussy as our forbears took to Brahms it should not be long before this music makes its appeal. As regards actual performance, the same conditions hold as in the thirteenth century—in other words, any combination of voices or suitable instruments was permitted by the composer, but whereas the motet tenors were probably more often played by instruments only, the upper parts were performed by voices and instruments either together or separately, and this applies to all the parts of a conductus. Once again it must be remembered that the number of those taking part was small. The instruments were those already mentioned in Chapters 2 and 3.

The thirteenth century was an astonishingly rich one. The Gothic cathedral reached its highest point of development and beauty; men were becoming intellectually independent, and while the Church's authority was still regarded as absolute, individuals such as Thomas Aquinas were reconciling Greek philosophy, particularly that of Aristotle, with Christian doctrine, in spite of the fact that in 1215 the Church condemned Aristotle's works; in science the solitary voice of Roger Bacon [*c.* 1214-1292] rejected the attitude which placed tradition, popular opinion, and outside authority above experimentally verified theories, and so pointed the way toward modern scientific methods; the end of the century saw the hitherto unsurpassed lyric poetry of Dante [1265-1321]—much of it influenced by the troubadour, Arnaut Daniel [d. 1199]— which culminated in the *Divine Comedy* written during the last twelve years of his life. In the world at large Constantinople, the capital of the Eastern Roman Empire, was taken during the Fourth Crusade (1202-4), but was regained by the Greeks in 1261, largely because the Church found it increasingly difficult to raise sufficient enthusiasm for the later Crusades; the power of the Church in fact was waning, and in England Edward I was beginning to draw his country away from complete subjugation to the Pope. In no single activity, however, whether spiritual, intellectual, political, or artistic, did such enormous changes take place or was there so great a variety of expression as in music: monophony and polyphony, Gregorian chant, organum, and clausula, trouvère song and conductus, motet and secular part-song, liturgical music and music for every aristocratic occasion, the beginnings of independence from the Gregorian tenor melodies, especially in the polyphonic rondeau, virelai, and ballade (cantilenae), the increasing flexibility of rhythm and melody and with it the rapid development of notation, from Pérotin's lack of differentiated shapes to Franco's classification of note values and their extension by Petrus de Cruce, the widespread use of instruments and the epoch-making re-discovery of the keyboard. As one writer has said: "The thirteenth century is one of the greatest in music history, being comparable with the sixteenth, eighteenth, and nineteenth."*

* G. Reese, *Music in the Middle Ages*, p. 329.

PERFORMANCE

(See also pp. 108, 116-18.)

Ex. 37. This may be sung with instruments or played by instruments alone.

Ex. 38. As for Ex. 37.

Ex. 39. As for Ex. 37.

Ex. 40. As for Ex. 37, except that the lowest part is better played than sung.

Ex. 41. As for Ex. 37.

5

THE NEW ART

The pope sits on his holy chair, which stood
For rock of Peter once, but now is wood.
He looks at Fauvel there in his presence,
To whom the assembled make great reverence,
And groom him constantly from morn till night.
The pope then stretches out his hand so white,
And by the bridle through his palace rooms
He gently leads him, blaming not the grooms.
And now, while softly rubbing Fauvel's head,
He says, 'A lovely beast, he must be fed.'
The cardinals, who wish to please anew,
Reply, 'O holy Father, thou speak'st true.'*

THIS quotation comes from a very famous French poem
called *Le Roman de Fauvel*§ ('The Fable of Fauvel') written in
1310 and 1314 by a certain Gervais de Bus. Its main purpose
was a violent attack on the Church, and although the above
passage may seem harmless enough at first sight, its sting will be
fully appreciated when it is realized that 'wood' was symbolical
of 'inconstancy' and that Fauvel was a fictitious horse or ass,
the name being derived from the initial letters of the following
vices: *Flatérie, Avarice, Vilanie* (depravity—'u' and 'v' were
interchangeable in the Middle Ages), *Variété* (fickleness)
Envie, and *Lascheté* (cowardice), so that when anybody groomed,
caressed, or praised Fauvel they were in fact revelling in
wickedness. Such a criticism would hardly have been possible
in earlier centuries, and *Le Roman de Fauvel* indicates in a
striking manner the disrespect with which the Church was
regarded during the fourteenth century by a great many
intelligent and cultured people.

The reason for this was not only due to the waxing interest in
pagan philosophy and science, but also to the waning authority
and saintliness of the Church herself. The trouble started near
the end of the eleventh century, when a succession of popes

* Freely translated from lines 105-16.

began to claim complete supremacy in the realm of Church *and* State—in other words, to insist that emperors and kings must bow to Papal rule. To enforce their claim, armies were either hired or offered indulgences—which to the mediaeval peasants meant free tickets to Heaven—and the amount of blood that the Church shed as a result, coupled with the widespread torture and death inflicted on those she regarded as heretics (e.g. the Albigensian Crusade) and the shocking corruption of most of her clergy, caused her prestige to sink rapidly until the crowning scandal of the Great Schism (1378-1417) was reached during which two Popes, one at Avignon (France) and one in Rome, simultaneously claimed to be God's highest representative on earth and used all the religious, political, and financial means at their disposal to obtain support for their respective claims. To make matters worse, all this happened while the so-called Hundred Years' War (1339-1453) was ravaging France (the battles of Crécy, 1346, and Agincourt, 1415), and it followed shortly after the virulent plague known as the Black Death had swept over Europe from the East, killing about 25 million people, including over half the population of Britain. At the very time when the Church should have been a source of hope and inspiration, she was found lacking; small wonder, therefore, that her hitherto unassailable position began to crumble and the seeds of religious revolt and secular power began to germinate; small wonder also that composers, following the general trend of the times, found a greater incentive and satisfaction in writing for the royal courts and the aristocracy which thronged them, where new ideas and experiments were encouraged and no clerical authority hampered their creative faculty, than for a Church discredited by corruption and split by rival factions and which actively discouraged the new developments in music.

We have already quoted the criticisms on church music by Aelred and John of Salisbury, but the climax came when John XXII, an Avignon Pope from 1316-34, issued a decree in 1324-5 which contains the following sentences: "Certain disciples of the new school, much occupying themselves with the measured dividing of time, display their method in notes which are new to us, preferring to devise ways of their own rather than to continue singing in the old manner; the music, therefore, of the divine offices is now performed with semibreves and minims, and with these notes of small value every composition is pestered. Moreover, they truncate the melodies with hockets, they deprave them with discantus, sometimes even they stuff them with upper parts made out of secular song [e.g. Ex. 40] . . . . Their voices are incessantly running to and fro, intoxicating the ear, not soothing it, while the men themselves endeavour to convey by their gestures the sentiment of the music which they utter . . . . We now hasten therefore to banish these methods . . . and to put them to flight more effectually than heretofore, far from the house of God. Wherefore . . . we straitly command that no one henceforward shall think himself at liberty to attempt these methods, or methods like them, in the aforesaid offices, and especially the canonical Hours or in the celebration of the Mass.

"And if any be disobedient, let him . . . be punished by a suspension from office of eight days. . . .

"Yet for all this, it is not our intention to forbid, occasionally . . . the use of some consonances, for example, the octave, fifth, and fourth, which heighten the beauty of the melody; such intervals, therefore, may be sung above the plain cantus ecclesiasticus, yet so that the integrity of the cantus itself may remain intact, and that nothing in the authoritative music be changed. . . ."*

In other words, Pope John XXII approved of Notre Dame organum, but not the motet, especially the modern kind, which was 'pestered' with semibreves and minims. The minim (Latin, *minima* = least) takes us back to *Le Roman de Fauvel*, for, apart from reflecting contemporary criticism of the Church, the manuscript on which the poem is written also contains an important anthology of popular music of the time. The pieces comprising this anthology were added in 1316 by a musician named Chaillou de Pestain, and they range from Gregorian chants to motets. Most of the latter are written in the style of Petrus de Cruce, but some of them show significant differences which indicate a development in notation, rhythm, and construction.

The main objection to Petronian notation was that although there were in practice note values from two-thirds to one-seventh of a breve, they were all shown by the same note shape

* Adapted from H. E. Woodridge, *Oxford History of Music*, I (2nd Ed.), 1929, pp. 294–6.

—the semibreve, and in order to lessen this ambiguity an anonymous scribe later added a downward stroke or tail to some of the semibreves in *Le Roman de Fauvel* motets, thus, ❢ , which equalled two-thirds of a breve (see Fig. 2). He also began to add upward tails to the 'shorter' semibreves, ↓ , but soon realised that this was a hopeless task because the values of these semibreves varied so much. This note shapé, however, became more important than any of the others that were invented round about 1300, and was called the minim. At about the same time, or, to be a little more precise, *c.* 1316–25, a Frenchman, Philippe de Vitri [1291–1361] was writing a remarkable treatise from which we have taken the title of this chapter. Indeed, it is now usually applied to the whole of the fourteenth century, but to begin with we shall limit outselves to discussing its effect on French music only.

De Vitri's 'Ars Nova', by expanding Franco's system, provided composers with a clear-cut and much more flexible notation, and one that had become an absolute necessity since the time of Petrus de Cruce. The three fundamental innovations of de Vitri's system are the placing of perfection and imperfection on an equal footing, the application of this to the semibreve (which at last could be used singly and which soon replaced the breve as tactus), and the introduction of the minim as a distinct and independent note value. Thus the dictatorship of triple time had ended and a far greater variety of rhythm was now possible (see Fig. 3).

In order to make the relationships between the notes quite clear de Vitri uses three words—*modus*, *tempus*, and *prolatio*, or 'mood' (a sixteenth-century English word which we prefer to the already overworked 'modé'), 'time', and 'prolation'. The mood is either great, when it refers to the number of longs in a double-long, or less, when it refers to the number of breves in a long. Time refers to the number of semibreves in a breve, and prolation to the number of minims in a semibreve. Each of these four relationships is either perfect or imperfect, and any combination of them was theoretically possible; in practice however, the great mood was never used owing to the length of the double-long (which roughly equalled the breve of today), and the less mood was almost invariably imperfect, so that instead of a possible sixteen combinations there were to all intents and purposes only four. In addition, de Vitri invented a number of signs, each of which stood for a particular combination, and thus showed the singer at a glance the values of the various notes; but they were hardly ever used by composers, possibly because of the fact that other musicians started inventing different ones. In order to simplify matters, those signs that were in common use in the fifteenth and sixteenth centuries and which developed out of de Vitri's are given in the following table, together with the four usual combinations and their modern time signature equivalents, with de Vitri's minim equalling our quaver (Ex. 43):

Ex. 43

Less Mood	Time	Prolation	Sign	Time Signature
Imperfect $(L=2\ B)$	Perfect $(B=3\ S)$	Perfect $(S=3\ M)$	⊙	$\frac{9}{8}$
,, ,,	Imperfect $(B=2\ S)$	,, ,,	₵	$\frac{6}{8}$
,, ,,	Perfect $(B=3\ S)$	Imperfect $(S=2\ M)$	O	$\frac{3}{4}$
,, ,,	Imperfect $(B=2\ S)$	,, ,,	C	$\frac{2}{4}$

As in Franco's system, the values of the notes also depend on their position (cf. Chapter 4, p. 113, Rule 4), this now being applied to the semibreve and minim as well. In order to make all this quite clear here is a series of note shapes with their values and grouping in modern notation in the four different combinations of time and prolation (Ex. 44):

Ex. 44

In the $\frac{9}{8}$ and $\frac{6}{8}$ examples the second minim has been 'altered', but it is quite possible for the last five notes to be sung thus: ♩ ♪ ♪ ♩ ♩., and in order to try and clarify this kind of situation composers expanded de Cruce's idea of using dots. This would have been admirable if they had all agreed on the way these dots should be used; as it is, however, the modern transcriber is often in difficulties as to the exact meaning of a dot and can sometimes only arrive at the correct solution by a process of trial and error, an unsatisfactory state of affairs which almost certainly existed for the fourteenth-century singer as well. In the succeeding centuries the number of dots was reduced, until by about 1650 only one remained—the one we use today, which adds to the note preceding it one-half of its value.

Some idea of the variety of rhythm which could be obtained from just three note shapes can clearly be seen in Ex. 44, but such was their desire for greater rhythmic freedom that composers began to use red notes as well. Apart from making the look of a musical manuscript considerably more attractive, red notes indicate certain differences in value and rhythm compared with their black brothers. They first appear in the tenor part of two motets in *Le Roman de Fauvel* (see Fig. 2), and for some time after their use was restricted to this part only.

Their value was similarly restricted at first, for redness implies the imperfecting of a note which is perfect if black, and when a number of them are grouped together they indicate a change of rhythm, as, for instance, in this example. (For reasons of economy, the original red notes are printed as white ones in Exx. 45-7) (Ex. 45):

Ex. 45

(See also Ex. 51, bb. 3-7, 13-17, and 23-7.) Later in the century red notes were used in the upper parts as well and their function became more varied, such as indicating ternary groups in binary rhythm (Ex. 46):

Ex. 46

or increasing the value of a note by a half (Ex. 47):

Ex. 47

or, if written as a white note with red outlines, making it equal to half its value when black. This last use meant that in performance there was a shorter note than the minim, and near the end of the century this received a black shape, ♪, and the name 'semiminim'.

Not content with the introduction of red notes and shorter notes, nor with the new patterns which binary rhythm made possible, composers began to experiment with the more subtle technique of syncopation. To us syncopation means the up-setting in various ways of a regularly recurring number of strong beats—e.g. $\frac{4}{4}$ ♩ ♩ ♩ | ♩ instead of $\frac{4}{4}$ ♩ ♩ ♩ ♩ | but regular strong beats were unknown in mediaeval music and therefore syncopation meant something quite different, and although the explanations in various theoretical works (the earliest being by an Englishman, *c.* 1326) are almost invariably abstruse, the general principle is as follows: into a normal binary or ternary group of notes is inserted another normal group— for example (in modern notation), instead of (Ex. 48)—

Ex. 48

the group enclosed in the square bracket was placed between the two notes of the first bar, thus (Ex. 49):

Ex 49

A more musical way of writing this and one which shows how the composer intended the notes to be grouped is (Ex. 50):

Ex 50

This example stands about halfway in complexity between the short, simple syncopated passages of the earlier part of the century and the long, complicated ones that can be found in some of the later pieces (see Ex. 61).

But although this development of rhythmical freedom which the composers of the fourteenth century enjoyed and exploited made a greater degree of melodic expressiveness possible, it

brought with it the danger of disintegration, for the more
rhythmically varied the parts become, particularly the upper
parts, the more independent are they of each other, and in
music as in society when the individual components have no
interrelationship or are not based on some unifying principle
something approaching anarchy results. In the motets of the
thirteenth century, except those written in the style of Petrus
de Cruce, the disintegration which the singing of different
words in each part might have brought was balanced by the
prevailing ternary rhythm and by the customary arrangement
of the tenor in repeated rhythmic patterns that were short
enough and simple enough to be heard. In the Petronian
motets, however, the unifying effect of ternary rhythm in all
parts is lessened by the use of semibreves of varying values, and
the highest part in particular becomes more independent in
every way, a state of affairs that is not adequately compensated
for by the organization of the tenor, and when in the next
century the scope of rhythmic variety increased rapidly, the
danger of the motet falling to pieces, as it were, became real.
De Vitri and many other composers seem to have been alive to
this danger and they tackled it as one would expect from a
rhythmic angle.

The two motet tenors in *Le Roman de Fauvel* that include red
notes are arranged in repeated rhythmic patterns which only
differ from those of Pérotin in being longer and more rhythmically varied; here is one of them. (The notes and rests enclosed
by brackets are red in the original: see Fig. 2) (Ex. 51*):

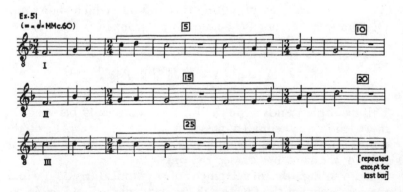

---

* Transcribed from W. Apel, *The Notation of Polyphonic Music, 900-1600*,
4th Ed., p. 331.

This organization of the tenor now goes under the fearsome name of 'isorhythm' (='the same rhythm'), and the repeated rhythmic patterns—called 'taleae' (Latin, *talea* ='a cutting') by fourteenth-century theorists—either fit the melody or 'color' exactly, as in the above example, in which there are three taleae, or else they overlap, in which case if the melody is repeated, which it usually is, it receives a different rhythmic interpretation, exactly as described in Chapter 2 (cf. pp. 57-8, and Exx. 24 and 25). This latter use of isorhythm became more popular than the former for the simple reason that it gives more rhythmic variety to the melody.

Isorhythm became the main structural device of the four-teenth-century motet, but so long as it was restricted to the tenor part only it hardly provided a sufficiently unifying effect on the composition as a whole with its different texts and varied rhythms in the upper parts, particularly as the longer and more complex the taleae became the less clearly audible were they to the listener—in other words, their unifying effect was felt rather than heard. In some of his motets therefore de Vitri applied the isorhythmic principle to the other parts as well, though not so strictly as in the tenor. This idea was increasingly adopted by later composers, some of whom made all the parts strictly isorhythmic, and round about 1400 this was carried a stage further when only the upper parts are isorhythmic, the tenor being free. It should be mentioned, however, that each of the upper parts, while naturally having a different melody or color from the others, always has a different rhythmic pattern; moreover, the talea of each part while sometimes of the same length as the others is often longer or shorter. Even so, the spread of the isorhythmic principle to most or all of the parts went a fair way to unifying the motet, which in fact can be regarded as a series of melodic variations on one or more rhythmic patterns. On the whole, however, it is probably true to say that the fourteenth-century motet is a less perfect art form than those written before Petrus de Cruce, because variety is not adequately balanced by unity.

Unlike most theorists, de Vitri was himself a composer of international repute, but unfortunately very few of his pieces have survived, and hence the man who most completely represents the French Ars Nova to us is Guillaume de Machaut§ [*c.* 1300–*c.* 1377]. Though a priest, Machaut undoubtedly appreciated the things of this world, an attitude which, as we have seen, was typical of the mediaeval ecclesiastic. He certainly saw and enjoyed a good deal of Europe, for as secretary to King John of Bohemia (brother of Pope John XXII), a monarch who was fond of travel, he met many influential people and visited countries as far apart as Italy and Lithuania. When John was killed at the Battle of Crécy, Machaut was employed by his daughter and later by such high-ranking personages as King Charles of Navarre, the Dauphin of France (later Charles V), and his brother Jean, Duc de Berry. The regard in which he was held, particularly by his noble patrons, is the main reason why so much of his music has been preserved, some of it in manuscripts of great beauty. His reputation, however, was by no means confined to music, for he was the chief literary figure in fourteenth-century France, undoubtedly influenced Chaucer [*c.* 1340-1400], and was compared by his countrymen to his great contemporary, the Italian poet Petrarch.

A true child of his century, Machaut wrote almost entirely secular music, in spite of the fact that he was in Holy Orders and reached the comparatively exalted position of Canon of Rheims in 1333, and of the 140 pieces that have survived only seven are liturgical—six motets and a mass, the rest consisting mainly of ballades (forty-two), virelais (thirty-three), rondeaux (twenty-one), lais (eighteen), and secular motets (seventeen).

Nearly all the motets§ have isorhythmic tenors, and in many of these Machaut heightens the interest towards the end by shortening the note values when the color is repeated but keeping the taleae intact (see Ex. 52), a procedure that later composers frequently adopted. In some of the motets isorhythm is freely applied to one or more of the upper parts, and in one motet this application is strict. In Ex. 52 the isorhythmic scheme of the tenor can be shown thus:

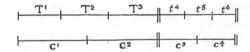

'C' stands for color and 'T' for talea; in the second section, where the note values are halved, the taleae ('t') are naturally half as long as in the first section. The two upper voices are also

isorhythmic (though not strictly so), but unlike the tenor only
the taleae repeat in each section, not the colores; furthermore,
the talea and color in the second section are quite different
from those in the first. This is a secular motet and a very lovely
one, but the tenor melody is sacred, being that portion of the
Gregorian chant, *Domine in tua misericordia speravi* (Introit for
the First Sunday after Pentecost), which is set to the word
'speravi' ('I have hoped [for]')—an obviously deliberate choice
considering the text of the triplum part (Ex. 52* pp. 132-7).

It will be noticed that the tenor has a B♭ in the signature
which is lacking in the two upper voices; such a practice was
very common in part-music from the thirteenth century to the
fifteenth, and various explanations have been advanced of
which the following is the most satisfactory.† The commonest
partial signature in the thirteenth and fourteenth centuries is,
from highest to lowest voice, ♮, ♭ in two-part compositions, and
♮, ♮, ♭ in three-part, as in Ex. 52. (For convenience we will
restrict the discussion to three-part pieces only, though what is
said below applies with equal force to two-part pieces.) The
mode of Ex. 52 was called Lydian by mediaeval musicians,
even though the tenor part, by which the mode of the whole
piece was judged, has a B♭ in the signature and hence is really
in the Ionian mode (see Chapter 1) transposed down a fifth.
(As the mode with F as final but with no B♭ in the signature
was also called Lydian (correctly) we shall indicate the F mode
with a B♭ thus: 'Lydian'. The Ionian mode, incidentally,
together with the Aeolian, was not recognized as an independent mode until the late fifteenth century.) The basic range of
the two upper parts in Ex. 52 is *c′-c″*; this is the exact range of
the duplum, whereas the triplum extends from the note below
(*b*) to the note above (*d″*). The theoretical range of the tenor is
f-f′, although only the notes *f-b♭* are actually used. Now,
nearly all compositions that have a partial signature are in
either the 'Lydian' mode—and there are comparatively few
pieces in the 'Lydian' mode that do not have a partial signature
—or else in the transposed Dorian mode, that is the tenor part
ends on a G final, a fifth lower than the D final of the untransposed Dorian. In both cases the basic range of the upper parts
is *c′-c″* when the tenor is in the 'Lydian' mode, and *d-d′* when

---

* Adapted from H. Gleason, *Examples of Music before 1400*, p. 88.
† Largely based on two articles by Richard H. Hoppin in the *Journal of the
American Musicological Society*, Vol. VI (1953), No. 3, and Vol. IX (1956), No. 2.

Ex.52 Motet-*De bon espoir - Puis que la douce - Speravi*   Machaut

EX. 52 (CONTD.)

EX. 52 (CONTD.)

EX. 52 (CONTD.)

EX. 52 (CONTD.)

EX. 52 (CONTD.)

the tenor is in the transposed Dorian mode, while the basic range of the tenor is a fifth lower, namely *f–f'* and *G–g* respectively. On the other hand in the great majority of compositions that have the same signature in all parts, e.g. ♮, ♮, ♮, or ♭, ♭, ♭, the range of the tenor is either within the same basic octave as the upper parts or else an octave below; in other words all the parts are in the same modal plane, whereas those pieces with partial signatures are 'bimodal', that is they are written in two modal planes. (It is important to realise that the term 'bimodal' does not mean in two *different* modes, e.g. Phrygian in the upper parts combined with Mixolydian in the tenor; it only means the combination of two forms of the *same* mode at the interval of a fifth. Furthermore the notes on which the duplum and triplum end are dictated primarily by the stock cadential figure of the period (see below), not by the mode of the voice concerned (this applies to all modal part-music), otherwise in each piece with a partial signature the upper voices would have to end on the fifth or its octave above the tenor final, and in all other pieces on the tenor final itself or its octave, thus ruling out the ⁸₅ chord and of course the later ⁵₃ chord.)

What has been stated above poses three questions. (1) Why did composers, when they wrote bimodally, nearly always use the 'Lydian' and transposed Dorian modes? (2) Why did they write on modal planes a fifth apart, and not a fourth or some other interval? (3) Why did they write bimodally at all?

Questions (1) and (2) can be taken together as they both revolve round the use of the note B♭. This was the first chromatic note to be placed on an equal footing with diatonic notes, for it is the only chromatic note to be found in Gregorian chant and, moreover, is an integral note in the Guidonian hexachord system. By far the commonest modes to employ B♭ in Gregorian chant are the Dorian and Lydian, the former because in the frequent and important melodic progression A–B–A, which hinges on the dominant of the mode, it was found that B♭ was easier to sing and sounded more graceful than B♮, and the latter because the augmented fourth or tritone F–B is avoided. By the middle of the thirteenth century it had become common practice to write a B♭ in the signature instead of in front of each B (as in Gregorian chant) for most compositions with F as final and for many with D as final, the modes still being termed Lydian and Dorian respectively, though in actual fact the

former is Ionian transposed (as we have seen) and the latter
Aeolian transposed. But real transposition by means of a B♭
signature, which results in the mode being transposed down a
fifth, was also recognized, and although the mode with final G
and a signature of B♭ was sometimes called Mixolydian because
of its final, it was more often called Dorian transposed, which
indeed it is. Transposition up a fifth by means of a key signature
was not used by the mediaeval composer because all he wanted
was the opportunity, when he desired, to write on two modal
planes, and while the simplest transposition, then as now (so
far as accidentals are concerned), is up or down a fifth, transposing up a fifth would have meant a new signature of F♯,
whereas the means for transposing down a fifth was already to
hand, namely the long-established B♭. (Not until the middle of
the seventeenth century did signatures of one or more sharps
become common.) The fact that the majority of bimodal
pieces are in the 'Lydian' and transposed Dorian modes is
almost certainly due to the traditional association of B♭ with
these modes in Gregorian chant.

The reason why a composer wrote bimodally at all was
undoubtedly because of his fondness for differentiating the
voices of a composition; this indeed is one of the main characteristics of most of the music written in the late thirteenth and
fourteenth centuries (see p. 153). Thus both the greater
animation of the triplum and to a lesser extent of the duplum
compared to the tenor in the latter half of the thirteenth
century (see Chapter 4), and the introduction of complex cross-
rhythms in the fourteenth century sprang not only from an
absorbing interest in rhythm itself, but also from the realisation
that rhythmic differences between parts assist greatly in
differentiating the parts one from another. Similarly bimodalism, in presenting two modal planes, helps to differentiate the
upper part or parts from the tenor.

An offshoot, as it were, of bimodalism is apparent in the
stock cadential figure of the fourteenth century that occurs in
both the untransposed and transposed Dorian, Lydian, and
Mixolydian modes. It can be seen at the end of Ex. 52, and
Ex. 53 overleaf is its simplest form.

The noteworthy feature of this cadence is that both the
dominant and the upper final are approached by a sub-
semitone or leading-note. In Chapter 1 we noted that the

subsemitonal approach to the final in the Lydian mode is usually avoided in Gregorian chant; indeed, this mode occurs much less frequently in Gregorian chant than either the Dorian or Mixolydian modes. In fourteenth-century cadences however,

Ex.53

Lydian cadence

the sub-semitonal approach to the upper final in all three modes is the rule rather than the exception, and results in the progressions C♯–D in the Dorian mode and F♯–G in the Mixolydian. Moreover the sub-semitonal approach to the dominant (B–C), which occurs 'naturally' in the Lydian cadence, was also applied to the Dorian and Mixolydian cadences, i.e. G♯–A in the former and C♯–D in the latter, thus creating, in a sense, two finals a fifth apart. This type of cadence in which both the final and dominant are approached by a leading-note is a characteristic of late mediaeval and much early Renaissance music; it is sometimes called the 'Burgundian cadence', an unfortunate name, because 'Burgundian' refers to certain composers of the mid-fifteenth century, whereas the cadence was already common in the time of Machaut (e.g. Ex. 52, bb. 16–17, 24–25, 76–77, and the final cadence). A better name is 'double leading-note cadence'. In the Phrygian mode, the only mode (apart from the discarded Locrian) in which the final is approached by a semitone above (F–E), the upper final and dominant were never preceded by a sub-semitone as this results in an augmented sixth (F–D♯) and augmented third (F–A♯) respectively (Ex. 54):

Ex. 54

Phrygian
cadence

Because of its unique supra-semitonal approach to the final, this is the only mediaeval modal cadence to survive to the present day.

The fact that Ars Nova composers liked the double leading-note cadence is one indication of the waning influence of the ecclesiastical modes, another being the greater use of chromatic

notes, because Gregorian chant, the largest and purest collection
of modal music in Europe, is essentially diatonic, even though
B♭ was admitted as a basic note quite early on, and certain
other chromatic notes were in fact sung as a result of transposing
a chant up a fourth or a fifth. Indeed, so far as chromaticism is
concerned the fourteenth century is less modal than the
fifteenth century, and it is no accident that secular music is
predominant in the former period, whereas in the latter
sacred music came increasingly to the fore, because sacred
music, particularly that for the liturgy, was, as we noted in
Chapter 1, profoundly influenced by Gregorian chant, and
hence is far more modal than secular music, in which composers
were less tied by tradition and hence freer to experiment,
especially in the fourteenth century, when ecclesiastical
authority, notably Pope John XXII, was so severe on new ideas.
This distinction between sacred and secular music applies also
to the thirteenth and sixteenth centuries; in the former the
songs of the troubadours and their offshoots and the dance
music of the period are quite frequently written in the Ionian
and Aeolian modes (which, as we have seen, were not then part
of the modal system), while contemporary liturgical music
uses them much less often, proving that these two modes—the
only two to survive to the present day—must have been popular
in the folk-music of earlier times. In the sixteenth century it was
the madrigal and chanson, not the mass and motet, that
destroyed most of the already crumbling walls of the modal
fortress.

But there is another reason for the double leading-note
cadence and the increased chromaticism—namely, that
fourteenth-century composers were more concerned with the
'vertical' aspect, i.e. the sonority of their music, than were
earlier composers. We observed in Chapter 2 that thirds and
sixths are richer sounds than the fourth, fifth, or octave, and
that this increased richness is due to a greater degree of
dissonance. We also observed that the ear has progressively
accepted as concordant or relatively concordant what was
previously heard as discordant. In the fourteenth century
composers were gradually beginning to accept thirds and
sixths as concords in their own right, and this new sense of
sonority, together with the preference for the leading-note, led
to such rules as (*a*) a third and sixth expanding stepwise to a

fifth and octave respectively should be major; (*b*) a third contracting to a unison should be minor; (*c*) a fifth and octave must be perfect; if the above intervals are not naturally major, minor, or perfect, they must be rendered so by chromatic alteration. The double leading-note cadence falls under (*a*), and its popularity was probably due to the bimodal flavour it imparted as well as to a liking for the sub-semitonal approach to a final and dominant and to a natural preference for the major third and sixth, which are less dissonant than the minor forms. Rule (*b*) was most likely dictated by the leading-note tendency, because, of the three 'natural' major thirds, C–E, F–A, and G–B, the first two usually, and the third often, had the lower note sharpened rather than the upper flattened when contracting to a unison. Rule (*c*) is really an outcome of rule (*a*), which underlines the restful, poised quality of the perfect fifth and octave following the expansion (always more emotionally intense than contraction) of a more dissonant interval.

The above rules do not apply to intervals of short duration, but only to those that have some significance, i.e. those that are approached by and consist of long notes or that are cadential; even so it is certain that composers did not regard the rules as inflexible, and it seems likely that performers took the same line (see 'musica ficta', pp. 167, 171). Moreover, it is perfectly clear that notes were quite often chromatically altered, not from any 'vertical' considerations, but simply in order to enhance the melody.

Machaut's motets display the composer's rhythmic technique and melodic sophistication at their height, but the lais, all but two of which are monodic, and the virelais,§ of which twenty-five are monodic, seem to be an attempt by the composer to recapture something of the spirit of the trouvères, of an age of chivalry long past; apart from the forms, however, and the fact that they are mostly monodic, there is little connexion between the two, except for the echoes of courtly love that can be heard in the poems. To this extent Machaut is akin to Brahms, for, like the latter, part of his output is in a style that reflects his sympathy with a tradition that was no longer the natural expression of the times in which he lived; chivalry had little place in the disillusioned atmosphere of the fourteenth century.

The same nostalgia, though to a lesser degree, can be sensed in Machaut's rondeaux§ and ballades.§ All of them, except one

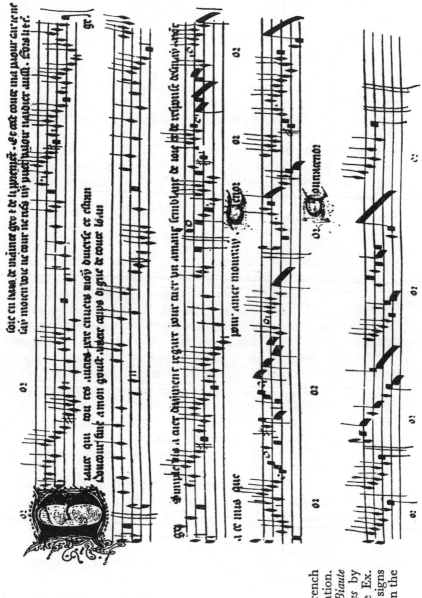

Fig. 3
French
Ars Nova notation.
The ballade *Biaute qui toutes autres* by Machaut. (See Ex. 55. Note the signs 'O', and 'C' in the tenor).

ballade, are in two to four parts and, like the lais and virelais, follow the thirteenth-century forms. The most famous rondeau, because of the subtlety of its construction, is that which has the refrain "*Ma fin est mon commencement, et mon commencement ma fin*"§ where the composer has indulged in word-painting, a rare occurence in the fourteenth century. Thus if the numbers 1–4 represent the tenor melody (the only part that sings the words) and the letters A, B represent the contratenor melody, the structure of the piece can be shown as follows and the link between the refrain and the actual music becomes obvious:

Cantus	.	.	.	4321 (instrumental)
Tenor .	.	.	.	1234 (vocal)
Contratenor .	.	.	ABBA (instrumental)

The two new voice names, 'cantus' and 'contratenor', came into use during the fourteenth century and gradually replaced the older duplum and triplum names. The contratenor, or 'countertenor', while usually having the same range as the tenor, was almost always composed last, and as a result is melodically less interesting as a rule than the other two parts. The cantus, however (sometimes called 'discantus', from which we get one meaning of the word 'descant' and which always indicates a high voice), became increasingly important as the century progressed, and in most of Machaut's ballades it has the main melody, the tenor and contratenor serving as supports, usually instrumental, as in the example shown opposite (Ex. 55*). (The form is that of Ex. 29 slightly varied, i.e. *ab ab cde F*: see Fig. 3.)

There are several things worth noting about this charming piece. To begin with, it is more sonorous than the motet of Ex. 52—in other words, there is a markedly greater percentage of triads, particularly at the beginning of each breve (=bar in the transcription). This is generally true of all Machaut's polyphonic ballades, rondeaux, and virelais compared to his motets, and represents a new unifying device that is first apparent in some of de Vitri's compositions. It also represents the beginning on the Continent of what is now known as 'tertiary harmony', i.e. harmony that is primarily based on the

---

* Transcribed from MS. Paris, Bibliothèque Nationale fr⁹ 9221 (fols. 152vo, 153). Facsimile in W. Apel, *The Notation of Polyphonic Music 900–1600*, 4th Ed. p. 359.

Ex. 55 Ballade - *Biaute qui toutes autres pere*   Machaut

EX. 55 (CONTD.)

† C♯ & B♮ should only be sung in the repeat.

EX. 55 (CONTD.)

third rather than on the fourth or fifth. In Britain, as we saw in Chapter 4, the acceptance of the third as a basic interval began a good deal earlier than in the rest of Europe, but the dominating influence of French music, with its stress on individualizing each part of a polyphonic composition, prevented the British conception of sonority from spreading for the richer or more sonorous the sound the more dissonant it is, and the harder it becomes for the ear to pick out the individual components. Thus the frequent use of thirds and sixths fuses the parts together more than if the less dissonant fourths and fifths are the main intervals.

Another point worth noting in Ex. 55 is the cross-rhythm in bars 9-14 and 30-35 between the tenor's syncopated breves (=minims in the transcription) in duple time and the ternary rhythm of the other parts. The change to duple time is indicated in the manuscript by the sign 'c' (cf. p. 125), one of the earliest instances of its use. These two closing passages of the two main sections are in fact rhythmically identical in the tenor and cantus parts, and the latter is almost identical melodically as well; this is known, for obvious reasons, as 'melodic rhyme' (see also Ex. 60, bb. 13–16 and 32–35, and Ex. 62). Note also the way the two motives A and B permeate the whole piece and thus give it unity, A occurring in bars 1-2, 10, 12, 14, 20, 26, 31, 33, and 35, and B in bars 4, 5, 7, 15, 16, 25, 36, and 37. This is a common feature of Machaut's music, although the delightful sequential use of motive A in the closing bars of each section is comparatively rare.

The melodic superiority of the cantus is very apparent in the above ballade, and this style of writing is usually called 'ballade style' today; a better name, however, is 'treble-dominated style', for this is a clearer definition and can be applied to other types of composition than the ballade without confusion. This style almost completely reversed the order of composition in the motet, for now the cantus was written first, the tenor next, and the contratenor last. It became enormously popular, lasting well into the fifteenth century (see Chapter 6), and when in the latter part of the fourteenth century composers began setting parts of the liturgy they often wrote in this style, thus flouting the authority of Pope John XXII. John's decree, in fact, had made things worse than before, because it encouraged composers to cultivate secular music, and when they returned to sacred composition they used a style which was, from the strict ecclesiastical point of view, far less suitable, not only in its complexity, but also in the fact that the main melody is in the top voice instead of the traditional tenor and, worse still, frequently has no connexion whatever with a Gregorian chant.

Machaut's church music, however, with one exception, is markedly more conservative in style than his secular pieces, all six of the motets being based on a Gregorian tenor and only Latin being used in the upper parts. The exception is the Mass,§ possibly the first complete setting of the Ordinary by one composer and the only one for nearly another 100 years, apart from the so-called 'Mass of Toulouse' and the so-called incomplete 'Mass of the Sorbonne' (sometimes mis-termed the 'Mass of Besançon'). Whether Machaut invented the idea or whether he knew either of the above two masses or the so-called Mass of Tournai (*c.* 1300), which is a collection of separate items in different styles and by different composers, will probably never be known, but in any case nothing can detract from the vigour, imagination, and technical ingenuity of the work. This Mass is sometimes and erroneously called 'Notre Dame' or 'Nostre Dame', and is often claimed to have been composed for the Coronation of Charles V (1364). It may have been, particularly as Charles had been a patron of Machaut, and the somewhat conservative style compared to his ballades, which might otherwise tend to date it as an early work, may have been deliberate for so solemn an occasion, but there is no proof.

The Mass is divided up into the usual five main sections, Kyrie, Gloria, Credo, Sanctus, and Agnus Dei, with a setting of Ite Missa Est at the end. The Kyrie, the 'Amen' at the end of the Credo and Gloria, most of the Sanctus, the Agnus Dei, and the Ite Missa Est are all in motet style with isorhythm in one or more of the parts, and all are based on a Gregorian chant in the tenor, except the two 'Amens'. The rest of the Mass is in conductus style, an obvious choice with regard to the Gloria and Credo because of the greater number of words, but the Credo is also based on a chant melody, not in the tenor however but in the motetus part, where it is highly ornamented. (The Credo of the Tournai Mass is similarly constructed.)

In order to give some idea of the way Machaut handles the motet and conductus style in his Mass, here are two short extracts, the first from the Christe Eleison and the second from the Credo (Exx. 56, 57* p. 150-2). (Translation for Ex. 57: 'And [I believe] in the Holy Ghost, the Lord and giver of life, who proceedeth from the Father and the Son, who with the Father and the Son together is worshipped and glorified, who spake by the prophets.')

This Mass anticipated that of the mid-fifteenth century and later in several ways, which it will be simplest to tabulate as follows:

1. In the Gloria and Credo movements the initial words 'Gloria in excelsis Deo' ('Glory be to God on high') and 'Credo in unum Deum' ('I believe in one God') are sung to Gregorian chant, the polyphonic setting beginning with the words 'Et in terra pax' ('And on earth peace'), and 'Patrem omnipotentem' ('The Father Almighty') respectively.

* Both examples are adapted from the edition of the Mass by J. Chailley.

2. The phrases 'Jesu Christe' in the Gloria and 'Maria Virgine' in the Credo are set to long notes, thus making them stand out from their context.
3. The Gloria and Credo are syllabically underlaid while the other movements are melismatic.
4. All the movements are linked together by a short motive, shown in the first two bars of the Triplum part in Ex. 56 (see also Triplum, b. 6, Motetus, b. 3, and in Ex. 57, Triplum, b. 13, Motetus, bb. 5–6, Tenor, b. 12); sometimes the motive is altered rhythmically.
5. Word-painting in the Credo on 'crucifixus', which is set to some unusually sharp discords. Later composers with a more refined sense of discord chose less emotional words or phrases to paint, such as 'descendit de coelis' ('came down from Heaven') and 'ascendit in coelum' ('ascended into Heaven'), making the voices fall and rise respectively.

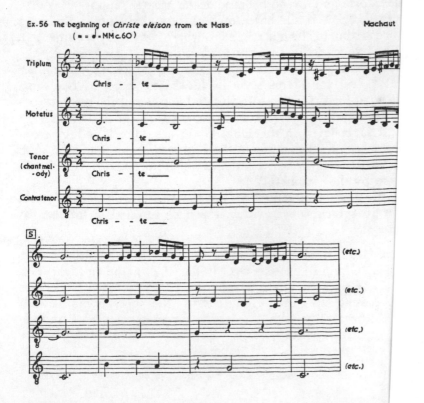

Ex. 56 The beginning of *Christe eleison* from the Mass.   Machaut

EX.   5

[10]

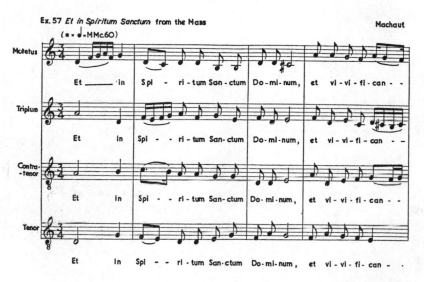

Ex. 57 *Et in Spiritum Sanctum* from the Mass

Machaut

EX. 57 (CONTD.)

[10]

cum Pa-tre et Fi-li--o   si-mul a-do--ra-tur, et con-glo-ri-fi-ca--

cum Pa-tre et Fi-li--o   si-mul a-do--ra-tur, et con-glo-ri-fi-ca--

cum Pa-tre et Fi-li--o   si-mul a-do--ra-tur, et con-glo-ri-fi-ca--

cum Pa-tre et Fi-li--o   si-mul a-do--ra-tur, et con-glo-ri-fi-ca--

-tur: qui lo-cu-tus   est   per   pro--phe--tas.   (etc.)

-tur: qui lo-cu-tus   est   per____   pro--phe--tas.   (etc.)

-tur: qui lo-cu-tus   est   per   pro--phe--tas.   (etc.)

-tur: qui lo-cu-tus   est   per   pro--phe--tas.   (etc.)

Machaut's Mass can be regarded as a summary of the French Ars Nova, for it contains nearly all the devices and styles practised by him and his compatriots—syncopation, hocket, florid melody, syllabic settings, both Gregorian and freely composed tenors, the elaboration of a chant in an upper part, the use of instruments to accompany one or more of the voices, and the four unifying devices—isorhythm, identical texts, imitation, and sonority. With reference to the last of these, there is the same distinction between the conductus style and the isorhythmic movements in the Mass that we noted between the ballades and the motets—in other words, there is a greater percentage of triads, especially on the first part of the breve, in the Gloria and Credo than in the other movements of the Mass.

As for imitation it is hardly used at all, because mediaeval composers were more interested in the differentiation of individual voices than in their integration, and imitation is the most powerful unifying device that music possesses. This desire to make each part independent of the others was natural enough if we consider that part-music was still in its infancy compared to monophony, and that, like a child with a new toy, composers wanted to, one could almost say were bound to, exploit the possibilities of this kind of music in which the more the parts are dissociated from each other the less like monophony they become.

The widespread use of instruments to contrast with the voice is another pointer in the same direction, for the similarity of range of the voices, which as a result frequently cross each other, would tend to obscure their melodic and rhythmic differences if unaccompanied, but when supported or doubled by instruments of different timbres each part stands out sharply from the others. Thus a purely vocal rendering of almost any French part-music written between *c.* 1200 and *c.* 1425 completely misrepresents the composer's intentions.

The Italian Ars Nova§ has usually been regarded as less important than the French, because for one thing its system of notation was less subtle and more cumbersome than the French and eventually became obsolete, and for another the school of composers that flourished from *c.* 1325 to *c.* 1425 left no followers, most of the fifteenth century being a blank so far as Italian composition is concerned. The music itself, however, which is quite different in many respects, surpassed that of France during the latter part of the century.

The 'New Art' in Italy began at about the same time as in France, and again it was a theorist, Marchettus of Padua [fl. first half of the fourteenth century], who, in his *Pomerium musicae mensuratae* ('The Fruits of Measured Music'), provided composers with a neatly classified system of notation which enabled them to exploit the new rhythmic freedom. The basis of this system is the breve, which never alters its value once this has been fixed, just as in Petronian notation, whereas in the French system the breve can be shortened or lengthened at any time by imperfection or alteration respectively (see p. 125). Like Petronian notation also, the groups of notes which make up the value of a breve are marked off by a long, a breve, a long or breve rest, a ligature, or, more frequently, a dot. Marchettus, however, expands the earlier system in two ways. He first of all divides both the ternary (perfect) and binary (imperfect) breve into four groups of smaller notes, the perfect breve consisting of three, six, nine, or twelve equal parts, and the imperfect of two, four, six, or eight equal parts. Each of these divisions is called by the number of parts it contains, e.g. 'ternaria' (three), 'senaria perfecta' (six arranged in three (i.e. 'perfect') groups of two), 'novenaria' (nine), and 'duodenaria' (twelve); 'binaria' (two), 'quaternaria' (four), 'senaria imperfecta' (six arranged in two (i.e. 'imperfect') groups of three), and 'octonaria' (eight), and in order to tell the performer which of these divisions was in operation composers sometimes, but alas by no means always, wrote the initial letters in the stave. Four of these divisions are exactly the same as de Vitri's four common arrangements of time and prolation given on p. 125, for in modern terms novenaria ('n') $=\frac{9}{8}=\odot$, senaria imperfecta ('si' or 'i') $=\frac{6}{8}=\mathbb{C}$, senaria perfecta ('sp' or 'p') $=\frac{3}{4}=$ O, and quaternaria ('q') $=\frac{2}{4}=\mathsf{C}$.

Marchettus's second expansion lay in the number of note shapes, and in this he went far beyond de Vitri, who was quite content with the addition of the minim, for some of the more complex Italian pieces bristle with shapes such as these ♈ ♭ ✔ all of which have different values, depending on which 'division' they occur in, but in any one division their value is fixed; two notes, however, the semibrevis and the semibrevis major ❢ (which also occurs in *Le Roman de Fauvel*, see p. 124), have no fixed value, like the Petronian semibreve.

It may seem from the above that Italian Ars Nova notation is needlessly complex and obscure, but in actual fact it is much less ambiguous than the French system and presents far fewer difficulties to the modern transcriber once the values of the notes in any particular 'division' are known, largely because of the inevitable grouping in breves. In fact, the music of the earlier part of the century is really nothing more than an ornamented conductus-style, for instead of the parts moving together at the same time as in the older conducti, the basic notes are broken up into notes of smaller value and so produce contrasting rhythms; thus syncopation can occur *within* the breve, but not *between* one breve and the next, and it is this limitation of the system that caused it to be severely modified from about 1350 onwards, when Italian composers came into contact with French music and saw how superior the French system was as regards rhythmical expression.

The notation which evolved in Italy during the latter half of the fourteenth century is best described as 'mixed notation', for while it adopted de Vitri's basic principles and scrapped the rigid division into breve groups, it still retained the multiplicity of note shapes—in fact, it even added to these as the century progressed, despite the frequent protests of French and English theorists. To make matters even more complex, not only do red notes occur in all the parts (in France they were still largely restricted to the tenor and contratenor), but white notes as well. Yet this notation was the one used by most of the Italian Ars Nova composers (see Fig. 4, p. 156).

The influence of France on Italy was not confined only to notation or even to music as a whole, for in society, learning, and literature French customs, ideas, and forms of expression played a considerable part in Italian life and culture. On the other hand, although Paris was still the intellectual and artistic centre of Europe, some Italian cities, particularly those in the north, were beginning to be independent of outside influence, and so far as music at any rate was concerned, Florence, Bologna, Padua, Rimini, Genoa, and, in central Italy, Caserta and Perugia all had flourishing schools of composers whose output, while still clearly influenced

FIG. 4   Italian Ars Nova 'mixed' notation. The ballata *Nessun ponga speranza* by Landini.   Squarcialupi Codex (see p. 167).   The tenor part starts at the beginning of the 5th stave and the contratenor at the beginning of the 8th stave.   Note the multiplicity of note shapes and the white breves and semibreves.   Facsimile in Apel, ibid. p. 393.

by the French Ars Nova, stressed a side of part-music that had till now been of only secondary importance—namely, *melody*.

Speaking generally, we can say that the development of music up to the end of the fourteenth century took place in France and that it was almost exclusively concerned with rhythm, both in the individual parts and as a means of providing some degree of unity (isorhythm). It is possible that this preoccupation with the most fundamental characteristic of music (for rhythm exists in nature without melody, but not vice versa) was inevitable, and that the melodic aspect of part-music could not be developed until the rhythmic aspect had been more or less fully worked out. Again speaking generally, it is true to say that the French have always been more interested in the intellectual side of artistic creation (rhythm and design) than in the emotional (melody and colour), whether in music, poetry, architecture, or painting, whereas with the Italians it has always been the other way round. (Could Gregorian chant, with its almost complete lack of interest in organized rhythm, have arisen in France rather than Italy?) This generalization is not contradicted by the fact that the first great flowering of secular melody arose in Provence, for this region of France was associated most closely, both geographically and culturally, with Italy, and the songs of the troubadours were in general more purely melodic than those of the northern French trouvères in the sense that they were less concerned with overall structure and hence with melodic repetition.

But the Italian genius, although it eclipsed the French during the latter half of the fourteenth century, was too much under the influence of the latter to show its natural melodic bent as consistently as it might have done, but the one purely Italian type of composition, the madrigal, does rely almost entirely on melody for its appeal, for it not only rejected the immensely popular device of isorhythm, but the melodies themselves are smoother, sweeter, and more typically vocal than those of Machaut and his compatriots. One might indeed compare the two chief composers of the fourteenth century, Machaut and Landini, with Bach and Handel respectively, in that both Machaut and Bach were mainly concerned with structure and their part-writing is frequently instrumental in character even when written for voices, whereas Landini and Handel stressed the more sensuous and emotional aspect of music and their melodies are predominantly vocal even when written for instruments.

The madrigal§ was one of the two types of composition that appeared in the early fourteenth century—that is, before French influence became strong. The name possibly derives from the Italian *mandria*, which means 'sheepfold', and later the term 'mandriale' was applied to any pastoral poem. It may, however, have come from the Latin *matricale*, 'belonging to the womb', and hence denoted poems written in the mother tongue or vernacular. Whatever the derivation, the texts of the Ars Nova madrigals are by no means always based on pastoral subjects, but they all consist of two or three verses, each with three lines and a final verse of two lines called a 'ritornello' (refrain); thus the total number of lines was either eleven or eight. The music for each verse is the same, but that for the ritornello is different and, moreover, usually written in a contrasting metre, as in this charming eight-line madrigal by Jacopo da Bologna§ [fl. first half of fourteenth century] (Ex. 58* opposite).

The rhythmic simplicity and melodic smoothness of this piece, despite the occasional use of hocket (e.g. bb. 6-7, 14-16), is typical of the madrigal, as is the use of imitation (bb. 10-11, 43-4), and it is this last feature that provides another important difference between fourteenth-century French and Italian music, because for the first time it was consistently stressed and made an integral part of composition by the Italian Ars Nova composers, particularly those of the early generation such as Jacopo da Bologna and Giovanni da Firenze (=Florence), or da Cascia§, as he is sometimes called [fl. first half of fourteenth century].

The second of the two early types of Italian composition is the 'caccia'§ (hunt), which shows imitation carried to its extreme, for it is either entirely or mainly written in strict canon. Like the madrigal, most cacce are in two sections, the second, shorter one being the ritornello, but whereas the first section is always a canon, usually for two voices with an accompanying instrumental tenor, the ritornello is much less consistent, and is even omitted at times. Italy was not the first

---

* Adapted from H. Gleason, op. cit., p. 99.

country to employ strict canon in composition, as the caccia almost certainly derived from the French 'chace'; the latter, however, did not become nearly so popular in France as the caccia did in Italy, because canon inevitably binds the parts together, and this as we have seen was completely opposed to the French conception of polyphony.

Ex.58 Madrigal - *Fenice fu*   Jacopo da Bologna

EX. 58 (CONTD.)

EX. 58 (CONTD.)

Although most cacce deal with hunting in some form or other, this is often a disguise for amorous pursuit, the hunter being the lover and the hunted his mistress. In addition, animated scenes, such as a fire or market day, were sometimes used, but whatever the subject the music reflects the general excitement of the setting. In the following caccia by Giovanni da Firenze quails are the quarry, although it would seem from the end of the second verse that the hunter was himself ensnared (Ex. 59*):

EX. 59 (CONTD.)

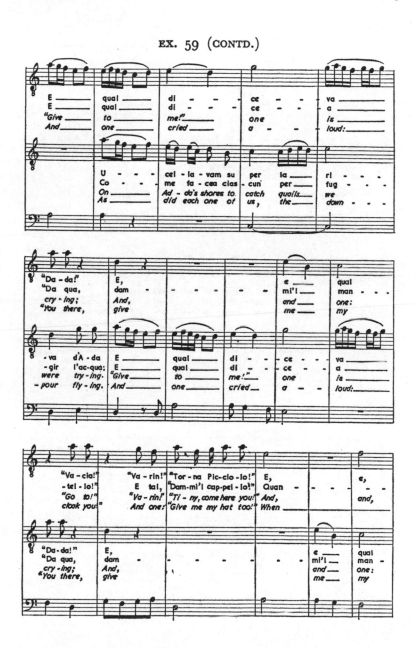

EX. 59 (CONTD.)

EX. 59 (CONTD.)

EX. 59 (CONT.)

Besides Giovanni da Firenze, Florence boasted a number of other composers, her most brilliant—indeed, the most outstanding composer of the Italian Ars Nova—being Francesco Landini§ [1325–1397] who, though blinded from smallpox while still a child, became not only a virtuoso organist, lutanist, and flautist, but was also widely acclaimed as a poet (like Machaut) and philosopher. It was his compositions, however, that brought him most fame, and those that have come down to us represent nearly one-third of the total number of Italian pieces of this period, a contemporary estimation of greatness that posterity for once has accepted.

Most of Landini's compositions are contained in a most beautifully written and illuminated manuscript, the Squarcia-lupi Codex, the largest collection of fourteenth-century Italian music that has been preserved. Twelve composers besides Landini are represented, and each is portrayed in a miniature placed at the beginning of the section devoted to his music.

Unlike Jacopo da Bologna and Giovanni da Firenze, Landini was considerably influenced by French music. This is clearly evident in his decided preference for the 'ballata'§ rather than the madrigal or caccia. The ballata is the exact parallel of the French virelai from which it is derived, but while the form is the same (*A bb a A*) the melodic character is quite different, being, as we should expect, smoother and more graceful. The following example has been described by one specialist of the period as "perhaps the most beautiful work of the century"; it is certainly an exquisite one (Ex. 60* overleaf).

The cadence in bars 8-9 with the inserted E between the F and the final G is very common in fourteenth-century music. It is often misleadingly called the 'Landini sixth cadence', 'sixth' because the inserted note is always a sixth—either major (as above) or minor—from the final, and 'Landini' because it was once thought (wrongly) that he was the first to use it. A better name is 'under-third cadence'. The seventh degree of the scale (F in this case) could be either sharp or flat (as in the above example), but it is possible that a contemporary singer would have sung F♯; if he did then the C in the contratenor would probably be sharpened also. This brings us to the vexed question of 'musica falsa' or 'musica ficta' (the terms are

* Adapted from H. Gleason, op. cit., p. 104.

Ex. 60 Ballata·*Gram piant' agli ochi*   Landini

EX. 60 (CONTD.)

EX. 60 (CONTD.)

synonymous). To the mediaeval musician this simply meant those notes that are not included in the enlarged scale of Guido (see Chapter 1, pp. 36 and 37), so that any note below *G* or above *e''*, or any chromatic note except B♭ (which is in the Guidonian system) was regarded theoretically as 'false' or 'fictitious'. Today, however, the term is limited to the chromatic alteration of certain notes (including B) which a modern editor thinks would have been made by a contemporary performer. All we know for certain is that the music as written down does not indicate all the accidentals, and that performers altered certain notes as they went along. Admittedly the theorists give us some help by stating, for example, that B is flattened in the melodic progression F–B–A or A–B–A, and F sharpened in the progression B–F–G or G–F–G, that the harmonic interval of a diminished fifth must be made perfect by altering one of the notes, and that a third expanding to a fifth or a sixth to an octave should both be perfect. This last rule ties up with the 'double leading-note' cadence mentioned on p. 140. Even so, none of the theorists provides a complete explanation of the practice, and even if some of them had done we could not apply their rules to all compositions, because it is quite clear that the practice varied according to the period, the nationality of the composer and performer, and even between one composer and another. Moreover, different manuscripts of the same period sometimes present the same composition with varying accidentals; thus it is unlikely that there ever was only one completely authentic way of performing a piece, a view which agrees with the lack of precise instructions as to which instruments should accompany or double the voice. The problems of musica ficta apply to most Renaissance music also, and in modern editions of early music the added accidentals are placed either in brackets before the notes or, better, above the stave.

The Italian Ars Nova composers are usually grouped into three generations, the more important ones in the first generation being Jacopo da Bologna and Giovanni da Firenze, in the second Landini, Niccolo da Perugia, Ghirardello da Firenze,§ and Paolo tenorista da Firenze, and in the third Matteo da Perugia, Antonello and Filippo da Caserta, Bartolomeo da Bologna, and the Belgian, Johannes Ciconia. The last group flourished during the end of the fourteenth and the beginning of the fifteenth century and represents, together with a number of French composers, the summit of mediaeval technique as well as some features typical of the Renaissance.

The main characteristic of mediaeval polyphony is, as we have seen, independence of parts, largely achieved by contrasting rhythms in the different voices. It was essentially a French idea and is more clearly shown in Machaut's music than in Landini's. But even Machaut provides some means of unification, either through isorhythm, the development of a rhythmic and melodic motive (see pp. 148, 150), or sonority. The climax came at the turn of the century, when a group of composers, most of them French, but including some Italians, created an art which for rhythmical and notational complexity has never been surpassed or even equalled, and which employs dissonances more freely than in any period before the twentieth century; the result is a texture composed of virtually unconnected strands of melody which at times all but disintegrates.

The leading composers of this group—often called the Mannered School§—whose output was almost entirely secular, were the Frenchmen, Solage, Jacques de Selesses (Senleches)§, Jean Trebor, and Jean Vaillant, and the Italians, Matteo da Perugia and Antonello and Filippo da Caserta. It seems likely that the last-named initiated this new style of composition, for he was a theorist as well as a composer, and his treatise deals at length with the complicated system of notation needed to express the rhythmic subtleties of the music, and just as in the case of de Vitri, whose Ars Nova satisfied the existing desire to enlarge the rhythmical horizon, so Filippo provided the means by which composers could pursue to the utmost their obsession with rhythm.

Space forbids detailed discussion or even a complete example of this ultra-refined art; suffice it to say that cross-rhythms far more extravagant than that shown in Ex. 55 and syncopations more complex than that of Ex. 49 abound. Example 61* (opposite) will give some idea of this extraordinary art.

Such music obviously requires not only first-rate musicians, but also the appreciation of a highly cultured circle intensely interested in secular art. Both existed in a few aristocratic establishments in the south of France, particularly at Avignon, the headquarters of the French Pope during the Great Schism.

---

* Adapted from W. Apel, *French Secular Music of the Late Fourteenth Century*, p. 36. The words in the top part have been omitted.

To this brilliant and distinguished court men came from all over Europe, and it became famous as an international meeting-place. This explains the presence of the Italian contingent and also the fact that most of the compositions have French texts and are either ballades, virelais, or rondeaux, the first of these forms predominating.

Ex. 61 From the Ballade *Du val prilleus*   Antonello da Caserta

The logical outcome of the mediaeval ideal had been reached, but alongside it there was developing a movement in the opposite direction, a movement which had already begun with the first generation of Italian composers and which aimed at a greater simplicity of rhythm, a smoother melodic line, and a more unified texture. The chief figures in this movement were Matteo da Perugia and Ciconia, most of whose works point towards the style of the mid-fifteenth century discussed in Chapter 6.

Apart from France, Italy, and Britain (see below), the rest of Europe contributed little to the development of part-music. There was tremendous musical activity in Spain,§ particularly in Aragon and Catalonia, the provinces bordering on to France, which reached its peak during the reign of John I of Aragon [1350-1396], but even though the cultural and political ties with France and Italy were strong and some French composers, including Selesses, visited John's court, actual composition, as in the thirteenth century (see Chapter 3, p. 90), was largely confined to solo songs in virelai-form rather than part-songs. Similarly in Germany, where Minnesang continued to flourish, but part-music was almost totally neglected, being much farther behind France and even Spain in both quality and quantity. Britain, however, whose main centre of composition seems to have been at Worcester,§ though stylistically out of date in that her composers preferred the conductus to the motet and rarely attempted the rhythmic complexities of Continental music, persisted in stressing the two features already referred to in Chapter 4 and which became all-important in the Renaissance—namely, sonority and imitation. The first is evident in the greater number of compositions in four or even five parts than on the Continent, and by the frequent use of $^6_3$ chords. This style is usually called 'English discant'§ today, and not only was it immensely popular in Britain from *c.* 1300 to *c.* 1450, but greatly influenced Continental music during the following century (*H.A.M.*, 57B). Imitation was almost entirely limited to voice-exchange, and it is rather surprising that canon was hardly used at all. Admittedly, the total number of British pieces that have survived is much smaller compared to France or Italy, but this does not fully explain the dearth of canonic writing, particularly after the *tour de force* of the Reading Rota (see Chapter 4, p. 112). Perhaps the explanation lies in the fact that it is harder to compose a canon using full triads than it is to write a sonorous piece in conductus style in which the parts exchange phrases.

Britain was also the probable home of the first harpsichord, the 'echiquier', and although we have no contemporary description or illustration it most likely consisted of a triangular-shaped sounding board with a number of strings of varying lengths stretched over it and plucked by 'jacks', which in turn were operated by pressing down a key. The appearance of these jacks ranged across the base of the triangle might very well have suggested a row of chessmen, for 'echiquier' means 'chess-board'.

The importance of instruments in the performance of fourteenth-century vocal music has already been stressed, and is further borne out by the frequent references in contemporary literature, the number of times they are portrayed in paintings and sculpture, and the great variety that existed. The almost complete lack of part-compositions intended solely for instrumental ensembles is certainly due to the widespread use of instruments in vocal music, much of which was undoubtedly performed without voices if so desired. Most of the remaining pieces that are definitely instrumental consist of dance and keyboard pieces; in the former the estampie§ is still the most common, and a special type called the 'saltarello'§ makes its first appearance. We know nothing about the actual dance steps of the saltarello, but the examples that have survived are (in modern terms) in $\frac{2}{4}$, $\frac{3}{4}$, or $\frac{6}{8}$, each having a number of 'puncti' with the usual ouvert and clos endings, and each employing melodic rhyme, as in the following delightful example (Ex. 62*):

Ex.62 *Saltarello*   Anon.
(♩.=MM c.80)

The fourteenth century is usually regarded as the period when dancing in the modern (i.e. fashionable) sense began as opposed to folk-dancing, which of course is as old as man. Unfortunately, very little dance music has survived, and what there is is nearly all monophonic, but we are better off as regards other instrumental music, most of which consists of arrangements for keyboard of vocal pieces. These are important because they show for the first time a clear distinction between vocal and keyboard styles, and the latter, by ornamenting the long notes and filling in the leaps of the original song, and by the use of rapid repeated notes and broken-chord patterns prepared the way for the keyboard variations of the sixteenth century. In Ex. 63, (i)* is the second part of a solo song with its keyboard transcription placed below, and (ii)† is an excerpt from a transcription of a hitherto untraced song. Only one example of variation-form from the fourteenth century has come down to us, and this is entitled *Di molen van pariis* ('The Windmills of Paris'; alternatively, the title may simply mean that the composition is by a certain Mr. Windmill of Paris).

None of the manuscripts of keyboard music gives any indication as to whether the contents are intended for the clavichord, harpsichord, or positive organ, or all three. (The great organ was obviously too clumsy, and the portative, as we have observed, was incapable of playing part-music.) Probably the occasion or the performer's personal preference for one or other of the instruments was the deciding factor.

Dance and instrumental music as well as singing played an important part in the fourteenth-century Mystery and Miracle Plays that developed from the earlier church operas. In Chapter 1 we saw how the popularity of these operas led to the increasing use of the vernacular instead of Latin, to the intrusion of secular music alongside Gregorian chant, and to performances in the market-place rather than the church, with professional and amateur actors replacing the clergy. Having ransacked the Bible for suitable material, and having created a unified series of playlets which dramatized the main events from the Creation to the Resurrection—the Mystery Plays§—men began to find more outlet for their dramatic talent in the miracles and lives

---

* Adapted from O. Plamenac, 'Keyboard Music of the Fourteenth Century in Codex Faenza 117' (*Journal of the American Musiological Society*, IV, 3, pp. 191-2).
   † Adapted from O. Plamenac, ibid., p. 193.

Ex 63(i) (a) Part II of the song *Jour a jour la vie* and (b) a transcription for keyboard.   Anon

Ex.63(ii) From Part II of *Bianca flour*   Anon.

($\bullet$ = $\bullet$ = MMc.45)

(etc.)

✝ A in MS.

of the saints. These Miracle Plays were performed singly, not in cycles, and whereas each Mystery Play became associated with a certain locality and was performed virtually unaltered every year for generation after generation, the Miracle Play, with its wider choice of subject matter, greater freedom of treatment, and lack of sacred tradition, provided an opportunity for dramatic experiments. During the fifteenth and sixteenth centuries the Miracle Plays changed in character and content, and by portraying contemporary society to a far greater extent than formerly reflected the realistic approach to life so typical of the Renaissance. Thus, instead of depicting the conversion of a sinner by a saint, together with other holy deeds by the latter, they presented everyday scenes and people with the saint replaced by personifications of the moralities—the Morality Plays. The experience gained through these Morality Plays in having to devise both theme and plot instead of relying on historical or legendary events and figures, and their greater dramatic scope in having actual characters representing 'Good', 'Evil', etc., had a profound influence on later drama which can be traced from Marlowe's *Doctor Faustus* (*c.* 1588) to T. S. Eliot's *Murder in the Cathedral* (1935).

Mystery, Miracle, and Morality Plays were acted and produced with tremendous gusto and often considerable elaboration. Processions, tableaux, dances, choral and solo songs, buffoonery, and pathos combined to form an entertainment so popular that the purely secular drama of the late Renaissance had some difficulty in ousting it. Only in Italy did the Morality Play not catch on, a fact which largely explains the comparative failure of Italian drama during the seventeenth and to a lesser extent eighteenth centuries.

Judged as a whole, the music of the fourteenth century lacks both variety and balance when compared to the century that preceded it, even though many compositions by men such as Machaut and Landini are as good as or better than anything produced in the thirteenth century. The lack of variety is due, in the first place, to the fact that secular music completely overshadows sacred, whereas in the thirteenth century the two fields are roughly on a par, and, secondly, because the absence of lyrical solo song, which resulted when the various national minstrel movements died out, is by no means adequately compensated for by the French treble-dominated style or even by the melodiousness of Italian part-music.

The lack of balance is due to the obsession with rhythm and voice-differentiation; and while admittedly these are also the main characteristics of thirteenth-century music, their application in this century is not so extreme, and is nearly always balanced by the structural devices of isorhythm or repetition (e.g. rondeau form). In the fourteenth century, however, preoccupation with rhythm increased, and in general is not adequately balanced by structural devices, nor by the new sonority, nor by the rare use (outside Italy and Britain) of imitation, and eventually reached a pitch where the texture all but disintegrates.

This lack of balance is much less true of Italian Ars Nova music than French, but France was the dominating influence in Europe for most of the century. Even so, the quality of Italian music and its differences compared to that of France make the fourteenth century similar in one respect to the eighteenth century. Thus the latter period saw both the end of the baroque movement (Bach and Handel) and the rise—indeed, fulfilment—of the Viennese classical style (Haydn and Mozart). Similarly in the fourteenth century, where Machaut and the Mannered School on the one hand represent the culmination of mediaeval ideals, i.e. the stress on rhythm and differentiation of parts, of which the treble-dominated style was one result and varied instrumentation another, while on the other hand many of the compositions of the Italian Ars Nova show traits characteristic of the music that flourished during most of the Renaissance, i.e. the melodic and rhythmic simplicity of individual parts, and a unified texture achieved to some extent through equality of part-writing in which no voice dominates the others, but more particularly through the consistent use of imitation.

The beginnings and endings of artistic movements have always caused a good deal of dissension and none more so than those of the Renaissance. The problem becomes simpler if we realize that there never can be a hard and fast line between one movement and another, that the later develops from the earlier, and that therefore the distinction of a particular movement from other movements lies in the importance attached to certain features, most or all of which will be found in the preceding period. Thus naturalism—or the portrayal of Nature as she appears to the artist after close observation—is one of the main characteristics of Renaissance art, yet as we saw in the last chapter this had already become significant in Gothic sculpture and, moreover, continued to play a vital part in movements following the Renaissance, the difference being that Renaissance naturalism is more realistic than Gothic, and that in those later movements in which naturalism is an important feature it is either even more detailed or else treated more emotionally. Again, the chief feature of mediaeval music—the differentiation of parts—continued through most of the early Renaissance, albeit considerably modified, virtually dying out during the late Renaissance, but reappearing as one of the most notable traits of the early baroque.

We should also remember that new movements affect different countries at different times and in varying degrees—indeed, some movements may hardly affect a particular country at all, as, for instance, the Gothic style in Italy (see Chapter 2, p. 70). Similarly, the Renaissance began in Italy earlier and affected Italian society more completely than in any other country. Moreover, the various arts are not necessarily influenced at the same time nor to the same extent by a change in outlook. Architecture, for example, was affected by the Renaissance much later and less strongly than was painting.

In what ways then did fourteenth-century music reflect the Renaissance? Before we can attempt an answer to this question we must clearly understand what the main features of this movement are.

Renaissance means 'rebirth', and what was reborn was the awareness that man as an individual was extremely important, that the present was very real, and that life should be investigated and enjoyed to the full. All this was largely opposed to the mediaeval conception in which the world was renounced, the future being the focus of all man's activities. It is dangerous to crystallize the ideals of any movement into a few words, but it may help to provide a rough distinction between one movement and another. Thus the mediaeval approach to life was essentially mystical or abstract, while that of the Renaissance was realistic or concrete. This latter approach had, of course, existed before (hence it was reborn), particularly in the civilizations of Greece and Rome, and the study of classical literature, philosophy, and art, largely made possible by the labours of the mediaeval scholar-monks (see Chapter 1, p. 11), played an ever-increasing part in fertilizing the seeds that had begun to germinate in the late Middle Ages.

The corruption and division of the Church, the growing independence of temporal power that sprang from the consciousness of man's importance, and the stress laid on earthly life inevitably resulted in a pronounced swing towards the secular in art. If the style of architecture was not affected at first, its uses certainly were, and as much attention was given to the designing and construction of palaces and public buildings as to cathedrals and churches. Similarly with music; indeed, from this aspect at any rate music reflected the Renaissance more faithfully in the fourteenth century than in either the fifteenth or sixteenth centuries, and more completely than any other art, with the possible exception of literature, for as we have seen very little was composed for the Church during the Ars Nova period, especially in Italy.

In literature the great figures of the century were Dante [1265-1321], Petrarch [1304-1374], and Boccaccio [1313-1375]. In his *Divine Comedy* Dante represents in a wonderfully penetrating and poetic manner the highest flights of mediaeval thought based on the ideals of Aristotle and Aquinas. But his outlook is essentially mystical and mediaeval in that his great poem traces the journey of a soul through Hell, Purgatory, and Heaven rather than portrays purely human experiences on earth. The *Divine Comedy* was enormously popular—so much so that the Tuscan dialect in which it was written ousted all other dialects and ultimately became the basis of modern Italian. But partly because it was such an unapproachable masterpiece and partly because it did not sufficiently represent the changing atmosphere of the times, it had far less influence than the lyric poems of Petrarch, especially those inspired by his love for a certain Laura, which are usually referred to as his *Rime* (literally 'rhymes'). Although these were considered trifles by their author, who regarded his Latin treatises and verse of more importance, they were imitated and translated all over Europe. The reason for this was not only the quality of the poems themselves, but also the prestige of the poet in the field of learning, for Petrarch's passion for antiquity, which led him to value highly and accept as true much of Greek and Roman moral philosophy, went far beyond that of Aquinas. In this he gave a lead to most thoughtful men of his time who could no longer find in the Church their only guide to personal conduct. Petrarch, in fact, was the first humanist, for by humanism we mean the desire to understand the Greek and Roman civilizations and the differences between them and mediaeval Christianity and heathenism, and the attempt to fuse classical with Christian doctrines without subordinating either of them to the other. It is this last which distinguishes the humanist of the Renaissance from the mediaeval classical scholar.

Petrarch's enthusiasm for classical culture was shared by his compatriot, Boccaccio, but whereas the former was a poet whose *Rime* show the influence of troubadour verse in their refined and sensitive expression of unrequited love, the latter excelled in prose, and in his most outstanding work, the collection of 100 short stories called the *Decameron*, he describes vividly, if somewhat crudely at times, and with penetrating psychological insight the men and women of his day. His characters live because they are based on acute observation, as are those of his great contemporary Chaucer, and in this Boccaccio can be likened to the first great Renaissance painter, Giotto [1276-1336]. In Giotto's works the portrayal of the subject is no longer largely dictated by the design of the whole as in Gothic architecture, for he achieves unity and form through the realistic grouping of comparatively lifelike figures and objects, based on a close observance of Nature (Plate IX), just as the Greeks had done in their incomparable statues.

Dante, Petrarch, Boccaccio, and Giotto were all born in Tuscany, the capital of which was Florence. This 'flower of cities', as it has been called, was the heart of the Renaissance. It was also the most important musical centre of the Italian Ars Nova, not only because Landini was born on its outskirts and spent most of his life there, but also because it had a larger and more brilliant group of composers than any other city. It is no surprise, therefore, to find Renaissance traits in the purely Italian madrigal and caccia, or even in the French-influenced ballata. Thus the greater melodiousness of Italian music compared to French can be likened to the lyricism of Petrarch's verse, one of which indeed was set as a madrigal by Jacopo da Bologna, the first of countless others by later composers, for Petrarch was easily the most popular poet of Renaissance music. Again, the true-to-life stories of Boccaccio and the naturalistic paintings of Giotto are paralleled partly in the lively realism of the caccia, but more importantly in the increasing use of imitation as a means of achieving unity, for the mediaeval device of isorhythm, which the Italians virtually rejected, is abstract in that it is felt rather than heard, whereas imitation is concrete, actual, its binding effect being clearly audible.

But imitation was too powerful a means of unification to

become general for composers whose chief concern was to differentiate one part from another, and even though this was less true of Italy than France, fourteenth-century music as a whole is undoubtedly more mediaeval than Renaissance-like in its aims and outlook.

PERFORMANCE

(See also p. 153.)

All the vocal examples, except 56 and 57, may be performed on instruments alone, provided they are of contrasting timbres, but when one or more voices participate the following arrangements are recommended.

Ex. 52.   The triplum and duplum parts should be sung by solo voices with instruments doubling one or both. The tenor part should be purely instrumental.

Ex. 55.   The top part should be sung by a solo voice with or without instruments while the two lower parts are played.

Ex. 56.   The triplum should be sung, the motetus may be sung provided that it is doubled by an instrument, and the tenor and contratenor should both be played by instruments of contrasting timbre.

Ex. 57.   This may be sung by unaccompanied voices, though it sounds better if the tenor and contratenor are doubled by contrasting instruments.

Ex. 58.   This may be sung by unaccompanied solo voices, or with the voices doubled.

Ex. 59.   The tenor part should be played by an instrument, but the two upper parts in canon may be sung by solo voices with or without instruments.

Ex. 60.   The top part should be sung by a solo voice, although instrumental doubling for the refrain is effective. The middle part should be instrumental, and the lowest part may be sung or played.

Ex. 62.   This may be played on a violin or viola, as written, or doubled at the octave by other instruments. The piece is much enhanced by playing the puncti on different solo instruments with the others joining in the repeat, and with the addition, in the repeats, of a triangle and/or small drum when the ending common to all the puncti begins (i.e. bar 3 to the end in the first punctum).

6

MUSIC IN THE EARLY RENAISSANCE

THE leadership in European music during the latter half of the fourteenth century passed from France to Italy, but during the early years of the fifteenth century English influence became predominant, and mainly through the genius of John Dunstable§ [d. 1453] profoundly affected later composers.

English music of this period, except for that of Dunstable, is mostly represented in a large collection known as the Old Hall MS., compiled *c.* 1420, containing nearly 150 pieces, most of which are mass settings. The styles of composition are conductus, treble-dominated, isorhythmic, and caccia-influenced— that is, two upper voices, either in canon or much more animated than the lower voice or voices. The first two styles are the most common, the conductus settings being either simple, as in the thirteenth-century type, or ornamental, as in the Italian Ars Nova madrigal, and the treble-dominated pieces occasionally indulge in the kind of rhythmic complexity discussed in the previous chapter. This latter, together with the use of isorhythm and canon, shows that England was less insular than is usually made out. The prevalence of conductus style, however, indicates a conservatism which the example of Dunstable did nothing to alter; indeed, he can hardly have been known in Britain, as practically all his work is contained in manuscripts scattered about the Continent, notably those at Aosta, Modena, and Trent (all in Italy), only one piece, the very beautiful motet, *Veni Sancte Spiritus—Veni Creator,*§ being in the Old Hall MS., where it is given as anonymous.

Of the composers mentioned in the MS. the chief are Leonel Power§ [d. 1445], Thomas Damett§ [d. 1436], John Cooke [d. 1419?], Byttering,§ Pycard, Nicholas Sturgeon [d. 1454], W. Typp, Oliver, and Robert Chirbury.§ The pieces by Power, Damett, Byttering, Chirbury, and the anonymous *Credo*§ all listed in Appendix B are in conductus style, Bytterings's motet* and Power's *Sanctus*§ showing the ornamental type. A good example of treble-dominated style is Power's *Gloria* (*The Old Hall Manuscript*, Vol. I, p. 65, ed. A. Ramsbotham), while

---

* Strictly speaking, this is an antiphon, but for convenience we shall include all settings of sacred words in Latin under the term 'motet', except for the hymn and, of course, the mass and Magnificat.

Pycard's *Gloria* (ibid., p. 92)—one of the most attractive pieces in the entire MS.—is both canonic and isorhythmic. The MS. also contains the earliest surviving part-music by an English monarch—Henry V [1387-1422].

Several of the composers in the MS., including Damett, Cooke, Sturgeon, and Chirbury, were clerks or 'singing men' of the Chapel Royal. This institution dates back to the twelfth century, when it was clearly an imitation of the Papal Chapel with its picked singers and composers. It was not confined to any one place, but accompanied the King wherever he went, and during the 200 years or so from Henry V to Charles II it included most of the leading English composers.

Although all the styles mentioned above had been and were being practised abroad, they show in general an important difference, a difference that was characteristically British— namely, a greater sonority based on the 'English discant' technique (see Chapter 5, p. 174) and evident also in the number of pieces *a*4 and even *a*5. It was this sonority which attracted Continental composers so much and inaugurated what the first great theorist of the century, Tinctoris, called a "new art". The third, and to a lesser extent the sixth, which had been gradually gaining acceptance in French and Italian compositions of the previous century, now became standard, but they did not yet seriously affect the supremacy of the fifth and octave, and in final chords especially the third was virtually excluded for many years to come, undoubtedly because it was less pleasing than the clear, open sound of the octave or octave and fifth combined (the $\frac{8}{5}$ chord).

The impact of British sonority abroad was largely affected by Dunstable, who was in France for a number of years as musician to John, Duke of Bedford—Henry V's brother and Regent of France from 1422 to 1435. It seems likely that the composer visited Italy also, judging from the number of his works that exist in Italian manuscripts. At any rate he was sufficiently renowned in France to be acclaimed by a contemporary French poet, Martin le Franc, who in 1441-2 wrote:

> The English guise they wear with grace
> They follow Dunstable aright,
> And thereby have they learned apace
> To make their music gay and bright.*

* Translated by G. Reese, *Music in the Renaissance*, p. 13 (see Plate XV).

'They' refers to the two leading composers on the Continent at that time, Dufay and Binchois (see Plate XV), of whom more anon.

The 'English guise' as presented by Dunstable was not only an increased sonority, but a more pronounced feeling for chords and chord progressions, a more refined treatment of discord, a fresher, more lyrical vocal line, and a greater equality of part-writing than had existed before, the chordal sense and equality of part-writing being a natural outcome of English discant and conductus style combined.

Although Dunstable might well be called the first great composer in the early Renaissance period, mediaeval features persist in much of his music—for instance, isorhythm (which, like most of the examples in the Old Hall MS., usually occurs in all the voices), polytextuality, and distinction between the parts, both through rhythmic differences and (more especially) through the use of voices and instruments, particularly in secular pieces, the most common layout being a vocal top part with two lower instrumental parts.

Apart from general style, Dunstable's music exhibits four noteworthy features. The first is his fondness for melodic figures—particularly at the beginnings of phrases in the top part and usually ascending—which are based on the notes of a chord, e.g. *O rosa bella*§ (voice entry) and *Sancta Maria*,§ such figures clearly deriving from the increased chordal sense mentioned earlier. This feature hardly occurs in the Old Hall MS., but is fairly typical of the early fifteenth-century English carol (see p. 214), and this fact, together with the lyrical freshness of much of Dunstable's music and found in most of the carols also, makes it likely that the composer's art, or at any rate his melodic line, stemmed more from the semi-popular, non-liturgical English tradition than from the masses and motets of the professional composers of the Chapel Royal.

The second feature, which is characteristic of the English school as a whole, is the free treatment of the borrowed chant melody. In the thirteenth and fourteenth centuries this was almost always in the tenor, and although it was mercilessly chopped up into rhythmic patterns the original pitch and notes were nearly always kept. In fifteenth-century England, however, the chant was sometimes altered in pitch (transposed), either bodily or in bits, and frequently tampered with both by inserting new notes and by omitting some of the original. Furthermore, it was placed in either the highest or middle voice, especially the latter, more often than in the traditional tenor, as in the three pieces by Power and the anonymous *Credo* in Appendix B, the chant being transposed up a fifth in the last-named and up a tone in Power's *Sanctus*. Sometimes the chant even wandered from voice to voice, as in Byttering's *Nesciens Mater*,§ a practice made easy and probably suggested by the rhythmic similarity of the parts in conductus style. In the following extract from a *Gloria* by Dunstable the beginning of the top part is compared with the corresponding portion of the chant melody on which it is based; it will be noticed that the composer has transposed the chant up a fourth (Ex. 64*):

Ex.64 *Gloria* (a) From Mass IX; (b) The top part from a setting 'a 5' by Dunstable.

This way of ornamenting the chant is now known as 'paraphrasing'; it had already occurred, very exceptionally, in Machaut's Mass (see Chapter 5, p. 149), and although it was not peculiar to English composers (as the idea of a 'wandering' chant seems to have been), they used it more frequently than any other nation, and Dunstable was undoubtedly responsible for its increasing adoption on the Continent.

The third feature of Dunstable's music, and of some other English composers also, concerns the mass and the motet. The latter, as we have seen, had become almost entirely secular, but it gained a new lease of life in England, where for the first time liturgical motets were written in which all the parts were newly

* (a) *Liber Usualis*, p. 40. (b) Adapted from M. Bukofzer, *John Dunstable: Complete Works*, No. 9, pp. 16-17.

composed, e.g. Damett's *Beata Dei genitrix*,§ and all Dunstable's motets in Appendix B except *Ave Regina* and *Veni Sancte Spiritus*. This technique had been occasionally applied to mass movements abroad (see Chapter 5, p. 148), but nothing like to the same extent as in England, and the majority of those in the Old Hall MS., e.g. Chirbury's *Sanctus*§ and *Agnus Dei*,§ half of Dunstable's mass movements, and nearly half of his motets are not based on a chant, another indication of the creative urge which flowed from this island to rejuvenate European music.

The predominance of liturgical music in the Old Hall MS. is apparent also in the output of Dunstable, and in that of his slightly older contemporary, Leonel Power, whose works are distributed more equally between English and Continental sources. An important and influential composer, Power was one of the first (with Dunstable) to link two mass movements together by using the same chant in each. Moreover, he may have been the originator of the cantus-firmus mass—that is, a mass in which all the movements are based on the same borrowed 'fixed melody'. In one Italian MS. two such masses, *Alma redemptoris Mater* and *Rex seculorum*,§ are credited to Power, but in another possibly more reliable source part of one of the latter has Dunstable's name attached. In any case the original idea and its expansion was undoubtedly English, and it is the fourth of the important features mentioned earlier.

Both the above masses omit the Kyrie, a characteristic of fifteenth-century British works of this kind, probably because the majority of the Kyrie chants in the Sarum Use (see Chapter 1, p. 34) were troped, the inserted texts referring to special feast days. Thus the use of such melodies as the basis of a polyphonic Kyrie would have limited the number of occasions on which it could have been sung, so composers very sensibly set the Gloria, Credo, Sanctus, and Agnus Dei only.

Complete settings of the mass (that is, including the Kyrie) began to be common on the Continent round about the 1420s, though not until later did the practice of linking all the movements together with the same melody become general. This reawakening of interest in liturgical music reflected the wave of religious feeling that occurred when the Great Schism ended in 1417. This wave grew during the century, but the Church never recaptured its old supremacy over mind and spirit; the humanism of the Renaissance had made that impossible.

The return to liturgical music is clearly shown in the works of the next great composer, Guillaume Dufay§ [*c.* 1400-1474], who wrote at least eight masses, well over thirty separate mass movements, two *Magnificats* (the earliest polyphonic settings of which are English), and a number of motets, hymns, etc. But the secular influence was still strong, and Dufay's chansons (nearly seventy of them) and a considerable proportion of his motets faithfully reflect this aspect of the times as well.

Dufay was a Frenchman, or, to be more precise, a Burgundian, Burgundy being a province comprising most of central and the whole of southern France (the rest belonging to the Crown) and, during the reign of Philip the Good [1419-1467], the countries of Friesland, North and South Holland, Zeeland, and what is now Belgium. Politically Philip was, on occasion, an unscrupulous and even an unpatriotic opportunist. Some of his possessions he acquired by purchase or inheritance, but some by force. In the year after he came to power he sided with the English in the Hundred Years' War, signing a treaty with them which disinherited the Dauphin (later Charles VII). Ten years later, in 1430, his army captured Joan of Arc [*c.* 1412-1431], and his commander, John of Luxembourg, sold her to the English for 10,000 gold crowns (about £50,000 today). In the previous year Joan had insisted that the Dauphin be crowned King of France, and in 1435 Philip executed a *volte-face* by recognizing Charles VII and helping him to drive the English from French soil in return for substantial concessions. But, despite his acquisitiveness, Philip was a tolerant and imaginative ruler of considerable culture, and at Dijon, the capital of Burgundy, he maintained a court which for magnificence was unequalled in Europe and which, like so many royal and aristocratic courts of the fourteenth and fifteenth centuries, emulated the Papal Chapel at Rome with its picked band of singers and composers. A keen musician himself, he employed a number of the best men of his time, including Dufay, and if the Prince re-established much of France's former power and prestige, Dufay regained for her her old dominant position in European music by fusing English, Italian and French elements into a style that eventually became international.

Dufay and his contemporary Binchois, are usually called the leaders of the 'Burgundian School' of composers, while the next two generations are sometimes referred to as the 'Flemish' and 'Franco-Flemish' schools respectively. There have been other suggested titles, but we shall simply use the name 'Burgundian' to include all three schools, remembering that Burgundy was more a cultural than a national unit. The greatest composers of the fifteenth century were born in this province, most of them spent the greater part of their lives in it and, most important of all, they belonged to the same musical tradition—a tradition which continued long after Burgundy had been split up, when the territories north of France passed to the Hapsburgs through the marriage in 1477 of the daughter of Charles the Bold (Philip the Good's son) to the Austrian Archduke who later became the Emperor Maximilian I [reigned 1493-1519], and when the Duchy itself became reunited with the French Crown in 1482.

Of the foreign elements which influenced Dufay's style, those from Britain have already been discussed. The Italian ones are best seen in the work of Matteo da Perugia and Johannes Ciconia§ [*c.* 1340-1411], particularly the latter. Matteo, while occasionally indulging in the rhythmic complexities of his generation, favoured a style in which the two lower voices, contratenor and tenor, act more as a support for an animated top part that is less virtuosic and more graceful, approaching the treble-dominated style of Dufay more nearly than do Machaut's ballades. Matteo also shows a greater chordal sense, and his use of discord is less arbitrary.

Ciconia, although born at Liége and spending most of his life there, stayed in Italy from 1404 to 1411, and most of his quite considerable output is found in Italian manuscripts. His style is similar to Matteo's, except that he employs imitation more frequently, this being restricted to the two upper voices and hence undoubtedly arising from the earlier canonic caccia. His setting of *O rosa bella*§ by the Italian poet Giustiniani (see p. 225) is one of the most exquisite compositions of the early Renaissance, superior even to the fine setting usually attributed to Dunstable.

The fact that canon was common some 200 years before the general acceptance of imitation is another instance of the way in which a technique once discovered is rigidly applied at first and then modified and developed; thus isorhythm, strict in the tenor part of the mid-fourteenth-century motet, was later freely applied to all parts; again, Pérotin kept the notes of a borrowed chant intact, but Dunstable omitted some and inserted others; similarly (to skip several centuries), Schoenberg's twelve-note system was less flexible when he first used it than at the end of his life. In the fifteenth century the strict canon of the Italian Ars Nova continued in use, but it was also treated more freely and new forms were invented. Imitation, however, is still comparatively rare in Dufay's generation, and when it does occur is almost always found in the upper parts only.

Literally, 'canon' means a 'law' or 'rule', and applies to any piece of music in which two or more parts in performance are derived from only one written part. In the caccia, for example, it was unnecessary to write both upper parts out completely, for only the endings differed in order that both should finish together, and a sign indicated where the following part began. This is easy enough, but fifteenth-century composers delighted in devising much more difficult ways, using obscure sentences (usually in Latin) which were intended to help(?) the singers, as in the Agnus Dei III of Dufay's *L'Homme Armé* Mass (*H.A.M.*, 66c). Another method which became very popular later on was to place two, three, or four mensuration signs before a part, the note values of the two, three, or four parts varying according to the sign which governed each one (see *H.A.M.*, 89). This is called a 'mensuration canon'.

Dufay not only adapted and expanded the strict canon of the Italian caccia, but also the smooth sonority of English discant, which in his hands became more expressive through having the main melody in the top part instead of the middle, and in not sticking so rigidly to chains of $^6_3$ chords. This was called 'fauxbourdon'§ ('false bass') because the lowest voice was no longer 'true' to tradition in being the most important one. This style became very popular in the fifteenth century, particularly as a means of improvising a third inner part to two written parts moving mainly in sixths, the improvised part, while not slavishly following the contours of the top part, being sung or played a fourth below it, as, for example, in Dufay's fauxbourdon setting of the hymn, *Vexilla regis*.§ In his later works Dufay's treatment of fauxbourdon became much freer, but its sonority influenced all his music and was the main cause of his greater feeling for tonality—that is, the stressing of one chord (the tonic) which is regarded as the central and most important one. The most emphatic way of doing this is to cadence on this chord more often than any other, and this is what Dufay increasingly tended to do. Moreover, the cadences themselves were altering, and in addition to that given in Ex. 53, which was still very common, the following (given in its simplest form) became more frequent (Ex. 65):

Ex.65

and later (Ex. 66):

Ex. 66

Both these are what we now call 'perfect' or, more strictly, 'authentic perfect' cadences, i.e. a tonic chord preceded by its dominant, but Ex. 65 is a transitional type showing the influence of the fourteenth century, in that the lowest note of the last chord is approached from the note above (the supertonic). The probable reason why the perfect cadence gained in popularity and finally ousted the mediaeval ones is that composers realized that if the lowest note or root of the final chord was approached by a leap it would stand out more clearly, and hence the whole chord would be more sharply defined, and the dominant note was the only one that would sound well with the other two, i.e. the leading-note and supertonic, both well established in the history of the cadence.

Another cadence that began to be more widely used round about 1450 was the 'plagal perfect' cadence (Ex. 67):

Ex.67

Dufay's tonal feeling, however, must not be overemphasized, for he continued to use the fourteenth-century 'double-leading-note' cadence with its bimodal implications.

The chordal approach affected not only cadences, but harmony as a whole, and Dufay in his more mature work shows a slight but definite preference for chords in root position, a preference which was to remain in music for centuries to come. Furthermore, the relationships between chords became less arbitrary—in other words, it began to be realized that certain chord progressions sounded more satisfactory than others because they are more closely related to a central chord. These two facts, plus the English habit of frequently placing the chant in the middle or highest part, almost certainly explains why Dufay (and all later composers) preferred to place the borrowed melody in an upper part, because this obviously enabled the lowest part to move with much greater freedom and widened the choice of chords. For instance, if we take a note—say, C—and make it the lowest one, the only concordant chords we can build on it are C-E-G and C-E-A; but if there is a lower part then we can get the same two chords (by writing a C either an octave below or in unison) plus the chords E-C-G, F-C-A, A-C-E, and A-C-F.

To move the borrowed melody up a voice would have been pointless in earlier centuries, because the range of each voice was usually much the same. In the fifteenth century, however, the range expanded first upwards and then downwards, with the result that differentiation between the voices was naturally achieved by pitch and timbre, not artificially by rhythm and the singing of different words. The equality of part-writing thus suited the new trend admirably, and the use of only one text for all voices (when more than one voice is meant to sing that is) became increasingly common.

The English cantus-firmus mass and paraphrase technique were also developed by Dufay. Of the eight masses§ that are definitely his, two are in three parts (a3) and six are a4. Five of the latter use a cantus firmus, which in two (possibly three) of the masses is a secular melody, an innovation that may have been his, and one that represents another and more profound break with tradition than the displacing of the melody from the bottom part. One of these masses uses the tenor part of the ballade *Se la face ay pale*§ by Dufay himself, and the other is based on a tune that was to become more popular than any other as a basis for fifteenth- and sixteenth-century masses— *L'Homme Armé.*§

That only one of Dufay's masses uses paraphrase may be explained by the fact that he was nurtured in the French tradition and therefore attached great importance to the overall structure of the mass and the means of binding it together, and it is obvious that a melody ornamented in different ways in different movements, even if it is in the top part, is less likely to be heard as a unifying device than if it is simply and uniformly presented, even though its position in the next to lowest voice tends to obscure it. Dufay and others seem to have been aware of this latter difficulty and partially over-came it by choosing a melody that was well known, making it the last voice to enter, and anticipating its opening notes in the top voice or voices. It is certain also that the melody was played on a suitable instrument, either solo or doubling the voice.

But Dufay was not content with the degree of unity achieved through the use of a cantus firmus alone, and in most of his masses, e.g. *Missa Caput*§ and *Missa se la face ay pale*, he intro-duced (but did not invent) a device now known as a 'head motive'. This is simply a melodic fragment ('motive') which occurs at the beginning ('head') of each movement, and at various important places *en route*, so to speak, and almost always in the highest voice where it is most clearly heard. It is usually varied each time it enters, but is always recognizable, and like imitation it is an external unifying device compared to the tenor cantus firmus which, like isorhythm, is an internal one, being more felt than heard. The head-motive device became standard in mass composition until *c.* 1500, when it was gradually replaced by the use of parody (see p. 204) and pervading imitation.

The use of a cantus firmus either to link together the different movements of the mass or as a structural basis for a motet was in fact a logical development of isorhythm, and, like Dunstable, Dufay used the older technique in a number of his motets§ together with polytextuality, usually in those written to celebrate an important event, such as a royal wedding, the election of a pope, or the signing of a treaty, the solemnity of the occasion being the probable reason why a style hallowed by tradition was employed rather than the 'modern' one (see Chapter 5, p. 149). Most of his motets and hymns,§ however, are composed in the new style, but this is shown most consis-tently in his purely secular work, his chansons. This term is a

general one covering all French secular compositions, but we
shall use it only in the plural, except for an individual work
that cannot be classified as a ballade, virelai, or rondeau. In
the fourteenth century the ballade had been the most popular
form, but in the early years of the fifteenth century the rondeau gradually displaced it, and in Dufay's chansons§ the
latter predominates. Although the fifteenth-century rondeau is
similar in structure to the mediaeval type, it is usually more
concise than that of the previous century as composers preferred syllabic underlay to melismatic. This meant fewer notes
per line of text and indeed less composition altogether compared to the ballade or for that matter the virelai, because the
ballade usually had five different units—a, b, c, d, e (see p. 80),
and the virelai three—a, b, c (*A bb a A* or *AB cc ab AB*), whereas
the rondeau had only two—a, b (*AB a A ab AB*). The popularity
of the rondeau probably sprang from this reduction in length
and content, and may be explained by the fact that composers
were feeling their way towards a new style and would therefore
naturally prefer to work on a small canvas, as it were. Monte-
verdi in the seventeenth century and Haydn in the eighteenth,
to mention only two later instances, both experimented with a
new musical language in the intimate and well-established
fields of vocal chamber music and string quartet respectively,
before applying their results to the larger forms of opera and
symphony, and it is a reasonable assumption that Dufay and
his generation did the same. Thus Dufay's chansons, nearly all
of which are *a*3, and some of his smaller sacred compositions
(e.g. the lovely motet, *Alma redemptoris Mater*§) are in general
more forward-looking as regards style than the masses and
larger motets.

Dufay's genius enriched the entire realm of vocal music and
reached its greatest heights in sacred music, but although his
versatility remained unchallenged until the advent of Josquin
des Prez, his chansons were equalled if not surpassed by his
fellow countryman, Gilles de Binche, usually called Binchois
[*c.* 1400-1460], who was also employed by Philip the Good and
in whose service he remained for about thirty years. Binchois'
chansons§ were greatly admired and reflected more clearly than
Dufay's the taste of the bourgeois merchants, whose influence—
in direct proportion to their wealth—in matters political, social,
and cultural was increasing rapidly, an influence which

counterbalanced the almost purely secular atmosphere of the aristocratic courts, and which supported the new wave of religious feeling already mentioned. The most obvious bourgeois element in Binchois' chansons is their simplicity, not only in being mainly *a*3 and in rondeau form, but also in the texture, for the top part predominates more than in Dufay and the melodies are more 'popular', as for instance in the delightful rondeau, *De plus en plus*§. The same lyrical rather than learned attitude is shown in his less frequent use of canon and, in his comparatively few sacred works,§ the rejection of the simple cantus-firmus technique in favour of paraphrase and treble-dominated style. He seems to have been the only major composer of the fifteenth century who wrote no complete setting of the Mass.

Binchois was born in the province of Hainaut in what is now Belgium, and some twenty years later the same province produced one of the most striking musicians of the Renaissance, Johannes Ockeghem§ [*c*. 1420–*c*. 1495] (see Plate XVII), a composer who, from 1454 onwards, served three kings of France, Charles VII [reigned 1429-1461], Louis XI [reigned 1461-1483], and Charles VIII [reigned 1483-1498], and whose reputation was such that at his death he was mourned all over Europe, notably by Erasmus, the great humanist and scholar, and by two leading French poets, Molinet and Crétin, the lament by the former being set to music by no less a composer than Josquin des Prez.

Like Dufay, Ockeghem was more at home in sacred than secular music, but for different reasons, for it was mainly Dufay's interest in structure that found its most satisfactory expression in the mass, but it was Ockeghem's creative vitality that found the chanson§ too limiting a form, and although a number of these were amongst the most popular of the century (e.g. the rondeau, *Fors seulement*§), he most truly reveals himself in his masses§ and motets, where his rich imagination had more scope, and it is these, particularly the masses, that we shall discuss.

Ockeghem has been more misrepresented than any other major composer of the early Renaissance. On the one hand he has been accused of dryness and pedantry because he happened to write a mass, the *Missa Cuiusvis toni*, that can be sung in any of the four church modes, and another, the *Missa Prolationum*,§

which is mostly in double canon, the canons being at all intervals from the unison to the octave, and on the other hand he has been acclaimed as the first composer to apply pervading imitation as a structural device on the evidence of a motet whose authorship is questionable. In actual fact he was no more learned than Bach, whose cycle of canons in the 'Goldberg' Variations is a distant relation of Ockeghem's Mass, and the motet, even if it is his, is so unlike the rest of his work in its consistent imitative writing that it must have been composed towards the end of his life under the influence of Josquin des Prez.

Ockeghem's greatness lies not in his technical ingenuity, which was tremendous but discreetly employed, nor in his use of imitation, which is much less frequent than in the works of his lesser contemporary, Busnois (see below), but in the sustained power and beauty of his vocal line. Melody, in fact, is all-important, not only in the top part but in all the parts, and the resultant multi-strand texture is frequently maintained with hardly a break throughout an entire movement or piece. This continuous polyphony is achieved by replacing the clear-cut phrases of Dufay and Binchois with 'overlapping' cadences— in other words, a voice begins a new phrase before the previous one has ended, a technique that became standard in later polyphonic as opposed to contrapuntal writing.

Ockeghem also differed from his predecessors (and his successors for that matter) in the ornateness and sweep of his melodies, and his soaring melismas contrast sharply with the simpler, more syllabically underlaid lines of Dufay and Binchois. The application of such melody to all parts could only be effective if the parts did not cross, otherwise a positive tangle of sound would result, and it is not surprising therefore to find Ockeghem keeping his voices intact as it were, and as an inevitable result spreading them over a wider range, especially downwards, for the upper regions had already been partially explored by Dufay's generation. But the greater distance between top and bottom would have meant a decrease in sonority if only three voices were used, and it is from Ockeghem onwards that four-part writing becomes normal in both sacred and secular compositions.

The fact that Ockeghem paraphrases his borrowed material far more often than does Dufay provides a further proof of his strong melodic bent, as does the number of his pieces which are newly composed throughout—for example, the fine *Missa Mi-mi*.§ In addition, he shows distinct originality in his treatment of traditional techniques, such as paraphrasing the highest part instead of the usual tenor of a previously composed chanson, or borrowing two parts and sharing them between all the voices, or changing the rhythm of the original melody from ternary to binary. This apparent delight in doing the unusual comes precious near to leg-pulling at times, as when he writes an original tenor part in long notes but places the borrowed chant, freely ornamented, in the top voice, thus kidding the listener into believing that the tenor is the chant and the top voice original.

While Ockeghem, like Dufay, enriched both sacred and secular music, he had, like the latter, a contemporary who excelled in chanson composition, and who in fact definitely surpassed him in this field. This was Antoine Busnois [d. 1492], the most important composer in the service of Charles the Bold [reigned 1467-1477], the son of Philip the Good. In his comparatively infrequent use of imitation, Ockeghem stands somewhat apart from the general line of development from Dufay to Josquin des Prez, but it is the greater application of just this feature that is so characteristic of Busnois. Most of his chansons are in rondeau form and *a*3, and, like Ockeghem, he explored the lower ranges of the voice, but his melodies are clearly in the Dufay-Binchois tradition in their simplicity and clear-cut phrasing. However, his feeling for tonality, while perhaps not stronger than Ockeghem's, is more obvious because of the greater number of times at which all the voices cadence together, whereas Ockeghem, as we have seen, prefers to overlap. This increased tonal sense is shown in the works of both men by the more frequent occurrence of perfect cadences, particularly the normal one (i.e. Ex. 66), which now definitely began to oust the 'double leading-note' cadence with its ambiguous tonality.

Another feature of Busnois's compositions (and indeed of Ockeghem's too) which became common later on is the rhythmical interplay between the voices. For instance, one voice may begin a phrase in ternary rhythm on the first beat, and another voice imitate this phrase beginning on the third beat, but this beat receives the same accent as the first beat of the original phrase; hence there arises a conflict of 'micro-rhythms', i.e. of the rhythms of individual voices. In most modern editions of mediaeval and Renaissance music bar-lines are used to help the singer, but it must always be remembered that the originals are unbarred (with a few exceptions), and that although beating time was essential in order to keep everyone together, this simply indicated the duration of a breve or semibreve and did not imply a regular and recurring strong accent. Accent in fact is determined in two ways—melodically and harmonically. Any note in a melody becomes relatively accented if the word or syllable to which it is set is a strong one, or if its position in a phrase is higher or its value substantially longer than the surrounding notes. In mediaeval and most of early Renaissance music, composers were largely unconcerned about the way syllables fitted the music, but from the latter part of the fifteenth century on much greater care was taken and the natural stresses of the text are more faithfully reflected in the melody. Harmonic accent can hardly be said to have existed before the fifteenth century, because it depends entirely on a refined use of discord and concord. A discord in a series of concords gives rise to a feeling of tension owing to its greater sonority (see Chapter 2, p. 43), and this tension demands the relief given by a succeeding concord. Now greater sonority produces an impression of greater accentuation; thus, for example, in a succession of thirds and fifths played absolutely evenly and of equal duration, the thirds will sound more accentuated than the fifths, and the same applies with even more force to a series of concords and discords. If the discord is of short duration compared to the surrounding concords, it has little influence on the harmonic accent, but if it is of comparable length, then it will produce a definite feeling of stress which will affect the 'macrorhythm', i.e. the rhythm of the piece as a whole. That this was increasingly realized from *c.* 1400 on is proved by the growing practice of placing the longest discords at intervals of two beats or multiples of two in binary rhythm, and of three or multiples of three in ternary rhythm, thus producing a macrorhythmic framework in which the harmonic stress, when it does occur, always comes on what we would call 'the first beat of a duple- or triple-time bar'. The usual length of these discords is a minim, and their treatment becomes more and more circumspect during the early Renaissance, until by the latter half of the fifteenth century by far the majority of discordant minims are approached and quitted in a very definite manner now known as 'suspension'. For example (Ex. 68):

The details varied, of course, but the three basic steps are always the same: (1) 'preparation', in which the note to be suspended is concordant with the other parts and occurs on a 'weak' beat; (2) 'suspension', in which the note is discordant with the other parts, thus producing a feeling of accent; and (3) 'resolution', in which the suspended note almost invariably falls a step on to a concord, falling rather than rising because lower notes are less tense than higher ones.

In the top part of Ex. 68 the accent most naturally falls on the F, the microrhythm of this part thus conflicting with the macrorhythm as determined by the harmonic accent, i.e. the suspension, and it is this subtle contrast between the fluid rhythm of the individual voices, with their irregularly placed stresses depending on the accentuation of the text or the shape of the melody, and the comparatively regular accents produced by suspensions which underline the prevailing binary or ternary rhythm of all the parts that is one of the chief characteristics and delights of later Renaissance music.

Other important composers of the latter half of the fifteenth century are Jacob Obrecht§ [1450-1505], Alexander Agricola [c. 1446-c. 1506], Antoine de Févin [c. 1480-c. 1512], Gaspar van Weerbecke [c. 1445-after 1514], Heinrich Isaac§ [c. 1450-1517], Johannes Martini [b. c. 1450?], Loyset Compère§ [d. 1518], Pierre de la Rue§ [d. 1518], Antoine Brumel§ [d. after 1520], and Jean Mouton§ [d. 1522], but head and shoulders above these was Josquin des Prez§ (see Plate XVI) [c. 1450-1521], who has been mentioned several times already in this chapter, and with good reason, for he was the greatest composer in the early Renaissance and one of the greatest of all time. His masses,§ motets,§ and chansons§ are as a whole superior to those of any other composer both of his time and before it, but despite a number of fine masses and chansons—

for example, the *Missa Pange lingua*§ (a superb work) and the chansons *Allegez moy* and *Mille regretz*§—it is in his motets that his genius is most fully shown. The reason for this is probably that only the motet provided both a wide variety of texts suitable for expressive treatment together with a form large enough to contain his tremendous creative vitality and sense of structure. Previously, expressive treatment had been mainly restricted to the chanson, and structural devices and melodic expansion to the mass; now, however, in Josquin's hands, the motet not only represented more richly than any other type a synthesis of what had gone before, but introduced a style of composing that became 'classic' for the rest of the Renaissance.

To discuss in detail the variety of elements which constitute Josquin's style would take up far too much space, and a summary of the most important features must suffice. Like Ockeghem, the ease with which Josquin wrote in canon has caused some writers to over-emphasize this side of his technique, but, as one scholar has aptly said, canon was as natural a form of expression to him as fugue was to Bach. To take only one instance (and one hard to equal, let alone surpass, in its combination of skill and beauty), the section beginning 'Ave vera Virginitas' from the motet, *Ave Maria*§—perhaps the most exquisite motet he wrote. This section is a canon at the fifth below between soprano and tenor, the latter following after only one minim beat, with alto and bass being free. The charming simplicity of the main melody and the clear tonality and full harmony of the whole quite overshadow the technical feat involved, while the accents in the tenor part, falling as they do one beat later than in the soprano, produce an effect of indescribable poignancy.

Much more important than canon, however, is Josquin's use of pervading imitation as a unifying device, governing most or all of an extended piece. The 'point' of imitation is often double—that is, two voices introduce it and two other voices later imitate it, sometimes inverting it so that what was the top part at first becomes the bottom part when repeated ('double counterpoint'). Occasionally imitation is 'tonal', not 'real'—in other words, if the first point begins by leaping a fifth up from, say, C to G, a later entry will underline the 'key' octave (in this case C-C) by answering with the complementary fourth, G-C, not another fifth, G-D. Josquin's feeling for tonality is also shown in the greater frequency of perfect cadences and in his purely chordal writing. This latter sometimes persists throughout an entire motet, but is more often contrasted with polyphonic sections, a technique that became standard in the sixteenth century and later. Contrast is obtained also by vocal scoring (see p. 214) which, as we shall see, was a typically English feature throughout the century, but which had been largely neglected on the Continent owing to the prevalence of three-part writing, for it can only be really effective in compositions for four or more parts. Writing *a*4 had become common with Ockeghem, but Josquin went further in not only composing for five and even eight voices, but in helping to establish a standard combination of four voices—namely, soprano (C clef on the bottom line of the stave, i.e. line 1), alto (C clef on line 3), tenor (C clef on line 4), and bass (F clef on line 4). Towards the middle of the sixteenth century the soprano clef was often replaced by the treble or violin G clef that we use today. Other clefs that occasionally replaced or were added to the standard combination were the mezzo-soprano (C clef on line 2), baritone (C clef on line 5 or F clef on line 3), and sub-bass (F clef on line 5).

Josquin's melodic line owes more to Busnois than to Ockeghem, although he clearly learnt the art of overlapping cadences from the latter. Also his melodies tend to reflect the text ('word painting') to a greater extent than earlier composers, and while this is normally restricted to such devices as ascending or descending passages when the text mentions 'rising' or 'falling', etc., an extreme example can be found in his chanson, *Nymphes des bois*, a deeply felt lament on Ockeghem's death (see p. 197), which is written entirely in black notes.

Apart from pervading imitation, Josquin employs all the structural devices in current use—paraphrase, cantus firmus, and isorhythm. In the first two the borrowed melody is either sacred or secular and placed either in one part or shared between them all. A fair proportion of his compositions are free, but in some of these he repeats a short melodic fragment achieving an ostinato effect, and in others he derives the main theme from the text, as in his *Missa Hercules Dux Ferrariae*, where the vowels 'e', 'u', 'e', 'u', 'e', 'a', 'i', 'e' (='ae') are regarded as solmisation syllables—namely, *re, ut, re, ut, re, fa, mi, re*, and these, in the initial statement of the theme, become the notes D, C, D, C, D, F, E, D. The use of borrowed material is not restricted, as it had largely been before, to the mass and motet, for a number of Josquin's chansons are based on previously composed melodies. Furthermore, canon now invades the secular domain almost as often as the sacred, and, in keeping with Josquin's freer treatment of traditional techniques and forms, strict canonic writing is sometimes replaced by free, as in the tenor and bass parts of the chanson, *Plus nulz regretz*;§ the chanson, in fact, has become a far richer and more expressive medium of composition than ever before, and represents not only a more complete cross-section of the composer's style than it had earlier, but also reflects the general tendency, already apparent in the mass and motet, of treating traditional structural devices more freely. Thus Josquin was possibly the first to break away from the strict rondeau, ballade, and virelai types and to create forms which, although using repetition also, are far more varied—for example, *Cueurs desolez*.§

In addition to the structural devices used in Josquin's motets, there is one that occurs in his masses only. It consists of borrowing not one but usually all the voice parts of a previously composed sacred or secular work, either by the composer himself or someone else. Sometimes the entire model is quoted verbatim, but more often it is divided up into sections which are distributed throughout the mass, with the voice parts slightly altered and one or more voices added. This type of mass was later called a 'parody' mass, and it became one of the most popular types of mass composition in the sixteenth century. Although Josquin was not the first to apply the parody technique to several movements of a mass, his four-part *Missa Mater Patris* (printed in 1514) is almost certainly the earliest example of a true parody mass, in that the parodying of Brumel's three-part motet, *Mater Patris*, provides the basic means of uniting all the movements.

But important as Josquin is in the development of composition technique, his brilliance in this sphere is hardly if any greater than Ockeghem's, and his early works, like those of Palestrina (and indeed many other composers), while amply demonstrating his mastery over his material, give little indication of his real stature. Between *c.* 1474 and some time after 1503 Josquin was almost continuously in Italy, first of all at Milan in the service of Cardinal Ascanio Sforza, later as a singer in the Papal Chapel at Rome, and finally as composer to Duke Hercules I at Ferarra, to whom the mass mentioned above is dedicated. The impact of Italian culture in general and the taste of his noble patrons in particular had a profound effect on the composer. It was as if the southern sun had warmed and stirred the closed bud of his genius, causing it to unfurl until the full flower was revealed. From now on, not only did he excel in all branches of vocal composition, but surpassed all other composers before the late sixteenth century in the range and quality of his feeling and imagination; from the exquisite tenderness of *Ave verum* to the sombre depths of *Miserere*§ (commissioned by Hercules I); from the dramatic power of the five-part *Cueurs desolez* to the light-hearted gaiety of *El grillo*.§ This emotional range, expressed through sensuous harmony and melodic lines that are often of great beauty and always perfectly moulded to suit the texture, together with a profound technical skill, particularly in the use of sequence and canon, make him, as we said earlier, one of the greatest composers of all time.

Josquin's supremacy was recognized both in his own day and later, and while Martin Luther's statement that "other composers do what they can with the notes; Josquin alone does what he wishes" is somewhat exaggerated, it does in fact indicate the general estimation in which he was held, as does the high opinion of the sixteenth-century theorist, Glareanus (see Part II), who included more examples by Josquin than by any other composer in his *Dodecachordon* (1547).

Both Luther and Glareanus were well acquainted with the galaxy (for galaxy it certainly was) of composers who were roughly contemporary with Josquin, and this lends added weight to their judgements. The brightest stars—but not all of the same magnitude—have already been given on p. 201, and some of them must be singled out for individual mention.

We stated earlier that Josquin was not the first to apply parody technique to several movements of a mass; indeed the technique was known in the fourteenth century as the Gloria and Sanctus of the so-called 'Mass of the Sorbonne' and the Ite Missa Est of the so-called 'Mass of Toulouse' demonstrate (see p. 148). So far as we know, however, these are isolated instances, and it seems likely that the first composer to use paroby at all frequently was Oberech, for in a number of his masses he introduces at various places all the voice parts of his model. Indeed, in his very fine *Missa Rosa playsant* each movement contains a reworking of the original chanson, but because the chief means of unifying all the movements is through the paraphrasing of the chanson tenor—in other words, through a cantus firmus—it is not a genuine parody mass.

More important than Obrecht's use of parody, however, is he very high quality of the actual music, particularly in his masses and motets, the imaginative treatment of the stereotyped secular forms, even though secular composition occupies but a small part of his total output, and his strong sense of tonality, notably at cadences where he often places the subdominant chord before the dominant, thus defining the tonic chord with greater precision. In all these ways Obrecht was progressive, and may well have influenced Josquin, who probably met him shortly before his death at Ferrara and who was almost certainly acquainted with his music. In other ways Obrecht was rather conservative, as in his infrequent use of imitation, and in the number of times he uses strict rather than paraphrased cantus firmi, and polytextuality, but all in all he is a very fine composer, surpassed by none of his contemporaries except Josquin.

Agricola, too, was both progressive and conservative, and to a greater extent than Obrecht, for on the one hand his chansons (of which he wrote more than did any of his contemporaries, including Josquin) are often based on previously composed material, this being considerably varied, and his melodic lines in general show marked originality, even a degree of restlessness, in rhythm and contour. On the other hand, the ornateness of his melody and the complexity of his texture hark back to Ockeghem, and his occasional use of $^6_3$ progressions and hocket to the early years of the century. The restlessness of Agricola's melodies is reflected in his life, for he was in Italy twice, working in Milan, Florence, and Mantua on his first visit, and later made two trips to Spain in the service of Philip the Handsome, son of Maximilian I. Philip had married Joanna, daughter of Ferdinand and Isabella (see p. 223), in 1496, and in 1504 he became Philip I, King of Castile.

Also in Philip's retinue, from the date of his marriage till his death in 1506, was La Rue, who wrote more masses than any of his contemporaries. This fact underlines the essentially serious quality of his music, and it is not surprising that his Requiem,§ apart from being the high-water mark of his own output, is one of the finest compositions of the period. Another fine work, the *Missa Ave sanctissima Maria*, is probably the first six-part setting of the Ordinary and definitely the first mass to use canon *a*6, in this case the canon being 6 in 3 at the fourth above—in other words, three parts are written, each producing another part which is sung a fourth higher. The astonishing thing is that this technical *tour de force* in no way impairs La Rue's melodic suppleness or harmonic variety. Both this mass and the Requiem show the composer's fondness for contrasting groups of voices, especially for passages *a*2.

La Rue does not appear to have ranked very high with his contemporaries, yet without doubt he is the equal of Obrecht and superior to Mouton, who was widely acclaimed, both at the courts of Louis XII and his successor, Francis I, and abroad. Like La Rue, Mouton wrote little secular music, and like him too he was a master in the use of canon. Two of his motets, *Nesciens Mater virum* and *Ave Maria, gemma virginum*, both fine works, are canons 8 in 4, and another exquisite motet, *Ave Maria, gratia plena*,§ has a 'mirror' canon between alto and bass —that is, the 'comes' (the part that 'follows') moves in contrary motion to the 'dux' (the part that 'leads'). Although the quality of Mouton's work entitles him to special mention, he is also important as the teacher of the most influential musician of the sixteenth century, Adrian Willaert, and was thus a significant link between the early and late Renaissance.

The impact on Italy of composers from the north did not produce any really marked effect until the period after Josquin, but during his lifetime the tide had already begun to flow southwards, and in addition to Josquin himself, all the leading composers mentioned on p. 201, except Févin, La Rue, and Mouton, crossed the Alps.

Perhaps the most striking of Josquin's contemporaries was Isaac, who for the last twenty years of his life was court composer to Maximilian I. While less brilliant and profound than Josquin, and not quite the equal of Obrecht and La Rue, he was the most versatile composer of the period, writing a number of secular songs with German and Italian as well as French texts, and also a fair amount (for those days) of instrumental music.§ The setting of texts in different languages does not of itself, of course, denote any remarkable versatility, and it is in the musical contrasts between his French chansons, German Lieder,§ and Italian frottole* that the range of Isaac's gifts is revealed. Thus while both chansons and Lieder are frequently based on a borrowed melody and are generally imitative in style, the former are more sectional and freely repetitive than the latter, in which a continuous polyphonic flow is usually maintained, with the borrowed melody nearly always in the tenor part, and in which canon occurs more frequently. The differences between chanson and Lied, however, are not nearly so marked as between them and the frottola, for in this the style in general is non-imitative, less polyphonic, and simpler in texture, with the main melody, which is hardly ever borrowed, lying in the top part, though like the chanson it is sectional and employs repetition.

During the middle fifty years or so of the fifteenth century, Italy produced practically no music, although there were plenty of vocal and instrumental performers. Of the latter the most famous was Antonio Squarcialupi [d. 1475], owner of the important collection which is our main source of Italian Ars Nova music—the Squarcialupi Codex (see Chapter 5, p. 167)—and organist of the renowned Santa Maria del Fiore at Florence. Round about 1484 Isaac obtained this post and remained in Florence under the patronage of Lorenzo de Medici [1449-1492]—nicknamed 'the Magnificent'—and his son, until the overthrow of the latter by the ardent reformer Savonarola in 1494. This Dominican monk vigorously criticized the corruption and worldliness of the Medicean rulers of Florence and advocated government on more democratic lines. The masses acclaimed him for a time, but soon tired of his high ideals, and eventually the fury of the aristocracy and the displeasure of the Pope, whom he had also censured, led to his execution in 1498. The Medicis returned in 1512, but the old magnificence and *joie de vivre* did not, for the country had since been invaded by foreign troops and the city's future was uncertain.

The highlights of the Florentine year were the carnivals before and after Lent, and under Lorenzo these reached a degree of extravagance and ingenuity unmatched before or since. Legends, classical figures, the city guilds, etc., were all symbolized in great torchlight processions of decorated cars and

* See below.

fantastic masks. Music naturally contributed to the festivities and the 'canti carnascialeschi',§ or carnival songs, extolled mythical heroes or the greatness of the Medicis, and described the various trades of the city or sections of the populace, usually by means of innuendo (*H.A.M.*, 96) or even on occasion frank obscenities.

Isaac is known to have composed carnival songs, none of which, however, have survived complete, but, judging by his other pieces with Italian texts, they were almost certainly typical of the current secular style in Italy. This style, as we have seen, is less complex and 'learned' than that of the typical Burgundian chanson or German Lied, and the main melody in the top part is not only simpler than in the chanson and Lied but more clear-cut than the lower, usually instrumental, parts.

The chief type of secular music was the frottola,§ which strictly speaking refers to only one class of composition, but which we shall use to cover all the various types which arose from the widespread practice of reciting poetry to an improvised instrumental accompaniment. The main centre of frottola composition was Mantua, where one of the most gifted and influential women of the Renaissance, Isabella d'Este [1474-1539], resided. An ardent and accomplished musician herself, she was more than a mere patron, and in literature and poetry as well as in music she was respected by many of the great artists of her day. To her court, round about the year 1495, came Bartolomeo Tromboncino§ [d. *c.* 1535] and Marco Cara§ [d. *c.* 1530], the first notable Italian composers of the Renaissance. The frottole of these two men, particularly of the former, were greatly admired by Isabella, to whom the musical setting of a poem in which the melody did not obscure the words was completely satisfying. The texts of most frottole, especially the earlier ones, are trivial, but the improvement in taste in the early years of the sixteenth century probably owed much to Isabella's influence.

Although the frottole are simpler in style and texture than Burgundian and German part-songs, the fact that they are mostly written a4 ,with the lowest three parts still being quasi-polyphonic, tends to produce a heaviness which ill suits the syllabically underlaid vocal line with its clear-cut phrases. Cara seems to have realized this to some extent, for he composed a frottola in which the accompaniment is restricted to a few simple chords. This experiment, so much more typical of the Italian genius than the madrigal, mass, or motet, would almost certainly have led to the creation of monody long before the 'New Music' of the early seventeenth century (see Part II), but Burgundian polyphony intervened, and for nearly 100 years Italy adapted her natural talent to the art from the north.

The rise of the frottola occurred at the same time as the invention of music printing, some thirty years after the first printed books had been issued. At first either the lines of the stave were engraved in a wooden block and printed in black or red ink, the notes, clef, etc., being added by hand, or else the other way round, the notes being cut and the lines added. In the latter method the notes were sometimes engraved in separate pieces of wood and stamped on to the page. Later the lines were printed and the notes stamped on to them. These three methods involved difficulties in aligning the notes on the stave correctly, and this was overcome by engraving all the music on to wooden blocks and eventually metal plates. Although this method ensured the exact placing of the notes on the stave, it was lengthy and wasteful, for every page of new music necessitated a new block, and it was soon replaced by double-impression printing. In this method the lines of the stave were scratched (engraved) on a metal plate (usually copper), the number of staves depending on the size of the page; the plate was then inked and wiped, but the ink remained in the lines and was transferred to a sheet of paper when this was firmly pressed on to the plate. This was the first impression and easily performed. The second was considerably more difficult, for each note, rest, etc., was cut from small pieces of lead (type) so that the raised parts represented the shape of the note. These were then placed in a 'bed' and very carefully arranged so that when the staved paper was impressed each type would be printed in the position required. It was this exact arranging of the type that was so laborious and finicky a job and which made the method so costly, but when perfectly done it was artistically far superior to the single-impression technique which replaced it (see Plate XIII). This technique, which was invented by a Frenchman, Pierre Haultin, in 1525, dispensed with the engraved plates for the stave, using only type, each piece of which contained a note or rest, etc., placed in a small portion of the stave, these being joined together to form any length of stave required (see Plate XIV). The speed with which a page of music could now be set up was comparable to that for an ordinary book, and whereas Petrucci (see below), who used the double-impression method, issued only about fifty music-books in twenty years, Attaignant (see Part II), employing the single-impression technique, published nearly twice this number in twenty-two years.

Ottaviano de Petrucci [1466–1539] was the first important printer of music, and his publications set a standard in accuracy and artistry which have never been surpassed and rarely equalled. He issued his first book in 1501 and his last in 1520, both in Venice, where he lived from *c*. 1490 to 1511 and from 1536 to his death, the intervening years being spent at Fossombrone. Fifty-two different collections of music from Petrucci's publishing house have survived, and while most of these represent the best of Burgundian music from Ockeghem and Busnois onwards, he issued as many as twelve books of frottole, three of them being reprinted.

The general reduction in length of fifteenth-century secular music, together with the melodic equality of all the parts, led to different arrangements on the page, and in a chanson *a*3 or *a*4, the parts follow each other down the page, one underneath the other, as in Plate XIII. In long pieces *a*4, however, two pages were used divided thus:

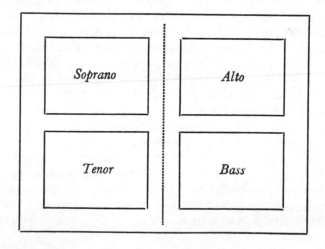

These arrangements are still basically the same as that used
for the thirteenth-century motet (see Chapter 4, p. 111)—in
other words, choir-book arrangement or cantus collateralis—
and Petrucci used both in his early publications, but whereas a
real choir-book was large enough for a small group to stand
round and see tolerably clearly, Petrucci's books measure only
about 8 inches long by 6¼ inches high with a stave of about the
same size as that used for piano music today. It would thus have
been very difficult if not impossible for four people to stand
round a single Petrucci print and sing from it, and buying two
or more copies was out of the question for the average music-
lover because of the expense. This brings up an extremely
interesting point that concerns manuscripts as well. Most of the
mediaeval and Renaissance manuscripts and sixteenth-century
printed music that have come down to us do not show the wear
and tear of frequent use. Performers then, as now, must have
made corrections or additions, or left finger-marks, etc., but
these are hardly ever to be found on the copies that have
survived. This leads one to suspect that these were either
presentation copies or made for reference only, the ones
actually used in performance always being in manuscript,
which were then thrown away when they became too dirty or
tattered, and fresh copies made. Furthermore, it is likely that
the practice of copying each part on to separate pieces of
parchment or paper was fairly common, for this would make it
unnecessary for the whole choir to cluster round a single copy
on which all the parts were written (see Plate XVII). Even the
huge choir-books with their outsize notes and placed on massive
lecterns were probably not sung from, because apart from their
remarkably clean condition, the treble part (where there is one)
is written at the top of the page, where it must have been very
difficult for boy choristers to read, especially in the semi-
darkness of the churches. On the other hand, placing the parts
one after the other on a page or pages is the most obvious
method if you want to present or preserve a piece intact.

The copying of each part on to separate pieces of parchment
or paper naturally led to binding the pieces of the same part
together, as in modern performing editions of string quartets.
This is known as 'part-book' arrangement, and was used by all
sixteenth-century printers, beginning with Petrucci, most of
whose publications are in this form. The earliest manuscript

part-books that have survived date from the last quarter of the fifteenth century, but for the reasons given above concerning wear and tear this does not contradict the argument that the idea originated very much earlier.

Although a great many manuscripts have come down to us from before 1600, hardly one of them is an autograph. This unfortunate state of affairs is explained by the fact that composers used blank sheets of parchment or paper called 'cartelles' on which the staves were indented, the notes, clef, etc., being written in ink or pencil. When the piece was completed it was copied by a scribe (often a pupil) and then wiped off, leaving the cartelle clean and ready for future use. The indented stave of the cartelle, and later the actual printing of music, explain why ledger lines occur so rarely, and as a result why there were so many different clef positions, for as the range of any individual part rarely exceeded an eleventh (the range of a five-line stave), it was obviously simpler to choose a clef which enabled the melody to be contained within the bounds of the stave than be constantly adding ledger lines.

The only example of music printing from the sixteenth century which rivals that of Petrucci is a collection of twenty three- and four-part songs published in London in 1530. Most unfortunately, it is incomplete and the printer's name is missing, but until recently it was thought (incorrectly) to have come from the press of Wynkyn de Worde, who came to London from Alsace *c.* 1477 as assistant to the famous printer William Caxton [*c.* 1422–*c.* 1491]. Nevertheless, it seems likely that the man responsible was also a foreigner, an increasing number of whom visited Britain from *c.* 1500 on. This foreign influx which, from the sixteenth to the nineteenth centuries, became such a marked feature of British culture and society, naturally affected her music to some extent, but not until the end of the sixteenth century did a body of native composers arise whose work, while it imitated, also rivalled that of the Continent.

Dunstable's influence seems to have been restricted to the Continent, as very few of his compositions are found in early Renaissance British sources, a surprising fact in view of his reputation abroad. The most important MS of late fifteenth-century British music is the Eton Choirbook§ (1490–1502); unfortunately over half the original contents are missing

(including the only motet by Dunstable) or incomplete
(including a setting of the Passion choruses from St. Matthew's
Gospel by R. Davy. The earliest polyphonic Passion settings
are British and date from before 1440). Among the twenty-five
composers listed are John Browne§ [d. 1498?], Richard Davy§
[*c.* 1467-*c.* 1516], William Cornysh [d. 1523] (a poet and play-
wright, and a great favourite of Henry VIII), and Robert
Fayrfax§ [1464-1521], who, as head of the Chapel Royal,
organized the musical festivities at the famous Field of the
Cloth of Gold in 1520. Apart from its seamless polyphony
(reminiscent of Ockeghem) the music is typically British in its
sonority (i.e. use of thirds—see Chapters 4, 5—and predominance of writing *a*5 and *a*6—see p. 186), and in its 'vocal
scoring' (i.e. use of groups differing in size and timbre; also
found in the Old Hall MS). But these two 'progressive' features
do not always compensate for the near-monotony and lack of
unity produced by a dearth of homophony, suspensions, and
imitation—also true of the mature style of Fayrfax, the most
notable composer between Dunstable and Taverner (see Vol.
II), except that he uses homophony and imitation more often
and parody once (his *Missa O bone Jesu* is possibly the first
British parody-mass). Elsewhere he, like the Eton Choirbook
composers, is old-fashioned in his preference for un-para-
phrased cantus firmi; indeed as an exact contemporary of
Josquin he is less 'up to date' than Browne, and this underlines
the slow development of British vocal music compared to
Burgundian. But being up to date has little to do with value,
and at its best the richness and tonal variety of Fayrfax's
music and that in the Eton MS redeem its weaknesses.

Although Fayrfax wrote a number of secular songs (all *a*3 or
*a*2), this side of music was largely neglected by his compatriots,
and the only considerable body of music that can be called
secular, in that it was not an integral part of the liturgy, is the
'carol',§ a form peculiar to England. Nowadays the carol is
usually associated with Christmas, but while this is still
generally true of the fifteenth-century type, it also included
other subjects, such as hymns to the Virgin, a petition to a
saint, a prayer for a king, or a thanksgiving for victory, e.g. the
famous 'Agincourt Song'.§ The common factor of all these
carols is not their subject-matter, but their structure, for all
consist of a 'burden' (B), which is sung at the beginning and

after each 'verse' (V), the burden being clearly separated from the verses, each of which may have the same 'refrain' (R), this being part of the verse. Thus the following scheme is typical B : V₁ R : B : V₂ R : B : V₃ R : B. The carols are almost all written in English discant-conductus style, and while comparing unfavourably with Continental chansons as regards technique and expressiveness, many of them are little gems that deserve wider recognition and more frequent performance.

Among Fayrfax's contemporaries was Hugh Aston [*c.* 1480-1522], who must be the only man in the history of any art to be ranked as important on the basis of a single work. This is a 'Hornpype' for virginal (a small harpsichord), and it shows a far more remarkable keyboard technique than anything on the Continent. Here is an extract (Ex. 69*):

Ex.69 From Aston's *Hornpype* (original note values)

It is unlikely that Aston's piece was as unique in its day as it appears to be now, for there must have been an earlier tradition, now unfortunately lost, showing a similar, though perhaps not so striking use of keyboard figuration. That very few British examples of fifteenth-century instrumental music have survived—a state of affairs that applies to every European

* From J. Wolf, *Music of Earlier Times*, p. 60.

country except one—must not blind us to the fact, made abundantly clear in contemporary writing, pictures, and sculpture, that the use of instruments on every conceivable occasion was even more widespread than in the fourteenth century.

The exception is Germany, whose makers, especially of wind instruments, and performers became internationally famous, and where instrumental music, particularly for the organ, seems to have been more intensely cultivated and practised than elsewhere. The earliest collection of importance is the *Buxheimer Orgelbuch* (*c.* 1460), a manuscript containing well over 200 pieces, including two by the first notable organist, Conrad Paumann§ [*c.* 1410–1473], a contemporary of Squarcialupi. Though blind from birth, Paumann was acclaimed all over Europe, but unfortunately most of the twenty or so pieces by him that have come down to us are elementary exercises for would-be organ composers. In the latter half of the century Arnolt Schlick§ [*c.* 1460–after 1517], Paul Hofhaimer§ [1459–1533], and Hans Buchner§ [1483–*c.* 1538], a pupil of Hofhaimer's, also achieved international fame. Schlick was a theorist as well, and his treatise on the organ (1511), the first to be published in German, gives valuable information on construction, tuning, etc., and embodies principles and suggestions, some of which hold good to this day. He also published in 1512 the first printed collection of keyboard music, including, in addition to fourteen organ pieces, some music for lute solo. We have less than half this number of organ pieces by Hofhaimer, although his reputation and influence were greater, judging by the number of his pupils. Many of these are represented in four great manuscript collections of the early sixteenth century, totalling nearly 400 pieces, and made by Buchner, Hans Kotter [*c.* 1485–1541], Fridolin Sicher [1490–1546], and Leonhard Kleber [*c.* 1490–1556].

The vast majority of German organ music is either based on a cantus firmus (usually sacred) around which the other parts weave more or less elaborate counter-melodies, or else consists of ornamental arrangements of masses, motets, and chansons. The style is essentially vocal, the only main exceptions being rapidly executed ornaments which occur most frequently at cadences.

More characteristically instrumental writing is found in the lute music of the period, for while the organ and (less success-fully) the harpsichord and clavichord can imitate the flow of vocal polyphony, a plucked instrument obviously cannot.

The lute was far and away the most popular of all the instruments in the fifteenth century, especially in Germany, Italy, and Spain, but as it was almost always used either in extemporizing an accompaniment to a song or, as in the case of many frottole, in playing as much of the lower parts as it could manage, very few solo pieces were written down, and inevitably even fewer have survived. The advent of music printing, however, and an increasing realization of the instru-ment's possibilities, led to a growing number of lute solos throughout the next century. Petrucci set the ball rolling by issuing four books in 1507-8 and another two in 1509 and 1511. Nearly all the pieces are transcriptions of vocal music, sacred and secular, but a few original pieces, such as dances and preludes, are included. The only other lute music printed during the same period was that contained in Schlick's 1512 collection.

All lute and much organ music of this period was written in 'tablature'—that is, a system of letters, figures, or signs some-times placed on four or six lines (like a stave), sometimes above. These letters, etc., either represent the alphabetical names of the notes to be played (organ tablature only), or else indicate the frets on which the lute player must put his fingers. Organ tablature was only used in Germany and Spain, particularly the former country, where it was even used on the rare occasion by as late a composer as Bach. Lute tablature, on the other hand, was universal, and though three systems were in use, the Italian-Spanish, German, and French, the last of these eventually ousted the others towards the end of the sixteenth century. In this system five horizontal lines represent the five highest strings, the sixth (lowest) string being shown by short ledger lines underneath. The letters 'a', 'b'. 'c', 'd', etc., are placed on the lines, 'a' meaning an open string, 'b' that a finger should be placed on the first fret, etc., the frets being roughly a semitone apart. The strings, the three lowest of which were in unison pairs, were tuned either G, c, f, a, d', g' or A, d, g, b, e', a', and were originally plucked by a small piece of wood, metal, or other substance (plectrum); by the end of the century, however, finger plucking was standard and remained so. The shape of the lute is the same as that described on p. 93, and the frets on the fingerboard not only serve as a rough guide to intonation, but, more important, provide a sharp edge on which to stop the string, thus making possible a clearer, more ringing tone with less difference between it and the open string than on, say, the violin, where the fleshy finger-tip presses the string on to a flat finger board and results in a markedly less brilliant timbre than that of an unstopped string.

The note values in tablature are indicated by short, vertical lines with or without one or more hooks, or else actual notes, and are placed above the 'stave'; only the shortest value is shown at any given point and this remains in force until replaced by another, so that, for example, a succession of eight minim 'chords' followed by a semibreve has only two signs, one over the first minim and one over the semibreve. This all sounds very complicated, but once the general principle has been mastered it is very easy, as any ukelele player will tell you, for he too uses a kind of tablature. The reason why lute tablature caught on so was that it not only instructed the player where to put his finger, but was also more economical of paper and far less expensive to print because it used standard type (letters or numbers) instead of complicated symbols like clefs, accidentals, and the different note shapes.

In the same year that Schlick published his organ treatise came the first printed book on instruments in general, by Sebastian Virdung. This describes and portrays through wood-cuts the clavichord, virginal, lute, viol, dulcimer, harp, oboe, flute, cornett, bagpipe, trombone, trumpet, organs (positive, portative, and regal), and various percussion instruments, as well as a few other types.

The fifteenth-century clavichord is rectangular in shape, and smaller than the virginal, and the strings, which vary little in length, are hit by small pieces of brass called 'tangents' fixed to one end of a pivoted lever, the other end being the key. The impact of these tangents is regulated by the finger pressure on the key, just as on the piano, and this not only makes possible abrupt dynamic changes, crescendos, and diminuendos, but also the prominence of an inner part. Moreover, by moving the finger to and fro on the key a discreet undulation of the note (vibrato) can be obtained. The action makes the clavichord more expressive than the virginal, but, owing to its small size (which in effect means a small sound-board), the volume is much less. The strings are tuned in unison pairs stretched parallel to the keyboard, and there are fewer pairs than keys, because each pair is assigned two, three, or even four tangents, the position of which determine the pitch of the note. Thus a tangent which hits a pair of strings in their middle and causes half their length to vibrate sounds a note an octave lower than that caused by a tangent which makes the pair vibrate only a quarter of their length. If the two tangents hit the pair of strings at the same time, only the higher note would sound and playing in octaves would be impossible, and in order to get round this the makers so arranged the tangents that only notes that were not normally played together (remembering the limited chords of the time) such as G♯ and C were obtained from the same pair of strings.

The virginal of this period was the same as a small harpsichord; it is single strung, each string corresponding to a different note. The body is usually harp-shaped, like a small grand piano, and the strings vary in length as well as in thickness, material, and tension. Each string is plucked by a 'plectrum' of quill or leather, which sticks out sideways from a hinged strip of wood—the 'tongue'—fitted into the 'jack', an upright piece of wood resting on one end of a pivoted lever. When the other end of this lever is depressed by the finger the jack rises and the plectrum plucks the string; when the finger is removed the jack falls, the tongue tilts back, thus preventing the plectrum from plucking the string a second time, and a piece of felt at the top of the jack stops the string vibrating. The distance between the plectrum and the string is much smaller than that between the tangent and its pair of strings on the clavichord, and hence it is only possible to get a very slight increase in volume by striking the key harder with the finger; the increase is sufficient, however, to enable the performer to distinguish between accented and unaccented notes. The greater volume of sound compared to the clavichord is due to the larger sound-board, which gives a bigger 'boost' to the sound actually produced from plucking, the sharper edge of the plectrum compared to the tangent, and the greater tension of the strings. These last two factors result in the characteristically brilliant timbre of the instrument, compared to which piano tone sounds dull and lifeless. During the early years of the sixteenth century a larger virginal was developed in Italy, the more usual name for which is 'harpsichord'. It has a second set of strings tuned in unison with the original set, thus gaining in brilliance and volume.

The four commonest viols were the treble, alto, tenor, and bass, each of which had six strings tuned in the same manner as the lute—namely (reckoning upwards), fourth, fourth, major third, fourth, fourth. The lowest strings were treble viol-*d*, alto-*c* (in England and France, but *A* in Italy), tenor-*G* (*A* in Italy), and bass-*D*. In addition, the violone or double-bass viol (tuned an octave lower than the bass viol) was occasionally used in consort. With the exception of this last, the viols were played sitting down, the instrument being placed on or between the knees, hence the Italian term, viola da gamba, or 'viol of the leg', a term which eventually implied the bass viol only, for this member of the family was easily the favourite, owing to the beauty of its tone and the ease of execution over a wider range than the others, extending from *D* to two octaves above its top string, i.e. *d'''*. The viol bow is held in exactly the opposite way to the violin, being above the hand, which faces palm upwards, and the stick, unlike the Tourte violin bow of today, is outcurved, not incurved. This method of bowing produces even less bite or accent than with violin bowing, and, together with the natural timbre of the instrument, which is edgier but less resonant and brilliant than that of the violin, determines the character of the music written for it, a character less virtuosic but more intimate and polyphonic than keyboard or lute music, the edgy tone making the individual strands of a polyphonic texture stand out clearly. The comparative lack of resonance and brilliance is due to the thinness of the wood and strings, and the lack of tension in the latter, and the edginess is accentuated by the frets on the finger-board placed at intervals of roughly a semitone, which, as on the lute, make a clear decisive tone, with less distinction between the sound of stopped and open strings than on the violin. During the latter part of the fifteenth century a number of pieces were written for viols only, thus underlining the general trend away from the mediaeval delight in variegated sound towards a more homogeneous one.

The regal, a small domestic organ invented *c.* 1460 that became very popular in the late Renaissance, was originally an all-reed pipe instrument—that is, every pipe was conical in shape and had a small strip or tongue of metal or wood attached to the lower end which vibrated in the wind from the bellows, as in the modern reed pipe. This strengthened the upper partials of the fundamental note and resulted in a characteristic 'reedy' timbre, like that of the bassoon or oboe. The other organs originally had only 'flue' pipes, which were cylindrical in shape and which gave a rounder, more open tone, like that of the flute; by the beginning of the sixteenth century, however, reed pipes were incorporated in the great and positive organs, while many regals had a few flue pipes.

Although Germany was pre-eminent in the production of instrumental music during the early Renaissance, the quantity and quality of her vocal polyphony, particularly sacred, continued to lag behind that of Burgundy, England, and Spain during most of this period, even though her musicians were fully aware of what was going on, as is clearly shown by the contents of the three important late fifteenth-century manuscript collections, the *Glogauer Liederbuch*§ (='Song Book'), the earliest surviving example of part-book arrangement (see p. 212), the *Schedelesches Liederbuch*, and the *Lochamer Liederbuch*§; these contain over 450 pieces, mostly copies or arrangements of secular works by Burgundian composers.

The only men who could in any way compare with the Burgundians were Heinrich Finck§ [*c.* 1445–1527] and Thomas Stoltzer§ [*c.* 1470-1526]. Finck's output is predominantly secular, and is 'up-to-date' in its use of pervading imitation, but his German songs (Lieder) show a feature that remained typical of this type during most of the sixteenth century, and which is old-fashioned compared to Italian or French secular music—namely, the placing of the main melody (nearly always a borrowed one) in the tenor rather than the treble. Stoltzer was German-born, but spent most of his life in Hungary. His output is greater than Finck's in both quantity and quality, and consists almost entirely of sacred music, the style of which shows a marked development in his later years, the seamless web of polyphony reminiscent of Ockeghem giving way to the regular imitation, careful word-setting, and harmonic feeling of Josquin. In his later years Stoltzer, like some other German composers, was considerably affected by the rise of Lutheranism, but more of this in the next volume.

The finest Lieder of the period were written by the Burgundian

Isaac, who, while adopting the feature mentioned above of making the tenor the main voice, treats the borrowed melody much more freely than his German contemporaries, preferring to paraphrase it rather than present it in long notes, and sometimes treating it canonically.

Isaac's masterpiece, however, is the *Choralis Constantinus*, written while he was at the court of Maximilian I at Innsbruck. This, the first polyphonic setting of the complete Propers of the Mass, was commissioned by the Cathedral at Constance (Switzerland) in 1508 and not quite completed before the composer's death. It is a tremendous if uneven work, containing the Propers for all the Sundays of the year, as well as for a number of feast and saints' days, and including at the end five settings of the Ordinary. The three books into which the work is divided, apart from demonstrating most of the mass and motet techniques that were current (parody does not occur and chordal passages are rare), also reveal the development in what we can conveniently call Isaac's 'Burgundian' style. Thus the voice parts (particularly the highest voice) are more florid in Books II and III than in Book I, but at the same time are more refined, and the same applies to his use of dissonance. Again, in Book III final chords include the third more frequently than in Books I and II. The first point shows an increasing mastery in writing individual lines of complex structure without their becoming angular or bizarre; the second point shows that Isaac was able to combine a number of these lines so that they offset each other rhythmically and melodically without clashing harmonically; and the last point underlines what we said earlier in this chapter about the slow acceptance of the third in final chords—on the Continent that is, for, as we have seen, contemporary British compositions end on a full triad far more frequently.

Part-music was not the only kind of vocal composition in Germany, nor indeed in other countries either, but the songs of the Meistersinger provide a larger body of monophonic song than existed anywhere else. The Meistersinger flourished from *c*. 1425 to *c*. 1600, establishing guilds in every important German town, and though they regarded themselves as the musical and poetic heirs of the Minnesinger, their art is quite different and inferior to the earlier poet-musicians. The main reason for this is that while the Minnesinger were wandering professionals mostly of noble birth and bound by no social ties, the Meister-singer were tradespeople who met together in their spare time and sang, and who as a result became highly organized. This naturally led to a system of rules, and with the spreading of the movement these rules grew in complexity and importance, thus impairing melodic spontaneity. To be a 'mastersinger' you had to compose both words and music of at least one song, but on no account had the melody to be reminiscent of any other 'master song', with the result that many of the songs are forced and artificial in their deliberate striving for originality§. Most of the other rules are concerned with textual faults, such as bad rhymes or incorrect scansion. The scene in Act II of Wagner's opera, *Die Meistersinger*, gives a very good idea of what a prospective 'mastersinger' had to put up with. The chief character in the opera, Hans Sachs§ [1494–1576], was the most famous of all 'mastersingers', composing over 6,000 songs, two-thirds of which are 'master songs'!

Despite the overall inferiority of their art, the Meistersinger performed a valuable and unique service, for only in Germany was music actually cultivated by the middle classes, and the organizing of amateur musical groups all over the country established a tradition of music-making and appreciation that bore rich fruit in later centuries.

In Spain, French and—later—Burgundian influence was all-powerful, so far as music was concerned at any rate, but during the first half of the century this did not produce much in the way of polyphony, as most of the comparatively few compositions actually written down are solo songs (Spanish music, like Italian, was more often improvised than in northern Europe). In the second half, however, a number of composers were active, chief of whom were Juan de Anchieta [*c.* 1462–1523] and, more particularly, Francisco de Peñalosa§ [*c.* 1470–1528]. The works of both these men show complete familiarity with the Burgundian style, and Peñalosa in particular reaped the benefits of a lengthy visit to Rome, *c.* 1517, where, as a member of the Papal Chapel, he met many highly trained musicians, mostly Burgundians. Both Anchieta and Peñalosa held positions at the court of Ferdinand V of Aragon [1452–1516] and his Queen, Isabella of Castile [1451-1504]. The reign of Ferdinand and Isabella has been called "the golden age of Spanish history", for they drove the last of the Moors from the Peninsula in 1492, sponsored the expedition of Columbus in the same year, and brought a period of economic and political stability unknown before. This, together with visits by a number of Burgundians, including Ockeghem and Agricola, and the fact that both Ferdinand and Isabella were keen music-lovers who laid particular stress on sacred music, may well account for the rejuvenation of native composition.

Despite the royal preference, however, a considerable body of secular music was written, the bulk being contained in four manuscript collections comprising nearly 700 pieces. The most important of these collections is the *Cancionero de Palacio* ('Songs of the Palace'), and most of the pieces (for two or more voices) are villancicos§—that is, songs in virelai-form, like the mediaeval cantigas (see Chapter 3, p. 90), with secular, i.e. non-liturgical, texts. Among the villancico composers represented in the *Cancionero de Palacio* are Johannes Cornago,§ Francisco de la Torre,§ and Escobar§ (which of the two known composers of this name is not certain), but the most important was Juan del Encina§ [*c.* 1468-*c.* 1529], a notable figure in the history of Spanish drama, even though he spent most of his life in Italy, whose songs are typical in that the main melody is in the treble and the style is that of Dufay and Binchois, with occasional use of imitation; the texts are mainly concerned with love, though, like the English carol, the subject-matter covers a fairly wide range.

That Burgundy was the dominating musical influence in fifteenth-century Spain, despite the latter's long and close association with Italy, is less surprising when we realize that of all the arts in the early Renaissance music was the only one in which Italy was not predominant, for in painting, sculpture, and literature she far outstripped the rest of Europe. One has only to compile a list of Italian artists and writers and then compare it with those of other countries to see how rich was the Italian genius in these fields. Florence was still the main centre, and her leading painters were Masaccio [1401-?1428], Fra Angelico [1387-1455], Uccello [1397-1475], Piero della Francesca [1416-1492], Botticelli [1445-1510], Leonardo da Vinci [1452-1519], and Raphael [1483-1520]; her sculptors Ghiberti [1378-1455], Donatello [1386-1466], and Luca della Robbia [1400-1482], while the greatest architect of the fifteenth century, Brunelleschi [1379-1446], was also a Florentine. So

also was the poet Politian [1454-1494], the scholar Pico della
Mirandola [d. 1494], and the greatest prose writer of the
Renaissance, Machiavelli [1469-1527]. But if Florence was still
the main cultural centre, Venice bid fair to usurp her prestige
through her popular lyric poet, Giustiniani [1388-1446] (the
author of *O rosa bella*), and more especially her painters, the
chief of whom were Giovanni Bellini [1428-1516], Mantegna
[1431-1506], Giorgione [*c.* 1478-1510], and Carpaccio [1460-
1522]. These men, by using rich, glowing colours with a
freedom only possible in the new medium of oil, stressed the
naturalism of their subjects to an even greater extent than did
the Florentines, who, mixing their pigments with white of egg
(tempera), or painting on plaster walls and ceilings (frescoes),
relied mainly on detailed drawings governed mainly by the
mathematical principles of perspective which they, in their
pursuit of realism, had discovered, with colour as a largely
inessential addition. But the Venetians were not only concerned
with realism, for the harmony of their colours produces a unity
of design which is not solely dependent on a geometrical pattern
achieved through the careful placing of objects, and it was
this use of colour, which conveys a more purely emotional
appeal than any other European school of the time, that
became intensified during the sixteenth century and was the
springboard of baroque art.

Compared to the Italian galaxy, the rest of Europe produced
only two important writers, the Englishman, Sir Thomas More
[1478-1535], and the Dutch humanist, philosopher, and scholar,
Erasmus [1466/7-1536], who through his breadth of mind,
clarity of thought, and sanity of judgment exerted a greater
influence on his generation (Catholics and Protestants alike)
than any other man of letters has ever done. As for artists, the
only ones of comparable stature were the Flemish (Burgundian)
painters, Hubert van Eyck [d. 1426] and his brother Jan [d.
1441], who served Philip the Good, van der Weyden [1399-
1464], who painted Charles the Bold, and Memlinc [1440-
1494], and the Germans, Dürer [1471-1528] and Grünewald
[b. before 1480-1528].

Dürer, who executed some fine oil paintings and exquisite
watercolours, is chiefly famous for his engravings and woodcuts.
In these his vivid detail, particularly of the human body, is
typical of the Renaissance, and was undoubtedly influenced by

Italian art, notably that of Leonardo da Vinci; Leonardo, in fact, made tremendous strides in the science of anatomy, and by dissecting human and animal bodies and carefully drawing his findings discovered an astonishing amount, none of which however became generally known, because nearly all his note-books, which were written backwards and partly in code, remained unpublished until the nineteenth century. These notebooks contain a mass of original and penetrating observa-tions on art, music, warfare, philosophy, and almost every aspect of the enormous realm of natural science, and show a thoroughly modern scientific approach in their clear realization that experiment is essential and must precede conclusions.

But Leonardo was a unique individual, perhaps the most unique in the whole history of western civilization, and not until the latter half of the sixteenth century did men really begin to throw off the double yoke of mediaeval speculation and reliance on ancient authority, especially that of Aristotle and Ptolemy. Even so a few daring spirits arose, including the Germans, Regiomontanus [1436-1476], who asserted, quite correctly, that Ptolemy was frequently inaccurate, and Nicolaus of Cusa [1401-1464], who maintained on purely philosophical grounds that the earth was not the centre of the universe and in fact revolved round the sun, a view that did not, in the tolerant atmosphere of the fifteenth century, prevent his being raised to the rank of cardinal, but which 150 years later, in the heat of the Counter-Reformation, was denounced as heretical.

The striking difference between the predominance of music in northern Europe and the predominance of the fine arts, literature, and science (such as it was) in Italy is explained by the fact (already mentioned) that the Renaissance, which grew more quickly and blossomed more richly in Italian soil than anywhere else, was primarily concerned with a reality based on the close observance of man and his world, the forms, colours, and details of which are readily and naturally transmitted to canvas or stone, or described in words. But realism is funda-mentally foreign to music which, in its essence, is abstract and incapable of conveying exact images, ideas, or feelings. To rejoice the ear by sheer sonority, or by weaving melody with melody into a simple or complex web of sound, yes; to express a general mood or feeling, yes; to satisfy the intellect through simple forms or delight it with structural subtlety, yes; but to portray precisely physical objects, mental concepts, or emotional states, no. The abstract mysticism and universality of outlook of the Middle Ages found music a perfect means of expression, but only in certain limited respects, some of them naïve, was the primary attitude of the Renaissance reflected in the works of her composers.

Basically the period from Dunstable to Josquin is still mediaeval (hence the title of this chapter as distinct from Early Renaissance Music), the cantus firmus, paraphrase, and parody techniques are simply developments of the borrowed Gregorian chant in the tenor of the thirteenth- and fourteenth-century motet; the predominantly linear polyphonic texture of sacred and secular music alike is only different from the earlier styles in its greater refinement of harmony, smoothness of line, and equality of rhythm, the last two being the natural application of conductus style to polyphony, while the first, being part and parcel of an increased feeling for tonality, shows the same development in part-music as that which took place in Christian chant, where the earlier semi-rhapsodic melodies were later pruned and became part of a clearly defined modal system; the optional or obligatory use of instruments, with their contrasting timbres to double or accompany the voice, is a direct continuation of mediaeval practice. Music is still the be-all and end-all, not yet the handmaiden of poetry nor the vehicle of passion; only through pervading imitation did she become in any fundamental sense Renaissance-like, for imitation is, as we observed in Chapter 5, a more realistic means of binding the parts together, but its use as the sole means of unification had still to be generally accepted. The increase in sonority achieved through the recognition of the third as a fundamental interval (though even at the end of the period final chords still frequently omitted it, except in British compositions), together with the expansion of the number and range of voices, were natural developments, the former for reasons already given (see Chapter 2, p. 43), and the latter because, as composers become more assured in any one tradition, they tend to enlarge their forces.

The most obvious realistic element in fifteenth-century music is the least important and naïve—word-painting. This can occasionally be found in mediaeval music (see Ex. 38 and the ritornello of *H.A.M.*, 52, where the voices imitate the sound of

perfection of style because his musical language is less refined, he is certainly as expressive and as profound. In other spheres, too, the early Renaissance can compare with the late—painting and architecture, for example, and while the scientific investigation of man and his universe was still in its infancy, the desire to explore the unknown parts of the world was as strong as in the period following. The journeys of the Polos to the Far East in the thirteenth century and Marco's account of them were the fifteenth-century explorers' chief stimuli, and the Portuguese Prince Henry the Navigator [1394-1460] planned a number of expeditions during which most of the north-western coast of Africa was discovered, including Rio de Oro (1436), Cape Verde (1445), Sierra Leone (1450), and the Gulf of Guinea (1460), together with the Madeira Islands (1419-20) and the Azores (1432-60). In 1487 the Cape of Good Hope was rounded, and in the same year India was reached by sea from Egypt, both by Portuguese sailors. The latter achievement fired the King of Portugal's ambition, and in 1497 he despatched one of the greatest navigators in history, Vasco da Gama [c. 1469-1525], to the Indian Peninsula, where a landing was effected ten months later and was followed by Portuguese settlements. The traditional route to India was open, and not long after parts of Malaya and the East Indies were conquered and even China reached (1516). In the meantime the southern Atlantic route had been blazed by the Spaniard, Christopher Columbus [1451-1506], who on his first two voyages of 1492 and 1493-6 conquered most of the West Indies, and in his third (1498) discovered Trinidad and the South American mainland. On his last voyage (1502-4) he searched in vain along the coast of Central America for a passage westwards; so did the Italians, Sebastian Cabot [c. 1483-1557] and Amerigo Vespucci [1451-1512]. The former, with his father, John [c. 1455-c.1498], both in the service of Henry VII of England, discovered the North American coast in 1487 and later entered Hudson Bay, and the latter, whose reputation far exceeded his achievements, even eclipsing that of Columbus, and whose Christian name as a result was given to South America, may have discovered Brazil (1499-1500), but certainly explored much of the South American coast. The passage through to the west was eventually found by the Portuguese, Magellan [c. 1470-1521], who, in the service of Spain, discovered the Straits that bear his name (1519), sailed across the Pacific Ocean (which he christened), and reached the Philippine Islands, where he was killed by the natives. His ship, however, continued the journey and returned to Spain in 1522, the first vessel to sail round the world. In the same year that Magellan found a way through to the Pacific Ocean, Mexico, with its ancient Inca civilization and enormous wealth, was conquered by the Spaniard, Cortez [1485-1547], and imperial expansion began in earnest.

The weeks, sometimes months, spent at sea with no or only uncharted land in sight resulted in a more scientific approach to navigation, in the improvement of the astrolabe and quadrant for measuring the angle of the sun and stars, and in the greater accuracy of maps, the first world map being published in 1507.

That Italy took comparatively little part in all this world expansion was probably due to her geographical position, for her only exit to the east or west was through the narrow and treacherous (in those days) Straits of Gibraltar. But whatever the explanation, it in no way affected the brilliance of her culture, a brilliance that shone over all Europe and drew men in all walks of life to study within her boundaries. Music was no exception, and although, as we have seen, there was little native composition during most of the period, the wealth of opportunities, compared to other countries, that were open to musicians, especially singers, in churches and aristocratic establishments attracted a host of foreigners, and, despite the lack of any Italian genius or school of composition, most of the leading composers from the north visited Italy at least once, although few stayed any length of time. In the sixteenth century, however, when the Renaissance reached its full flowering many of the outstanding Continental musicians from across the Alps settled in the peninsula for several years, some of them holding positions of considerable importance. Their effect on Italian music and vice versa takes us into the late Renaissance and Part II of this history.

PERFORMANCE

(See also pp. 195, 209, 215, 228-30.)

The expanding vocal range during the century, and the resultant natural distinction between voices through their timbres, and, in the latter half of the period, the achieving of a more homogeneous texture by means of pervading imitation make performance by voices alone less objectionable than in the Middle Ages. Nevertheless, it is quite certain that instrumental doubling or accompaniment was the rule, especially in those works that are based on an unparaphrased borrowed melody, for this should be clearly heard, and hence should be played on an instrument with or without vocal doubling. Many motets and most if not all of the movements in the mass should be varied at suitable places by altering both the number and combination of voices and instruments. In motets and masses the number of voices per part should not exceed four unless the top part is sung by boys' voices, when the number should be six or seven; instruments may be doubled or even trebled, depending on the timbre and the importance of the part played. Secular pieces should in the main be performed by soloists, whether vocal or instrumental, although where there is a refrain or burden and the texture is very simple, as in some frottole and many carols, the number of voices and instruments may be increased. In any case, considerable variety should be aimed at in all pieces employing repetition, the verses being shared by each soloist—who should sing his or her normal part, whether it be top, inner, or bottom—and the refrain being sung by all the voices, but with the instrumentation varied each time. The instruments used have already been listed in this and previous chapters, and there seems to have been less distinction than in earlier centuries as to which were suitable in church and which were not

Underlaying continues to be rather haphazard, and in melismatic passages it is usually impossible to discover the composer's exact intentions as to how the words should fit the notes, if indeed he had any such intentions. Musica ficta also is still very much of a problem, and in compositions with partial signatures too many editors and conductors remove the false relations that occur between the parts by adding an unnecessary number of accidentals. Successive false relations (e.g. when a B♭ in one part is immediately followed or preceded by a B♮ in another) are typical of the period, and even simultaneous false relations should not be removed if of short duration. In general, editorial accidentals are only permissible in order (*a*) to avoid the melodic intervals of the augmented fourth and diminished fifth (though at times even these seem to have been desired by the composer), and also to remove simultaneous false relations of a minim's length or more provided this does not result in awkward vocal line; and (*b*) to ensure that the leading note is sharpened, but only if it is the last leading note of the melodic phrase in which it occurs, is the resolution of a suspension, and does not result in a false relation of the augmented sixth with one of the other parts.

The subject of tempo has already been dealt with, but that of dynamics remains to be discussed. Violent changes in loudness and softness should never occur; crescendos should be gentle and infrequent, but a diminuendo is often effective at a sectional or final cadence where the words permit. There should of course be both dynamic contrasts and emotional warmth in performance, but in general the approach should be one of restraint.

VOLUME I

GENERAL INDEX

ABELARD, Peter, 53
Adam de la Halle, 84, 117
Adam of St. Victor, 22, 72
Aelred of Rievaulx, 69, 71, 117, 124
Africa, 232
'Agincourt Song', 214
Agnus Dei (Chirbury,) 189
Agricola, Alexander, 201, 206, 224
Alba, 83
Albigensian Crusade, 84, 122
Alcuin, 21
Aldhelm, 41
Alexandria, 33
Alfonso X ('The Wise'), 90
Allegez moi (Josquin), 202
Alleluia, 4, 21f.
Alle-psallite cum-luya, 112
Alma redemptoris Mater (Dufay), 196
Ambrosian Chant, *See* St. Ambrose
Anchieta, Juan de, 223
Andrieu contredit d'Arras, 81
Anonymus IV, 58, 59
Antiphon, 6, 10
Antonella da Caserta, 171f.
Apel, W., 54*n*, 57*n*, 58*n*, 61*n*, 128*n*, 144*n*,
    156*n*, 172*n*.
Architecture, 181, 231. *See also* Gothic,
    Romanesque
Aristotle, 53, 119, 182, 226
Ars Cantus Mensurabilis (Franco), 113f.
Ars Nova (de Vitri), 124f.
Aston, Hugh, 215
Attaignant, Pierre, 211, 242
Aulos, 13, 68
Aurelian of Réomé, 21
Austria, 40
Ave Maria . . . benedicta tu (Mouton),
    207
Ave Maria, gemma virginum (Mouton),
    207
Ave Maria . . . virgo serena (Josquin), 202
Ave Regina (Dunstable), 189
Ave verum (Josquin), 205
Azores, 232

BACON, Roger, 119
Bagpipes, 93, 218
Ballade, 79–83, 117, 119, 130, 142–9,
    153, 172, 191, 194, 196, 204
Ballade style. *See* Treble-dominated
    style
Ballata, 80, 167
Barbarossa, Frederick, 86
Baroque, 180f., 225; fugue, 52; opera,
    24, 52
Bartolomeo de Bologna, 171
Basilicas, 38

Beata Dei genitrix (Damett), 189
Beatrix of Burgundy, 86
Beethoven, 95, 96
Belgium, 190, 197
Bellini, Giovanni, 225
Bells, 68
Benedicamus Domini chant, 52; discantus
    57; organum, 46; trope, 22
Bernart de Ventadorn, 84, 90
Berno of Reichenau, 21
Bimodalism, 138f., 142
Binchois, Gilles, 187, 190, 196–9, 224
Black Death, 86, 122
Blondel de Nesles, 84
Boccaccio, 182f.
Boethius, 11f., 16, 19
Bologna, 8, 155
Botticelli, 224
Brahms, 51, 118, 142
Britain, 7, 34, 75f., 90f., 97–103, 112,
    147, 173f., 180, 185f., 189, 191,
    213–15, 222, 227, *See also* England
Browne, John, 214f.,
Brumel, Antoine, 210—4
Brunelleschi, 224
Buchner, Hans, 216
Bukler, C., 89*n*.
Bukofzer, Manfred, 188*n*.
Bulletin Hispanique, 90*n*.
Burgundy, 190f.
Busnois, Antoine, 198f., 211
Buxheimer Orgelbuch, 216
Byttering, 815, 188
Byzantine chant, 20, 29; Church, 4

CABOT, John, 232; Sebastian, 232
Caccia, 158, 161, 183, 185, 192
Cadence, 81, 139–42, 167, 171, 193f.,
    198f., 202f., 206, 213
Cancionera de Palacio, 224
Canon, 60, 158f., 174, 185f., 191f., 197f.,
    202, 204f., 207f., 221
Canti carnascialeschi, 209
Cantiga, 90, 224
Cantillation, 6
Cantus Collateralis. *See* Choirbook
    arrangement
Cantus firmus, 189, 194f., 203f., 206,
    214, 216, 227
Cara, Marco, 209
Carnivals, 298f.
Carol, 187, 214, 224
Carpaccio, 225
Cartelle, 213
Caserta, 155
Cassiodorus, 11, 16
Castanets, 93